About this book Peter Greenaway, one of the most original
directors to emerge in the last two decades, has secured his
reputation by combining in such works as *The Draughtsman's
Contract*, *Drowning by Numbers* and *Prospero's Books* a sumptuous
visual style with peculiarly artificial structural principles.
Cinematic images derived from Italian quattrocento perspective
studies, the Renaissance nude, Dutch still-life, German Baroque
allegories, French visionary architecture, English landscape
painting, and even the Land Art movement are placed in new
contexts, artificially lit with an almost obsessive attention to
detail, which exaggerates the eccentric and illuminates the
overlooked. Greenaway's films, animated by a powerful sense of
irony but still exhibiting a powerful consistency in their
approaches and preoccupations, invite us to reconsider notions of
visual culture. Their organizing principles – lists, number
systems, catalogues, texts – are designed to offer bizarre and
arcane routes through the many artefacts obsessively displayed in
his 'celluloid museum'; yet these structures also draw attention to
new forms of cinematic expression, new ways of seeing,
alternative enlightenments.

   This book represents the first attempt at a close formal analysis
of the relationship between painted and motion pictures, art
history and film, in Greenaway's work. Drawing on a wide range
of recent scholarship in several related fields, David Pascoe
examines the director's own paintings and drawings as well as
his films' many allusions to the Old Masters to suggest that lying
beneath his extraordinary style, in its development from the early
experimentalism to the dazzling imagery and rich visual texture
of his recent ventures, is a fascination with the ironies involved in
the mechanical reproduction of the world about us; and, in
particular, with the debilitating effects of artificial frames on the
human body.

About the author David Pascoe is a Lecturer in English Literature
at the University of Glasgow, and was previously College
Lecturer and Tutor at Oriel College, Oxford. He has written
widely on the Victorian and Modern period, and on Renaissance
drama, and among his many publications are editions of novels
by Thackeray and Robert Louis Stevenson, of the journalism of
Charles Dickens, and the plays of John Marston.

ESSAYS IN ART AND CULTURE

The Landscape Vision of Paul Nash
by Roger Cardinal

Looking at the Overlooked: Four Essays on Still Life Painting
by Norman Bryson

Charles Sheeler and the Cult of the Machine
by Karen Lucic

Portraiture
by Richard Brilliant

C. R. Mackintosh: The Poetics of Workmanship
by David Brett

Image on the Edge: The Margins of Medieval Art
by Michael Camille

Illustration
by J. Hillis Miller

Francis Bacon and the Loss of Self
by Ernst van Alphen

Paul Delvaux: Surrealizing the Nude
by David Scott

Manet's Silence and the Poetics of Bouquets
by James H. Rubin

The Symptom of Beauty
by Francette Pacteau

Figuring Jasper Johns
by Fred Orton

Political Landscape
by Martin Warnke

Visionary Experience in the Golden Age of Spanish Art
by Victor I. Stoichita

The Double Screen: Medium and Representation in Chinese Painting
by Wu Hung

Painting the Soul: Icons, Death Masks and Shrouds
by Robin Cormack

A Short History of the Shadow
by Victor I. Stoichita

Peter Greenaway

Museums and Moving Images

David Pascoe

REAKTION BOOKS

Published by Reaktion Books Ltd
11 Rathbone Place, London W1P 1DE, UK

First published in 1997

Cover and text designed by Humphrey Stone

Photoset by BAS Printers Ltd
Printed and bound in Great Britain by
BAS Printers Ltd, Over Wallop, Hampshire

British Library Cataloguing in Publication Data:
Pascoe, David
  Peter Greenaway: museums and moving images. – (Essays in
  art and culture)
  1. Greenaway, Peter – Criticism and interpretation
  2. Painting, Modern – 20th century – Great Britain 3. Museum
  curators – Great Britain 4. Collectors and collecting –
  Great Britain
  I. Title
  709.2

ISBN 1 86189 005 2

Contents

1   Artificial Light   7

2   Art and Language   42

3   Fields of Vision   67

4   Medical Experiments and Art Theory   92

5   Mechanical Reproduction   121

6   The Book Depository   158

7   Making an Exhibition   193

    Acknowledgements   223

    Filmography and Bibliography   224

    References   228

    List of Illustrations   239

1 'Escargot', from *A Zed and Two Noughts* (1985).

1 Artificial Light

In the final moments of Peter Greenaway's *A Zed and Two Noughts* (1986), a pair of brothers – Oliver and Oswald Deuce – lie down in the dark and stage their own deaths in front of a whirring camera. Throughout this strange and difficult film the men have been shown attempting to comprehend the recent deaths of their wives in a car accident, an 'Act of God', whose circumstances are so bizarre (a mute swan has smashed into a white Ford Mercury, registration number NID 26 B/W, driven by a woman wearing white feathers named Alba Bewick) that Oliver and Oswald have sought intellectual satisfaction from the work of Charles Darwin rather than the Book of Genesis, undertaking experiments on dead things, following life to its point of origin in dust and carbon, by recording in time-lapse footage the putrefaction of apples, prawns, fish, a crocodile, a swan, a Dalmatian, a gorilla and a pregnant Grevy's Zebra.

In venturing this project, they have followed Darwin's stages of Evolution to the letter, until finally (and so that their investigation can be taken to its logical conclusion) only one experiment remains to be done: the filming of the decomposition of human bodies. And so, at the conclusion of the film they set out to film their own decay, first constructing an elaborate film set in a rural idyll named Escargot (illus. 1):

> A warm mellow night in summer. The scaffolding built by the Deuce brothers stands in the centre of a wild garden of greenery. The wooden platform has a black floor, ruled off in six-inch squares by thin white lines. The platform is roofed with wood and canvas, as is the camera on its elaborate tripod. The camera is angled down on to the black squared floor. Numerous electric cables and leads trail off towards the house, which is lost in the greenery and long grass.[1]

The brothers lie down, inject themselves with drugs and die to the strains of the 'The Teddy Bears' Picnic'. But the big surprise in the woods on this day is that the time-lapse technique on which they have come to rely is itself subjected to a kind of formal de-composition; with a black irony, it is the experiment, rather than the twins' bodies, that is subject to the post-mortem processes. An influx of snails crawls over the equipment and the set – that word itself perhaps attempting to counter or to conceal the moving contingencies of the filmic world – in sufficient numbers to create a short-circuit, a breakdown, a power cut, which also, necessarily, provides the final cut of Greenaway's film:

> They die quickly. The record finishes. One has his mouth open and his eyes shut, the other has his eyes open and his mouth shut. The snails come in the failing light. They glide up the camera tripod, crawl across the naked bodies along the arm of the record player which regularly lifts and falls, up the hanging suit. The snail bodies glisten in the intermittent light-flash. A snail crawls into Oliver's mouth. The flashes come regularly at the beats of the record music. A snail crawls around the lens of the camera and across the electrical equipment, eventually fusing the apparatus. The lights begin to flicker and stutter. As dawn breaks they finally go out. The final experiment requiring the brothers' self-sacrifice has come to nought.

The story board (illus. 2), which Greenaway exhibited in 1996 as *The Snails*, shows the slow victory of the gastropods in explicit detail; in the village of Escargot they are, after all, simply reclaiming their *terroir*.[2] Their stately but ineluctable progress across the frame becomes a cinematic performance, engaging and challenging the viewer's own response; but just as these dense clusters of slime and shell seem pregnant with forms and images that never emerge singly, uniquely, so the drama conveyed in these last moments is implicit rather than articulated: a sense of an urgent faltering discourse – of 'flicker and stutter' – followed by the termination of the twins' grieving process as all comes to nought, an O for oblivion (illus. 3). After this point, only daybreak – the natural light of dawn – closes down the film, and not the artificial light cast by the strobes and the arc lights. All the sounds of the sunrise – most obviously, the dawn chorus – make themselves heard on the film now, and then persist for several seconds after the darkening of the screen. It is a reminder that the natural world can never be affected by artifice, or, more precisely, by the kind of film-making the twins have undertaken over the previous months.

This sequence and the suggestions it generates are typical of much of Greenaway's oeuvre: arcanely formal and staged, as the twins die against the backdrop of a carefully drawn grid; gruesomely and blackly comic, ending with that killing pun on 'come to nought'; meticulously detailed, especially in respect of the choreographing of music – in this case both children's song and Michael Nyman's driving score – with image; and, most obviously, archly ironic, with regard both to the medium of cinema itself and to Greenaway's own role as director. He is gleefully drawing attention to the foolishness of the medium in which he works, constantly reminding his viewers of the limitations of narrative ordering, which began with another pair of brothers, the Lumières, whose films were advertised as 'all the movements which have succeeded one another over a given period of time in front of the camera and the subsequent reproduction of these movements by the projection of their images, life-size on a screen'.[3]

This ironizing is at the heart of his work, as he observed in 1992:

> What is also constant – then and now – is the irony – irony as tolerance, as non-dogma, that 'this is only cinema, not life', that there are no longer any certainties – if indeed there ever were – and surely no single meanings – except to the very simple-minded who endearingly want things kept straightforward and clear-cut.[4]

The Deuce twins are such people, seeking from their time-lapse photography a 'straightforward and clear-cut' version of the relations between life and death. Elsewhere in his films, characters habitually contrive various forms of spurious order to insulate themselves against chaos, be they the maps in *A Walk Through H*, the directory in *The Falls*, the architectural drawings in *The Draughtsman's Contract*, the exhibition in *The Belly of an Architect*, the games in *Drowning by Numbers*, haute cuisine in *The Cook, the Thief, his Wife and her Lover*, the library in *Prospero's Books*, the Catholic theology in *The Baby of Mâcon* or the calligraphy in *The Pillow Book*. But in each case, such devices come to nought, as Greenaway is keen to emphasize:

> If a numerical, alphabetical or colour-coding system is employed, it is done deliberately as a device, a construct, to

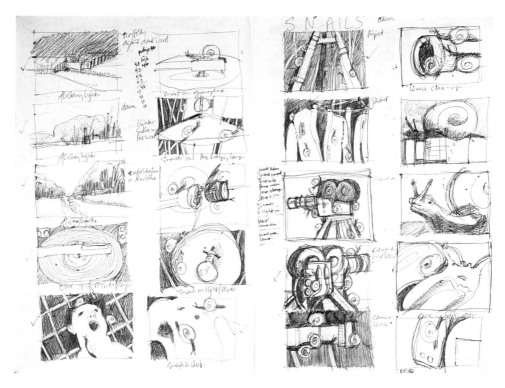

counteract, dilute, augment or complement the all-pervading obsessive cinema interest in plot, in narrative, in the 'I'm now going to tell you a story' school of film-making, which nine times out of ten begins life as literature, an origin with very different concerns, ambitions and characteristics from those of the cinema.[5]

2 'The Snails', from the storyboard for *A Zed and Two Noughts* (1985).

Why has the cinema associated itself with the business of story-telling? Could it not profitably exist without it? Greenaway's cinematic experiments with numerical systems, alphabetical sequence or colour-coding have all been attempts to dislodge this apparently unquestioned presumption that narrative is necessary and essential for cinema to convey its preoccupations.

As a recent critic has suggested, 'The recurring allegory, metaphor or subtext in all his films, underlying their more immediate and superficial action, is the inevitable failure of whatever ordering principles his protagonists engage in';[6] and this is especially true if they are involved in film. Naturally this seeming reductivism leads to the usual charges against him.

3 'The Snails on the Grid', from *A Zed and Two Noughts* (1985).

10

'Flaunting their erudition and relishing overt staginess, [his] films divide audiences. There are those who are prepared to entertain his conceits and play the game, and others for whom a Greenaway film is about as exciting as a guided tour through an ancient museum where the catalogue has been lost.'[7] In that closing sequence from *Z&OO*, however, what kind of catalogue has been lost or discarded?

It's possible that, for the twins at least, the world of Escargot may have come to represent a kind of Eden, a world radiant in its first light. As a literal goal, of course, this cannot be achieved in a world which has suffered the Fall; and all that any film-maker can do is to portray as closely as possible through artifice the site of his prelapsarian desire. For if the paradigm of the Deuce twins' creation and decay was the Garden of Eden (crossed, of course, with the Darwinian prerogative), the field of the film-maker's art is the studio; and, in the final moments of the film, that stage set created by the twins becomes, in Greenaway's hands, a kind of private theatre. The objects depicted – the stages, the cameras, the lights, the cables – have the instability of props, of things whose use and meaning are defined by a sovereign personal drama: that of the twins' last experiment. Antecedent to any work performed in it, this studio in the open air is already a perfect extension of the film-maker's will, in short, a creation. It is a space unlike any other, into which – like Eden or, better, in this film about zoos, Noah's Ark – nothing has entered by accident; a space whose artifice and whose taxonomy, down to the smallest detail, are the product of wilful choice. And to choose is to accept and reject; and that, in turn, is to fabricate. The studio is, absolutely, in place; and yet, at the same time, its only purpose is humbling, since photography, lighting and sound exist only as a means of moving towards something else. Charged with effect, defined as potential, the objects of this set are powerfully but precariously present – dependent, as are all created things, on the presence of their framer; Peter Greenaway, in this case.

Of course, this analogy of the studio with Eden cannot be sustained without some irony. Whereas Eden might imply the plenitude of a divine creator, the studio reflects human contingencies. To sustain that creative act, the artist's personal drive and perpetual exertion of will are necessary, as well as the producer's finances. Naturally, Eden is always full; but the studio or the filmset, however stuffed with objects, is, finally, perpetu-

4 Publicity shot for
*A Zed and Two
Noughts* (1985).

ally empty, and unless continually replenished its idle tools –
lights and camera – are a mockery of that creativity.

The analogy emerges in a publicity still from *Z&OO*, reproduced in the published text of the film, which presents a typical
shot of Alba in bed symmetrically flanked by the two Deuce
brothers (illus. 4). At the apex of the pyramidal composition is
a framed portrait – or is it a mirror? – in which Greenaway's disembodied head floats eerily over the scene, providing a virtual
signature (or sovereign stamp of authority) for the highly artificial symmetry of the tableau. Such self-referential inclusion
suggests it is right to call Greenaway an *auteur*; he, certainly, is
happy to be regarded as such:

> The word 'auteur' has acquired – perhaps from those who are
> frightened of it – dangerous overtones of indulgence. After
> all, it means no more than 'author'. You can – without fear of
> argument – use the word to describe the maker of a novel. I
> have a set of characteristics that, welded together, I suppose,
> can be recognized as a specific personal style – though they
> are not maniplated to be stylish. They arise naturally out of

13

personal interests – both in content and form. I would say that it is very difficult to put raw neat autobiography on to the screen. By nature it's messy, unstructured, self-obsessed and I don't think anybody's really interested. But to iron away all the idiosyncracies, interests and obsessions of a personal voice is probably certain to make a bland product.[8]

From the beginning of his career, he has been keen to be recognized as an an artist whose peculiar vision of life infuses his work, and has given scores of interviews in which he enjoys asserting his own distinctive views. Indeed, as we shall see, his frequent explanations of autobiographical allusions in his works, his openness about his source material and his freely given statements of intention often make it difficult to separate the personality of the creator from the creation of that personality by the films; at times, it is hard to separate the truth from the many fictions. Certainly, 'bland' is an adjective that does not apply to his work; it is strong stuff, and for some critics just too strong. Pauline Kael once described him as 'a cultural omnivore who eats with his mouth open'; and, following her, others have criticized him on the grounds of intellectual vulgarity: 'Style is all Greenaway has to offer . . . [he is] Stoppard without the wit.'[9] In 1993 Peter Matthews deftly summarized the case against the fim-maker, but in doing so, had to acknowledge his unique strengths:

> No one in contemporary cinema has a more distinctive style than Peter Greenaway, but few have ever wanted to imitate it. That's because, as everyone knows, Greenaway designs great petrified rebus puzzles instead of movies; you are expected to scan the huge painterly tableaux for clues. . . . There is no shading, no mystery, but Greenaway takes inert literal-minded academicism so far it becomes ghoulishly fascinating and that's something. And though he drives his talent down an ever narrower cul-de-sac, on his own terms he seems totally incorruptible, and that's something too.[10]

Probably the most striking aspect of Greenaway's work is that viewers who have seen only two or three of his 'painterly tableaux' feel confident they can isolate his 'distinctive style', which necessarily involves such avowedly cinematic elements as set design, lighting, the movement of the camera and the rhythm both of editing shots within a sequence, and of editing those sequences within the structure of the entire film. Yet it is probably more interesting and more useful to observe that the impetus behind Greenaway's drive down the ever narrower cul de sac is *ostranenie*; the desire to 'defamiliarize' us, as 'inert, literal-minded' Russian Formalist critics would put it, from our world and have us see it afresh as something exciting and mysterious, something that cannot quite be contained in the standard framing devices. In his well-known essay 'Art as Technique', Viktor Shklovsky puts the matter this way: 'The technique of art is to make objects unfamiliar, to make forms difficult, to increase the difficulty and length of perception because the process of perception is an aesthetic end in itself.'[11] Shklovsky feels that the function of art is to remove objects from the conventional forms of presentation so that our perception of them is not automatic and minimal, but attentive and searching. Greenaway would seem to go a stage further and would have us notice an ineffable illusionistic quality that cannot be grasped or even suggested by conventional forms. Indeed, from the commencement of his career in film-making, Greenaway's 'ambitions were to see if I could make films that acknowledged cinema's artifices and illusion, and demonstrate that – however fascinating – that was what they were'.[12] Consequently, he occupies an ambiguous position: a director who, making use of familiar cinematic discourses, abjures the larger possibilities of art and instead advertises the impossibility of ever forgetting that film is artifice. This formalist bent, which consists of foregrounding an artifice and then giving it a function, necessarily draws attention to the various elements of film-making. Cutting and montage, for instance, are present in the practice of Mr Neville, the Draughtsman contracted to fix on a white surface the portions of space that he captures in the frame of his optical device. The arrangement of objects and then people in large volumes of space is witnessed in the nine-month quest of Stourley Kracklite, the Architect. And the *mise-en-scène* of fabulous and artificial worlds is reflected in the magic wand – in fact, a quill – of Prospero.

'A little colouring goes a long way. Artificial colouring can be dangerous,' says Hardy in *Drowning By Numbers*, indicating the bright yellow iced lolly with which he is pleasuring his wife.[13] Yet the dangers are celebrated throughout Greenaway's work, from the green of the lawns of the Herbert property, achieved through special filters; the flashing neon lights that illuminate so much of *Z&OO*; the lights of photocopiers in *The Belly of an*

Architect; the primary colours that bathe the kitchens of the Hollandais restaurant; the Gaultier costumes that alter their hue as the camera follows characters from room to room in *The Cook, the Thief*; to the frames of *Prospero's Books*, *A TV Dante* and *The Pillow Book*, which juxtapose monochrome and colour images in the same bibliographical *cadre*. Greenaway, then, is fascinated by the abstract possibilities of artificial light; and in this regard he often recalls some of the earliest theorists of the cinema, such as Germaine Dulac, who claimed in 1925 that, 'For cinema, which is moving, changing, interrelated light, nothing but light, genuine and restless light can be its true setting.'[14] Some of the greatest stylists of the previous generation also emerge in Greenaway's thinking about artificial light. Alain Resnais, for instance, is a crucial figure, and his *L'Année Dernière à Marienbad* has provided Greenaway with much inspiration over the years, from the shots of the shadowless garden, which are recalled in *The Draughtsman's Contract*, to *Marienbad*'s unique formal structure:

> It is happy to manipulate chronology, happy to repeat and reprise, to take multiple views of the same phenomena, and to do it with elegant and witty self-reflection. It comfortably says, without stress or strain, 'I am a film. Nothing else'.[15]

And saying this, the film ensures that is only ever a film.

In this respect, an interesting conversation takes place in *The Cook, the Thief*. Michael and Georgina, the lovers, attempting to elude her brutal husband, Spica, are lying naked in the plucking room of the Hollandais restaurant, surrounded by game.

MICHAEL: I once saw a film where the main character didn't speak for the first half an hour.
GEORGINA: . . . like us? Counting up the minutes – have we spent half an hour together?
MICHAEL: . . . I was completely absorbed as to what would happen because anything was possible.
GEORGINA (after a pause): . . . and then?
MICHAEL (with a self-deprecating smile): He spoilt it – he spoke.
GEORGINA: . . . and?
MICHAEL: . . . and within five minutes I'd lost interest.
GEORGINA: Now you've opened your mouth, do you expect me to lose interest?
MICHAEL (smiling): It was only a film.[16]

'Anything was possible' precisely because 'it was only a film'; and this is always what Greenaway seeks to remind his audience: 'Cinema is nothing if not a beam of projected light striking a surface with a framed rectangle of brightness into which shadows are introduced to simulate illusions of movement.'[17] In defining the medium in this way, he lays claim to a cinema which owes nothing to realism and everything to illusion; and which habitually dissolves the artificial means by which it has been put into place. As he observed on the centenary of the birth of film:

> Whilst it is curious that the 'cinematograph' patented in 1895 by the Lumière Brothers etymologically stressed movement, the lift-off to true cinematic illusion was made possible by the discovery of how to throw light successfully – to project images. It could be said that artificially projected light is the key to cinema's great public success, because it permits large pictures to be viewed by large audiences.[18]

However, since Lumière, the cinema has attempted to dodge its origins in artifice, the means by which it captures and reconstitutes reality and replaces it with an illusory secondary world that will hide the first. It can do so because, in contrast to the photograph, the projected image lacks a surface; only the screen on which the image is thrown possesses such a face. However, the movement of the projected image lends a particular kind of presence to that surfaceless image. As Christian Metz noted in an early essay, the image of movement and movement itself are synonymous; there is no image of recorded movement in the cinema, there is only a moving image.[19] However, in Greenaway's view, that moving image must always be circumscribed by an awareness of a meta-image, a frame. Because the image is moving, objects within it appear to enter and leave the frame, and the frame itself moves. In comparison to the photograph, the viewer's awareness of the possibility of off-screen space in the cinema is greatly enhanced, and can be understood as an extension of the dramatic space of the image, solidly a part of this world, that we may look upon through the image when it is revealed to us. However, this self-referentiality of the work of art acts as a proof of the impossibility of any innocent signification, for when this awareness of off-screen space is combined with the perception of movement that appears present to us, and is supported by a soundtrack that emphasizes both the presence of the image and the continuum between on- and off-screen space, the preconditions for projective illusion are established.

Admittedly, cinema itself, with irony and amusement, often makes reference to its own passion for the power and illusion of the projected beam of light. Take Greenaway's deployment of the image of the projection room early in *Z&OO*, where the cinematic gaze is directed to the rays of light emanating from the the projection facilities at the rear; we are watching an audience watching, but, by implication, we are watching ourselves too. This is something of a cliché, as he acknowledges. Consider 'the cinema audiences rapt in attention beneath the smoke-filled projector-beam in more than one Fellini film, the shadow-play in Wenders' *Kings of the Road*, the swaying projector searchlight searching for its screen in *Cinema Paradiso*, Godard's amateur soldiers lifting up the edges of the screen to understand where the action has gone in *Les Carabiniers*.'[20] And that last sequence, coming after Michel-Ange's anouncement, 'Je suis allé pour la première fois au cinématographe', seems to be often on Greenaway's mind.[21]

At the Mexico Cinema, Michel-Ange sees a train arriving at a station, the locomotive growing in size as it approaches the platform on which the camera stands. Just as did those who attended the Grand Café on 28 December 1895 and witnessed the Lumière presentation of a train, so Michel-Ange curls up in his seat and places his hands over his eyes. Only a film, of course. Later in the presentation, he sees *Le Bain de la femme du monde*. A pretty blonde woman enters, runs a bath and begins to undress. In bra and petticoat, the woman moves towards the left of the screen and then leaves the frame. Michel-Ange, aroused, tries to follow her by moving position, watching with his head inclined to one side and finally climbing on to his seat to obtain a better view of the rippling water in the bathtub. Finally, he moves towards the screen itself, climbs on to the stage set, flattens himself against the screen on to which the image is being projected, and jumps up and down to catch a glimpse of the naked flesh out of the frame. Of course he can't help being caressed by the image that is cast over him; and in his keenness to penetrate further into the bathroom he pulls down the screen, but the projection only continues against the brick wall behind.

This behaviour, though extreme, may be typical of a larger point about the cinematic gaze, suggests Greenaway:

Every film-space itself is a framed peephole for us, the voyeurs of the audience, to be witness to other people's privacy, secrets, joys, miseries, embarrassments. It is voyeuristic because, in the very nature of cinema, the players on the screen are deemed to be ignorant of the fact that they are being watched by us. It is a perversely ironic state of affairs, of course, that this is not the whole truth, for cinema requires actors who know – and indeed it is the most essential part of their contract, to know – that they will be watched. They are paid to assume the innocence that their activities are not being watched. [22]

This is perhaps why voyeurism (particularly glimpses of restricted areas) is so strongly signalled in his work. The issue of representation is touched on in an exchange from *The Cook, the Thief*, which takes place after Michael has been murdered. His lover, still in shock, reminisces about their relationship with the Cook, Richard, who confesses that he once watched them making love in the plucking room, just as we in the audience did too.

GEORGINA: Tell me what you saw.

RICHARD: What I saw was what you let me see.

GEORGINA: Of course it was – how else could I know that it was real? – unless someone else was looking. Tell me what you saw or are you ashamed to tell me?

RICHARD: No. I saw him kissing you on the mouth – on the neck . . . behind your ear . . . I saw him undressing you. I saw him kissing your breasts. I saw him put his hands between your legs.

GEORGINA: And what did you see me do?

RICHARD: I saw you kiss him on the mouth. I saw you lying under him on the floor of the pantry. I saw him take you from behind. I saw you take his penis in your mouth. I saw you . . . (*She weeps*)

GEORGINA: Have you ever seen lovers behave like that before?

RICHARD (*after a pause*): My parents behaved like that.

GEORGINA (*surprised and delighted*): They did?! You saw them?

RICHARD: . . . and lovers in the cinema sometimes behave like that.

GEORGINA: That doesn't count.

RICHARD: . . . and in my fantasies . . . lovers always behave like that.[23]

Richard's statement, 'What I saw was what you let me see' implies that she is directing the situation; but her reply, 'Of course it was – how else could I know that it was real? – unless someone else was looking' suggests that there are no answers beyond the subjective gaze of the viewer. Of Richard's three responses in this dialogue to the question of the verisimilitude of the lovers' behaviour – that his parents did, that lovers in films sometimes do, that lovers in his fantasies always do – Georgie rejects only the second; and it is this that Greenaway seeks to discard too. His cinema habitually draws attention to its contingencies, its artifice, especially with regard to the pressing issues of sex and death. *The Baby of Mâcon*, his most controversial and least critically successful film, culminates with a judicial rape of a young actress carried out on stage by 208 members of the militia, and the killing and dismemberment of the eponymous child, and does so since

> the film attempts to convince a cinema audience of two phenomena I have never been able to suspend disbelief about in the cinema – copulation and death; at least not copulation outside of the pornography genre, and death outside the documentary. I have never seen a snuff-movie. I do not believe in the death of Olivier as Richard III or Welles as Othello or Brando as the Godfather. And neither of course do you. At least after the film is over, you don't. And yet the actor's obligation to simulate dying, death and the dead is commonplace in cinema – one might say it is almost an actor's most regular activity. It is rare also to contemplate a cinema which does not very frequently require actors and actresses to play at being lovers, which today may very well require them to simulate the act of copulation. *The Baby of Mâcon* plays with these impossibilities and with an audience's suspension of disbelief about these impossibilities.[24]

Recently, however, Greenaway has become increasingly suspicious of the medium in which he works, precisely because it is so rigidly exclusive. In 1994 he wrote:

> I feel, on perusal of the finished artefact, that I, too, am being strangely and curiously short-changed. I want the illusion of the moving cinematic image, but I also want the delights of

the original ideas, formats, strategies and texts, the excitements of the expertise of the collaborators, the reality of the props and the sets. And as a consequence I would wish to find ways and means of communicating to others and re-communicating to myself these fascinations.[25]

Above all, Greenaway's films offer an inventory of the tools for representation; and his 'fascinations' are the artificial orders and structures that a film-maker necessarily creates. Hence, the drawings in *The Draughtsman's Contract*, the letters in *Z&OO*, the figures in *Drowning by Numbers* or the colours of *The Cook, the Thief* are simply the means to create a representation of an individual thing, each addressing human possibility while remaining in themselves nothing. Hence, the mood of Greenaway's work is ludic and also elegiac; as though he is constantly aware that even with the camera, the set, the script, the props, the actors – the materials out of which any film can be made – you actually have nothing at all but the potential. In February 1996, as part of the *Spellbound* exhibition at the Hayward, he exhibited an installation, 'In the Dark', designed to break down the cinematic experience into its constituent parts. Ever the taxonomist, he separated out the main elements of film – light, sound, script, props, actors, and audience – and left the visitor to invent his own scenarios with the materials provided. He seemed to be encouraging a DIY approach, perhaps the kind of approach that led the Deuce brothers to build a set, which became the final stage of their decay; their condition either preceded representation or was just too late, pointing out how a civilization used to go about these things. Typically, Greenaway's works exist between this stance of forecasting unlimited possibilities and the other, of monumentalizing and effacing a no longer active past. The twins were destroyed by the very system of representing the world they so punctiliously established; their investigation ends in failure because the world refuses to be constrained by artificial discourses, and nature overcomes the limits of their devices and desires.

Greenaway's films, however, are only half the story. Indeed, he is an artist of international stature, the 'content' of whose work in several media manifests a consistent concern for certain recurring themes and ideas – the human body; mortality; reproduction, both artistic and biological; the problems of illusionism; the need to create taxonomies, and the obligation, equally pressing, to destroy them – and the form of whose work is made increasingly manifest in an obsession with the artificiality and contingency of the cinematic imagery with which he secured his reputation in the first place.

CINEMA AND PAINTING

Born in 1942, Greenaway is of that English generation that referred to an evening at the cinema as 'going to the pictures', an expression that suggests that film and painting are by no means mutually exclusive. 'I started my career a painter,' says Greenaway, 'and painting is still, for me, the supreme visual means of communication. Its freedoms, its attitudes, its history, its potential. And if you look at twentieth-century painting, it's been ten thousand times more radical than the cinema has. . . cinema is a grossly conservative medium. It's by allusion to painting that I try to further my passion for painting. Painting stimulates me more than any other cultural activity.'[26] Consequently, Greenaway's cinema invests heavily in art history, and he invariably hangs his films on paintings. His own canvases and collages punctuate the early experimental film *A Walk Through H*; Georges de La Tour and Januarius Zick provide the key to *The Draughtsman's Contract*; Vermeer presides over *Z&OO*, Bronzino and Piero della Francesca over *The Belly of an Architect*, the Pre-Raphaelites over *Drowning by Numbers*, Frans Hals and the genre of Dutch still-life over *The Cook, the Thief.* Titian, Giorgione, Botticelli and Bellini, among many others, feature in *Prospero's Books*; artists as obscure and various as da Crevalcore, Desiderio and Bellini are used in *The Baby of Mâcon*; and most recently *The Pillow Book* borrows from Utamaro and Hokusai, to depict lovers of the 'floating world'. Greenaway claims the rationale of this borrowing is simple:

> I like to make reference to painting as an example of perfection, a metaphor of vision and of looking; it's my acknowledgement of two thousand years of European painting of which cinema is the most recent heir; a recognition that painting and, I hope, cinema are vehicles of reasoning and speculation and, finally, the expression of a pure pleasure before such objects, such icons.

One such example of perfection and of the convergence of poetry and painting is a work by the late-eighteenth-century English artist Joseph Wright of Derby, who made it his entire business, closeted with the new technicians, to render the glint, shine, glisten and glow of artificial light on every metal, surface and texture he could lay his hands on. In keeping with the characteristics of his reputation as an 'industrial tenebrist', and because it offered a comment on his profession, he painted a version of *The Origin of Painting* in which

> a young woman of Corinth, anxious about the departure of her lover, traces the silhouette of his shadow on a wall as a remembrance of his true likeness. A shadow on a wall. A true likeness. The fixing of shadows. A remembrance. Perhaps there could not be a more suitable iconography to begin the history of cinema as well as the history of painting.[27]

Clearly, there are Platonic ideals working within Wright's distinctively lit canvas; most particularly, the parable of the Cave in Book 7 of *The Republic*. However, that phrase, 'the fixing of shadows', conveys Greenaway's own sense of the obligations incumbent on an artist painting with artificial light.

Nevertheless, Greenaway is keen to distinguish between his own practices and those of other directors who work with paintings.

> Most so-called painterly referencing in cinema is limited to copying superficial resemblances in a spot-the-reference kind of way, and film appreciation, such as it is in this area, is usually confined to such adjectives as 'painterly', which, I suspect, is usually merely a lazy synonym for 'picturesque'.[28]

Jean-Luc Godard tested the principle of the 'picturesque' in *Passion* (1981), in which a director – in order to announce his not being Delacroix, Ingres, Poussin or Rubens – tries to recompose some of their most famous canvases as *tableaux vivants*, in the hope of finding the origins of masterpieces. However, it is all in vain; how can the essentials – the natural world, the gestures of people – be painted anew even in a different medium? Greenaway makes a similar point:

> It strikes me that all the problems that have ever been set by somebody else for a painter to solve, or any problems that any painter has set for himself and solved, have been done time and time again in the 2,000 years of European visual history. Those same problems come up in terms of cinema.

There's obviously a slight difference as you have to contend with ideas like sound and movement which a painter doesn't have in his vocabulary – but constantly for me, the whole 2,000 years of European painting is a vast encyclopaedia for dipping in, for making comparisons, for seeing what other people have done under the same circumstances.[29]

What problems has he in mind? As well as sound and movement, which he mentions, what of perspective, representation, mannerism, illusionism? His 'obviously a slight difference' is a brushing away of the claim that cinema, being a medium of expressly broad and fast strokes, has little time for the still and quiet patience and stasis of representational art. 'Since film is not painting – and not simply because one moves and the other doesn't – I wanted to explore their connections and differences – stretching the formal interests to questions of editing, pacing, studying the formal properties of time intervals, repetitions, variations on a theme and so on.' But Greenaway here also draws attention to the fact that often film is set up and sets out to conceal the chronology of its own making – the time of its takes, the period that elapsed in its making. This is a theme in much recent film theory. Most influentially, Gilles Deleuze, taking Henri Bergson as a point of departure, argues that the distinction of film lies in the possibility of reproducing pure 'movement extracted from bodies or moving things', a 'movement image', which is the function of a series of equidistant instants reproduced in a sequence of shots. Ultimately, 'the cinema is the system which reproduces movement as a function of any-instant whatever'.[30]

In this respect, cinema *has* revolutionized painting: 'The Lumière brothers' passenger train, sailing into the sensorium straight out of the vanishing point of perspective, punctures the frontal picture plane against which painting had gradually flattened itself during nearly a century,' observed Hollis Frampton.[31] Before the brothers' cinematographic projections, one of the boasts of the painter was that he could capture evanescence: wind, clouds, water, rain, rainbows, even trains. Consider Turner's *Rain, Steam and Speed – The Great Western Railway* (illus. 5), where the smears and smudges of the oils reproduce water, steam and velocity; but even the steep foreshortening of the viaduct out of which the bright blur of the locomotive's headlamp emerges is not enough to convey the sense of fright-

ening speed that could be achieved by frames passing before a
projector's light source. Jacques Aumont has suggested that,
after Lumière had filmed the impalpable, the immaterial, the
play of light in clouds of vapour, 'il n'y aura plus de nuages en
peinture, de nuages naifs. Ils deviendront ironiques, chez Dali,
parodiques, chez Magritte'('There will no longer be any naive-
ly painted clouds. They will become ironic, in the hands of Dali,
or parodic in the hands of Magritte.').[32] Or, as Godard put it, 'les
changements de lumière amènent les changements d'idées'
('changes in light lead to changes in thought'). Hence, earlier in
his career, Godard dared to 'cinematize' (the word is Eisenstein's) painting in order to announce the new superiority of
film as a medium, which was easily capable not just of recasting, say, a landscape by Turner or, as we shall see, a light effect
by Vermeer, but also of bringing an added sensation to bear, a
recovering of sensuality.[33]

In 1972, Greenaway executed a diptych entitled 'If Only Film
Could Do the Same' (illus. 6). This is a work of sensual overlapping forms, of oils and collage, in colours mainly of deep pink,
blue and brown, the colours, respectively, of 'the human skin
under stress, bruising and the sun', Greenaway noted as an
afterthought.[34] There are traces of organic forms and natural
forces, of human arms and trunks and of human identity, as
well as unnatural ones – valves, electrical equipment, a list of
'D's and possibly a mushroom cloud, partly obscuring the

6 *If Only Film Could Do the Same . . .*, 1974.

phrase 'the wrongway'. He exploits optical possibilities: the mesmerizing power of a tantalizing pattern or grid lines fading and disppearing just off the canvas. Greenaway avoids facile violence and symmetry and varies his motifs and designs inventively, with dramas of clear-cut forms set against the haze of colours. The shapes are cut out from various materials – cardboard, newsprint, wallpaper, a monthly calendar – and contain, among other things, fragmented day-date watches, the buckles on a school satchel, a razor. There is a running headline in bold type, **ISSUE**; an arbitrary sum, £670; Death Valley pasted on a female torso above a pair of bikini bottoms and, in Greenaway's own cursive hand, the word 'madness' followed by a question mark. What might be the answer to this arrangement? Time certainly, especially as manifested in the strict routines of hygiene and education; the contingencies of the body; and perhaps even the burning heat of Death Valley converging with the big heat of Hollywood, and especially the Valley of the Dolls. Greenaway concludes, abstractedly: 'the dim and the sharp, the flat and the faded, the assertive and the self-effacing . . . if only film could do the same . . . but we expect content and narrative continuity of film and could never conceive of shape and colour being responsible enough to provide coherence.'[35]

However, Greenaway's meditation on art history goes much deeper to the heart of cinema than this painting allows. For him, it is a question of animation, a question of negotiating between two basics of the film image: the stillness it shares with painting and photography, and the motion that decisively distinguishes it from the earlier visual arts. Godard claimed famously that 'le cinéma, c'est vingt-quatre fois la vérité par seconde' ('cinema is truth, twenty-four times per second'). It is not simply that film is endowed with sound, or that it knows how to record the clouds, or that women in swimsuits make a splash when they enter the water; it is also that 'cinéma a un point commun avec la peinture: la caméra, comme le chevalet, tient sur trois pieds. Or, on ne tient pas debut sur trois pieds. Il faut trouver le quatrième' ('Cinema has one thing in common with painting: the camera, like an easel, stands on three legs. Now, one cannot remain standing on three legs. One has to find the fourth.') There are similarities; but in both forms a leg has been lost. Greenaway's conscious effort to allude to the styles of specific painters within his own frames draws attention to these compromised structures by, in effect, recasting them. When brought together, two visual styles – the stillness of painting and the motion of film – create a play of artifice, even if, separately, each aims at creating an illusion of 'reality'. In other words, they annul each other's illusory space and so stress their existence as *fabricated* images.

A glaring instance of this fabrication occurs in *The Belly of an Architect*, when Flavia, a professional photographer, says to the hero, Stourley Kracklite, in the course of a shoot at her studio, 'I don't know how to paint, but I can take photos'. She has invited him to assume the pose of the model in Bronzino's portrait of Andrea Doria painted as Neptune, and is herself filmed from behind, working the shutter of the camera as she checks the reproduction of the portrait in her right hand (illus. 7). This convergence of the three modes of representation – painting, photography, cinema – operates by a process of collation. One shot shows the face of Doria painted as Neptune; this is immediately followed by another of Kracklite in an identical pose, complete with false beard, and standing stone-still; and then, when the model blinks, comes the realization that the image, seemingly static, in fact forms part of a filmed sequence (illus. 8). Here Flavia is a thinly veiled metaphor for the film-maker, since

7 Agnolo Bronzino, *Andrea Doria as Neptune*, 1556.

she has assumed the role of the manipulator, who is simultaneously an almost neutral observer, dependent upon an antecedent source. It is a good example of the method of work that Greenaway likes to employ so often: creating doubles of himself, fictional personages, pursuing their own ends through references to painting. But, in the end, all may come to nought through betrayal.

Consider, in this regard, André Bazin's influential essay on 'Painting and Cinema' in which he argues:

> Not only is the film a betrayal of the painter, it is also a betrayal of the painting, and for this reason: the viewer, believing that he is seeing picture as painted, is actually looking at it through the instrumentality of an art form that profoundly changes its nature. . . the sequence of a film gives it a unity in time that is horizontal and, so to speak, geographical, whereas time in painting, so far as the notion applies, develops geographically and in depth.[36]

The disposition of these comments about the flatness of cinema as opposed to the depth of painting also reflects the larger Modernist consciousness of form and convention, the understanding that reality and its reproduction are, in one sense, not separate events. 'Reality' is produced whenever it is rendered in a given form, and that form perceived in its turn; and yet it is only the conventions of form that permit perceptual discrimination of the 'realities' of the 'real world' from the photograph, painting or film. Filmic conventions developed out of an ideological need to create illusions of an unmediated 'realistic' world as it might be 'directly' perceived; and although the cinema's use of dramatic conventions and movement within the frame, along with montage, separated it from the static contemplation of 'reality' inherent in, say, seventeenth-century Italian, Dutch or French painting, as has been pointed out by a number of critics, the articulation of space in classic narrative film and the construction of the spectator's relationship to that space follow the basic conventions of post-perspective, representational painting.[37]

Although, in Bazin's view, 'perspective was the original sin of Western painting', it was 'redeemed by Niéce and Lumière', in other words, by photography and cinema, which he regards as 'discoveries that satisfy, once and for all and in its very essence, our obsession with realism'. The work of painters, no matter how skilfully it might incorporate the rules of perspective, 'was always in fee to an inescapable subjectivity'. Greenaway puts the point more forcefully and more cynically:

> A painter can cheat. Canaletto painting Venice. Saenredam painting Amsterdam churches. Piranesi drawing Rome. Even Sickert drawing Camden Town. The painter easily invents multiple vanishing points. He is cavalier with scale. He keeps an arbitrary palette. His ubiquitous vision is enviable. He can see – with apparent conviction – both sides of the same wall at once.[38]

However, for Bazin, photography, unlike painting, 'completely satisf[ies] our appetite for illusion by a mechanical reproduction in the making of which man plays no part'.[39]

Many of these points are reiterated when Bazin uses what he terms the 'ontology of the photographic image' as a basis for another famous essay, 'The Myth of Total Cinema', in which he presents cinema as the inevitable goal towards which 'all the techniques of the mechanical reproduction of reality in the nineteenth century' were tending, 'namely an integral realism, a re-creation of the world in its own image, an image unbur-

dened by the freedom of interpretation of the artist or the irreversibility of time.'[40] This 'guiding myth', as he describes it, is the consequence of complementary outlooks towards seeing and reproducing what is seen, which have made the cinematic image a powerful and yet peculiarly limited visualization of sight. For Bazin, as for the dominant film industry (and many critics and theorists who otherwise have little sympathy with Bazin's defence of realism), the sheer potency of the cinematic image derives from its (generally unrecognized) limitations – that is, from its exclusion of any kind of seeing that is not amenable to mechanical, optical and photochemical reproductions of Renaissance pictorial perspective.

By incorporating painterly perspective into its image-making apparatus, cinema has maintained the 'cultural concepts' that give each member of the audience the sense of seeing the image from a privileged and unique point of view, while remaining distanced from it. This is what Stephen Heath calls 'the positioning of the spectator–subject in an identification with the camera as the point of a sure and centrally embracing view'.[41] The problem is that the view provided by the camera is not 'sure' and 'embracing' at all. It tallies with the norms of pictorial perspective and imposes them on the cinematic image, and it denies the 'spectator–subject' the possibility of experiencing a truly individual perception – just as it stands between the artist and his or her desire to create images true to an individual perception of the world. Film extends a franchise by effacing its very structure of representation and so, in a sense, inviting the spectator perceptually to enter its space and substitute it for the everyday 'reality' that is itself effaced in the silence and darkness of the cinema. However, all too often, after this process is over, cinema just leaves us in the dark.

Greenaway, always looking to draw attention to the contingencies of twenty-four frames per second, is keen to suggest that the fixed image is ever redistilled by the onward rush of the film. The frame, carefully weighed up by Greenaway, both in the sense of a portion of filmic space – twenty-four of them per second passing through the gate – and of a sign of delimitation around an image, exists to fictionalize and fabricate the real – not to capture it and enclose it but, instead, to free it into a spectacle that the eye is unable to apprehend merely passively.

As Bazin contends in 'Painting and Cinema':

> The outer edges of the screen are not, as the technical jargon would seem to imply, the frame of the film image. They are the edges of a piece of masking that shows only a portion of reality. The picture frame polarizes space inwards. On the contrary, what the screen shows us seems to be part of something prolonged indefinitely into the universe. A frame is centripetal, the screen centrifugal. Whence it follows that if we reverse the pictorial process and place the screen within the picture frame, that is, if we show a section of a painting on a screen, the space of a painting loses its orientation and its limits and is presented to the imagination without any boundaries.

This distinction between 'centripetal' and 'centrifugal' is crucial. A long static shot taken by a fixed camera head-on is the most obvious manifestation of this pictorial language; and it is Greenaway's trademark. Before such a fixed shot, the visual elements are arranged in its lines, its fixed ratios; and, just as the fixed frame lends power to the constant and ongoing process of transformation, so the viewer's gaze, inscribed in the lapse of time, demands and receives a period of contemplation. Yet the fixed image is frequently juxtaposed with the moving image in Greenaway's cinema, the lens of the still camera insinuating itself into the very folds of the action that unrolls before the turning camera, and so doubling and contradicting the moving image. In *The Belly of An Architect*, for instance, the illicit liaisons of Louisa Kracklite and Caspasian are not caught on moving image but are trapped in endless stasis in a series of snapshots recorded in long tracking shots. This is where the truth of the affair emerges; the fixed image offers secrets to which the moving image was not privy. As Comolli suggests, cinema is most fully aware of itself as a 'machine for simulation' that achieves only a 'mechanical and deathly reproduction of the living'.[42] Hence, in *Z&OO*, the flashes that come so regularly capture, in the first instance, the imperceptible movement of decay in the corpses on which the twins experiment; and yet the (de)composition then played back as a moving picture offers frenetic movement, as the body putrefies. In effect, it is a narrative of sudden loss, normally invisible to us and yet ubiquitous. It may be that, as John Berger writes, 'Everything converges on to the eye as to the vanishing point of infinity. The visible world is arranged for the spectator as the universe was once thought to be arranged for God.'[43] Thus individual consciousness believes itself to be the maker of the discourse it sees, everything falling into place according to the individual's point of view. Although this may suit the bourgeois ideology of individualism, it does not mean that, in fact, individuals are experiencing their own perceptions of the world. These thousands of single images, which the brothers take so carefully, are above all questions without answers; at the end of the film, in the movement from stasis to action, the insoluble mystery remains. Nothing has been solved by this attempt to frame their grief.

A FRAMED LIFE

It seems to me that dominant cinema seems to require an empathy or a sympathy between the film and the audience which is basically to do with the manipulation of the emotions, and it seems to me again – and this is a very subjective position – that most cinema seems to trivialize the emotions, sentimentalizing or romanticizing them. Now, the relationship a viewer has with a painting is somewhat different. You don't go into the National Gallery of any famous capital city and cry, sob, laugh, fall about on the floor, become very angry – it's a completely different reaction. It's a reaction which is to do with a much more composed sense of regarding an image; it's a reaction with a thought process as opposed to an immediate emotional reaction. It's my contention that there is no reason why we cannot bring this sort of reaction over into cinema.[44]

This is a plea for disengagement from the emotional simplicities of the cinema in order to regard images in a more 'composed' fashion; and, as with so many of his pronouncements, Greenaway's word is subtly and mischievously ambiguous, since it suggests the need for greater self-control and more artifice in the act of seeing – what he sometimes calls the 'stares'. This sense that the look is an unstable act in our time often surfaces in his work, and his films raise the issue by means of their making paradoxical demands that we undertake several acts of seeing simultaneously; following maps, say, or reading manuscripts, or looking at ornate calligraphy on screen while, at the same time, watching a film. But is this doubling of activities any different from the ordinary division between looking at the painting's surface for its effects of touch, stroke, colour and shape while also looking at what is represented within the frame, and even beyond it?

Take Burne-Jones's painting *The Hireling Shepherd*, which Greenaway claimed as a source for *Drowning by Numbers* (illus. 9). In the primer for that film, he describes the canvas in detail:

> [It] depicts a delectable slice of English late summer landscape with sheep and corn and willows. In the foreground are a young man and a young woman engaged in some form of

9 William Holman Hunt, *The Hireling Shepherd*, 1851–2.

tryst – he apparently importuning her. That is a fair description of the picture at first perusal. And it is enough if you wish it to be.[45]

Certainly, Hunt claimed that his first intention was to concentrate on the representation of nature: 'my first object as an artist was to paint, not Dresden china bergers, but a real Shepherd, and a real Shepherdess, and a landscape in full sunlight, with all the color of luscious summer without the faintest fear of the precedents of any landscape painter who has rendered nature before.'[46] F. G. Stephens writes that in this picture Hunt was 'absolutely the first figure painter who gave true colour to sun shadows, made them partake of the tint of the object on which they were cast, and deepened such shadows to pure blue where he found them to be so'. In doing this, says Stephens, Hunt relied on the latest scientific thinking, particularly 'Davy and Brewster'.[47] Absolute visual truth becomes the basis of his art; style and meaning are synonymous. Consequently, Greenaway now pushes on further and reads the picture as an abstract composition within a Victorian frame:

> The painting 'works' well. The sense of place – however artificial – is totally convincing. It is excellently composed – a complex of abstract structures – two-dimensionally up and down and across the picture-space, and three-dimensionally from the foreground grass to the horizon – it securely holds together. It has great 'presence' – there are strong sensations of warmth, shade, stuff and substance. The sleeping sheep is heavy, the green apples are bitter, the grass in the ditch is wet, the woman's feet are palpable. With no trouble at all you can walk about the painting like you can walk about a landscape – there is enough evidence to name all the plants.

That word again, 'composed'; and under its influence, Greenaway's account of this 'complex of abstract structures' makes the act of looking a familiar kind of double act. A greenish area with a certain set of shapes is also a ditch – one of Greenaway's preferred places, incidentally[48] – a flock of sheep, an open hand, a keg slung from the hip, some apples, a spread cloth. In a wider sense, it is also part of a human act of seduction in a certain social scene. Every coloured shape is, from another side, once again seen two ways: first, as a flat design on a surface; second, as a feature of illusionistic space in front of or behind, parallel to or receding from the surface. Greenaway continues:

All this could be enough – we would leave an Impressionist painting at this stage – probably much earlier – and leave it possibly with great satisfaction. But of course there is much more. The painting is an allegory – and the signs are numerous. Whilst the shepherd idles with the girl, the sheep have got into the corn . . . there is a nursery rhyme for the occasion . . . the shepherd shows the girl a death's-head moth – emblem of mortality. Eve's green apples are on the girl's crimson dress. In the beautiful landscape: carelessness, mortality and wantonness stalk the beautiful Eden. Delight in the painting for the painting's sake is now coupled with enjoyment of the significances of the imagery . . .

As this imagery clusters at the painting's margins, looking beyond itself for completion, it creates a set of hinges to the significances beyond itself. The young girl is enticed, and, not unwilling, she is about to fall into the hireling's arms. However, if he seduces her, he will not stay to answer for the temporal consequences – pregnancy – any more than he will stay to answer for the straying sheep. The permanent consequences, however, cannot be eluded. The death's-head moth symbolizes the situation; though neither of the participants looks at it in their absorption in each other, the insect is the dark heart of the picture. To them, it functions merely as the flimsy excuse for their embrace; but they ignore its true meaning at their peril. The moth is as ephemeral as their sin will seem but, like the sinner, the insect is self-destructive; and this one even carries on its back the grim symbol of death, the consequence of sin. The apples in the central foreground cannot help recalling the Temptation and the Fall; the flowers on the right are marshmallows, themselves perhaps a symbol of desolation, but also an indication of the marshy nature of the ground. Indeed, the whole field is a morass caused by the choking up of the stream which runs from the right of the couple back into the picture between the willow trees that border the field. The girl's bare feet rest on the marshy ground, but it offers no foundation, and she sits on the edge of calamity. Indeed, the shadow of a tree is already falling across her legs, though the couple has not yet left the true light. By existing as a conspicuous arrangement of parts, both physically in the composition and artistically in the different symbolic systems, the work presents itself as an aggregation, opening itself out tolerantly to wider significances:

But of course there is more. Hunt first exhibited the painting with a quotation from King Lear:

> Sleepest or wakest thou, jolly shepherd?
> Thy sheep be in the corn;
> And for one blast of thy minnikin mouth,
> Thy sheep shall take no harm.

The painting rides on Holman Hunt's major hobby-horse – 'anger and dismay at the neglect of the spiritual values . . . the shepherd represents a muddle-headed pastor who, instead of guarding the sheep, having found a symbol of evil, discusses questions of no value with people who could not care and are only interested in distracting him more . . .'

The less perspicacious viewer now might find himself becoming a little impatient and antagonistic to the picture.

In other words, beyond the frame exist significances, allusions to mid-nineteenth-century religious controversies.[49] Words, painting and objects work together, but only when this highly intellectual set of perceptions lets us overcome their stubborn diversity. Order is either organic, as in a row of neatly arranged trees, which draw our gaze deep into the damp ditch across which a sheep is escaping; or it is obscure and theological: Christ's flock in need of spiritual guidance. The pressure that binds together this painting is a pressure of intellection and not an act of painting:

> This painting does not reside high among the greatest paintings of the world - but it is a work that is complex enough to allow numerous layers of interpretation to be peeled back without endangering the original reasons why it attracted attention. In some ways it works more mechanically as a vehicle for lateral examination than some of the great Dutch moralist painting.

For Greenaway, the very act of seeing provides the script; and the clues for seeing a work of art can be brought into the open only by working out the similarities and differences between what goes on in the presence of the work of art and what goes on in a variety of quite different discourses, different frames.

And it is the realization of this that has enabled Greenaway to discard the image in his films and depict what so unexpectedly lies beyond it; the frame becomes not the unique locus of objectivity in a world of subjects but a subject in itself. He repeatedly returns to frames because they are all we have: the content of

10 Pages from *A Framed Life*, 1988–9.

11 Pages from *A Framed Life*, 1988–9.

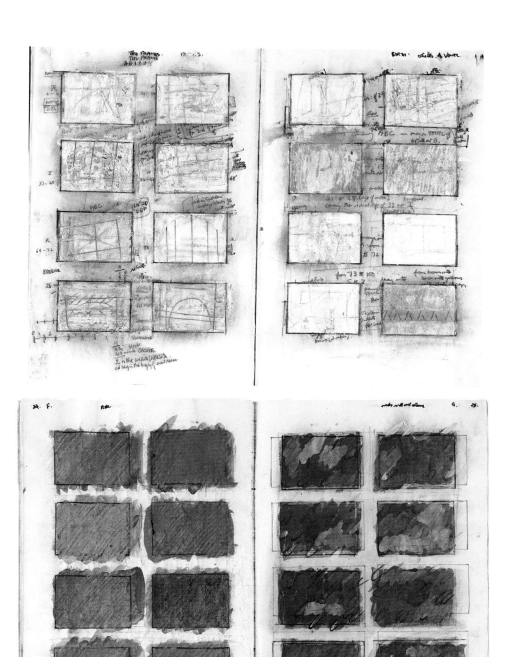

37

the world we possess and the only clues to the lost Eden we intuit. The frame reveals everything and nothing; it is the mystery of a total banality, a surface that is nothing more than raw exposure, unhealed wound. There is nothing more to seek; what lies beneath is a void. This fascination led him to undertake a major sequence of paintings entitled *A Framed Life*, which attempted, he claimed, to 'squeeze a life into a frame' (illuses. 10–13):

> Conception, birth, childhood, puberty, sex, love, marriage, adultery, maturity, illness, senility, death – all held together in a fixed rectangle. For a time these frames – often organized in sequences of eight with a common characteristic, a common colour-base, a common shared texture, a common shared medium – provided me with a minimal base for several projects.[50]

In these isolated members Greenaway achieves an extraordinary visual expression of one of the prime truths of our perceptual experience: that what appears to us as whole is nonetheless incomplete, and what appears incomplete is nonetheless whole. Rectangles in negative on the white of the unadulterated paper are deployed like a grid, and within these frames he grafts together various kinds of representational languages – the expressive mark, the diagram, the tracing, the map, a manuscript – and cleaves slates of vision, planes of perception, from air and earth. In a dusting of fading words he marks the path of sight, settling slowly in the mind, and precisely evidences feeling by fastidiously avoiding any suggestion that it captures or represents the totality of experience. That would be a necessarily fraudulent aim and claim. Greenaway's frames witness the experience of life, yet they do not report or document it; instead, their enigmatic ellipses provide the essential space for the imagination to illuminate, albeit artificially.

In strictly pictorial terms, an interplay occurs between the surface orientation of the frames of the grid and images of varying degrees of illusion within. The grid disciplines the eye; the gaze oscillates from the external extremity (the margin of the image) to the internal boundaries of colour and cadre. Hence, the painted frames are charged with an unoriented, empty energy, and gain all the more strength from their articulation on this grid which holds in the flicker, the deep pulsations, aerating them and rendering them visible. Each frame, however

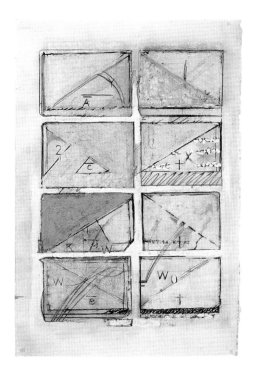

apparently simple, is thus an enigma, because it points (but never goes) beyond itself. It is both a thing and a symbol, itself and other, not in some static equipoise but on the perpetual verge of metamorphosis. Each frame – or in the terms of art, each image – thus presents itself under the absolute pressure of its own transformation, so that the only way to represent an object is as that which is about to become another, and yet remains itself. As he explains:

> They are all alive in their own right by slight shifts of colour, texture, and substance. As your eye slides up and down and back and forth across the frames they animate the rectangle. Working on the principle of retinal remembrance, the eye believes either that there is movement – as in a flick-book, a Muybridge photographic sequence, a Maray multiple-image sequence, a bande dessiné, a storyboard, ultimately a film sequence – or the eye believes in a steady state image and that all eight rectangles in one sequence are all the same rectangle, producing a single, times-eight, superimposed image of great richness. These two effects, it is hoped, may one day be elaborated into true cinematic or televisual movement.[51]

Consequently, there is a sense both of shrinkage and of growth; sometimes the image seems to spread into the frame, sometimes the frame seeps into the picture; and this confusion of thresholds has emotional implications. The experience, one might say, is edgy; though denying a definite external threshold, the smaller images insist upon their own autonomy. And Greenaway insists on it too; for despite being minimally representational, these frames are highly illusionistic, providing a distinctive three-dimensional effect, achieved through shape and colour, where one stripe or smear floats or rises in front of another, and the layers of planes recede into a depth of field.

Yet beyond the formal aspects of their structure, the grids also provide Greenaway with non-illusionistic breaks. Their delineated spaces can be used to convey comparison and variation, and to give the instant of a painting a duration – for narrative purposes – by compelling the eye to proceed from panel to panel, unfolding ideas, and so mimicking the narrative process of motion pictures. One might say that, like the Deuce twins or the Lumière brothers, Greenaway in these paintings and elsewhere in his work undertakes the act of framing not singly or discretely, but in a dense aggregation of different discourses. As he explains: 'There are many different vocabularies at work here – a filmic vocabulary of fading and mixing, an animator's vocabulary of clipping and pasting, a compositor's vocabulary of spacing and margins and perhaps even a sheet metal worker's vocabulary of welding and drilling.' The cluster of associations objectified in the central impasto of *A Framed Life* is also a compound of many frames; but these, realized in the mass of artifice, are no longer separately identifiable or recoverable from it. Hence, throughout his work, Greenaway comes closest to the underlying formal ideal of a coherence without objectification, a space defined by light as much as by shape, by the margins of the frame as much as the subject matter. In a wider sense, he is fulfilling a certain illusionistic aspiration of Western art, first visible in Piero della Francesca, then Vermeer, and more abstractly stated in Turner: the triumph of colour over image, of light over linear structure itself. In Greenaway's work, it is as if the most painterly effects of these Old Masters, originally wedded only to illustration or adornment, have become at last a full and irreducible subject for the cinema.

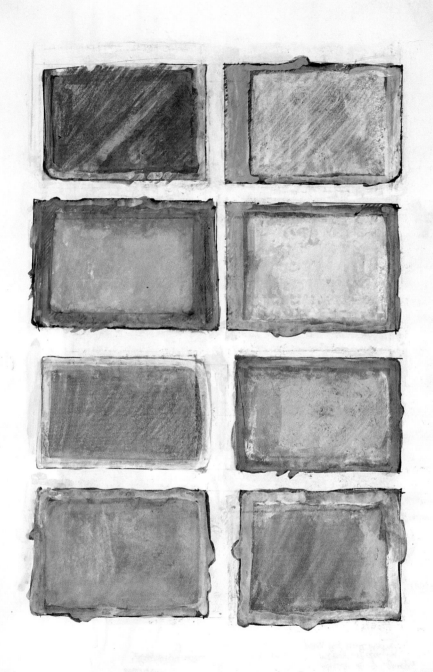

2 Art and Language

From the outset of his career, Greenaway deliberately sought to ground his projects in contemporary painters rather than cinematic *auteurs*; so that even now, as an established film-maker, he often walks around the film set 'with a book of R. B. Kitaj's paintings under my arm, whether we are shooting seventeenth-century melodrama or twentieth-century architecture – he is a painter in whom I have not a single misgiving and I could not say that about any film-maker'.[1] His indebtedness is so deep because, quite simply, Kitaj by making reference to the grammar of Modernism in the surfaces, structure and literary references of his work, yet simultaneously drawing on an idiolectic vocabulary of imagery culled from the library and the museum, showed Greenaway the vast artistic potential of the arcane. As Peter Wollen puts it:

> Like Greenaway, Kitaj maintains an impenetrably enigmatic relation to his sources. Like Greenaway, too, he is drawn to the arcana of old engravings, incunabula, emblems or maps . . . At heart, Greenaway, like Kitaj, is a collagist, juxtaposing images drawing from some fantastic archive, tracing erudite coincidental narratives within his material, bringing together Balthus and Borges in a bizarre collocation of bizarre eroticism and *trompe-l'oeil* high modernism.[2]

In the early 1960s, Greenaway attended Walthamstow College of Art, but for much of the time he was feeling curiously aimless in his work:

> I didn't really know what I was doing – I was repeatedly told my paintings were too literary, I was not interested in observational work or being a dispassionate documenter, or even a passionate one. Art schools are so successful at breaking your confidence.[3]

Greenaway reacquired his confidence in 1963, when he visited the Marlborough New London Gallery, saw Kitaj's work for the first time and witnessed a 'deliberate display of artifice aligned to powerful meaning, all made attractive and entertaining in the most positive way'.[4] Of course, he was not unique in feeling this about the American's work, which 'presaged the development of many young artists not just in his commandment to representation but to passionate convictions about particular themes and to a freewheeling synthesis of separate elements filtered through the artist's sensibility and related to a coherent subject-matter'.[5] But Greenaway told an audience at Sotheby's in 1990:

> I suddenly saw this body of work that legitimized all I had hopes of one day doing. Kitaj legitimized text, he legitimized arcane and elitist information, he drew and painted as many as ten different ways on the same canvas, he threw ideas around like confetti, ideas that were both pure painterliness and direct Warburg quotation; there was unashamed political passion and extravagantly bold sexual imagery. His ideas were international, far from English timidity and English jokiness and that English timid and jokey pop art.[6]

Kitaj famously asserted in 1964 that 'some books have pictures and some pictures have books'.[7] While some of the paintings exhibited at the Marlborough Gallery contained representations of common objects and figures and seemed to be complex expressions of repressed impulses, others were swift, fierce sketches of chthonic potency, expressed in no more than a stroke or two. Yet, in each case, Kitaj was attempting to find a viable pictorial matrix in his art for the intellection he had derived from the *Journal of the Warburg and Courtauld Institutes*; or to map the ground from which point line and space seemed to generate each other simultaneously, so that no element was there before any other. Often, this amounted to text itself being imported into the frame of the work, this use of the written word, as Marco Livingstone has noted, 'unparalleled in the art of his contemporaries'.[8]

Take, for instance, 'Specimen Musings of a Democrat', which includes a bibliography and whose scenic disposition was in fact based on Frances Yates's account of an alphabet table devised by Ramon Lull, a medieval Catalan philosopher. In the same way that Lull invented a system in which 'ten questions are to be asked of the "subjects" with which the Art deals', so Kitaj, in the grid structure of his painting, intended to show the changes of various image-types under six separate influences.[9]

Greenaway considers the structure of this painting in his Sotheby's lecture:

> As in much twentieth-century painting from Mondrian to Le Wit, here is the grid again, a hard background discipline directly related to the picture's rectangular framing and ratio and flat surface – a space for organizing and filling with disparate information – to suggest a legitimate, homogenous whole.

The dimension of the grid is particularly significant in evaluating these early works; as their spatial boundaries were arbitrarily fixed by the frame of the canvas, so their structural ones were determined by Kitaj's decision to break off a given relation of experience or knowledge at any point and replace it with a grid, 'variable in the ratio of one side to another, but rectangular in essentials, a composite cross-structure of horizontals and verticals'.[10] Consider *Trout for Factitious Bait* (1965) (illus. 14), a canvas clearly influenced by the abrupt, montage-style construction of the screen prints Kitaj had been creating at the time, and whose title was taken from Ezra Pound's 'Hugh Selwyn Mauberley'. Kitaj glossed the image with the following comments:

> A lot of old stories are malingering in *Trout* . . . old formalist persuasion, old briefcases and houses, old colours and arrangements . . . worn-out conjunctions . . . battling a modernist legacy. It can't have much of a future, that picture.[11]

14 R. B. Kitaj, *Trout For Factitious Bait*, 1965.

44

15 *Under the Ice*, 1994.

Yet this gamey picture found a future in Greenaway. The briefcase, for instance, may belong to his alter ego, 'Tulse Luper'; the oddly dislocated house may emerge in *H is for House*; and the ladder in the *Draughtsman*'s drawings or *The Stairs* exhibitions mounted in Geneva. The painting's imagery, its 'old formalist persuasion', manifested in the seemingly random clutter of grids and containers, draws the eye not so much to smudged single images but to the connections and juxtapositions between them. This technique, which Kitaj has termed 'plural energies', still has a bearing on Greenaway's own art.

A recent painting by Greenaway, *Under the Ice* (illus. 15), part of a series of works based on various aspects of the Daedalus myth entitled *Flying Over Water*, seems to borrow much from Kitaj's concept of plural energies. In its colouring and shading, it conveys effectively the possibilities of frozen water, of blocks of solidifying liquid, and simultaneously develops an approach to painting based on the principles of colour theory, which effectively excludes both subjective and emotional elements. Through the constant repetition of one primary spatial concept,

45

the rectangle – and by permitting only variations of size and colour within it – the absolute form of ice is ineluctably linked with the relative qualities of the colours, from blue to white. By means of a strictly rational artistic exercise, which can produce results of a spiritual and meditative character, Greenaway ensures that his image shifts the rational principle imperceptibly yet unequivocally towards the irrational.

As he freely admits, 'I think both the device of the grid for picture-making, and the list for text, are essential to my cinema practice – naked demonstrative ways of organizing information in some sort of coherence'. Indeed, most of Greenaway's early films are indebted to the grids, hieroglyphs, cryptic signs and suggestive letters of the type that exist in Kitaj's own early works. Retaining the significance that they were first accorded by Greenaway at the Marlborough Gallery, the American's scattered signs certainly represent a broken pre-text evoking a primary artistic process; but they are too undeniably antecedent to be shunted aside, appearing instead as the framework around which a finished film narrative is structured. Consequently, in the films Greenaway made between 1966 and 1980, primitive drawings, decorated maps and encoded systems of signs guard hidden worlds of secrecy and intrigue familiar from Kitaj; but, equally importantly, they also draw attention to the relationship between image and text, the quotidian and the bizarre, the arbitrary face of the landscape set against the face of an arbitrary culture.

Take *Vertical Features Remake*, a film Greenaway made in 1978, which recounts the secret history of the 'vertical features' that the strange 'Institute of Reclamation and Restoration' found around Glasbury on Wye in Herefordshire following the instructions left by one Tulse Luper. The commentary of this fake documentary – one of the most beautiful experimental films of the 1970s and Greenaway's most considerable work to date – suggests with an absurd seriousness and careful logic a labyrinthine structure of chilling intrigue; but at the same time the film's mock erudition is brilliantly matched by the director's own sense of locale and landscape. Real places, not just artefacts, vanish before they can really be seen or, in Greenaway's terms, known. The 'vertical features', images of trees, posts, fences, rugby posts, etc., are arranged in sequences of eleven, choreographed with Michael Nyman's pulsating chords in three separate dimensions of landscape. They emerge with the light of dawn, live during the day, decay in the dusk and are then revived again in any and every order, so that they may ascend into oblivion with the last frame of film. Greenaway's vertical features arise in a compelling abandonment to particular nature, and in this are not only more than formally classical, but also relate to a radically human way of marking out the world. Throughout the world human beings marginally, respectfully, and magically inscribe their ways with beaten tracks, stone-paved paths, cairns and shrines; and the film chimes with these. In a world mundanely sacred, commonplace materials can remind us where we are and what there is. Greenaway's discriminating restraint, his momentary insertion of formality into nature, also draws into the mind's resonance overtones of a sculptural transfiguration of nature within an accessible object of contemplation.

'None of these objects was ever manipulated,' Greenaway has said. 'Everything was found'; all were *objets trouvés*. In other words, the film implicitly asks how an author might reconcile his own time and space with those of his avowedly fictional representations without seeming hopelessly recherché or even phoney. The issue is encapsulated in one of the research images made by the archivists and theoreticians, and which appears in the film (illus. 16). A network of fine lines incised into the colour describes and reorders a world made up of water and pigment. The drawing spreads out in horizontal strata, at once penetrating and giving a structure to the opaque matter of the background. Little reality filters into the painting in the form of annotations; yet it is extremely arcane and formal. Hence the place and the journey are reinterpreted in the gleam of the intellect, given over and worked upon by memory and reminiscence. In these spaces formed by imagining information and indicators, Greenaway, through his fictional investigators, seems to restore, but in transcendent form, the landscape, creating it anew, abstractly. As the title of the film indicates, such research evokes a kind of ascending perspective. With considerable control over the distribution of colour and line, he achieves a division of the different levels and has them flicker among themselves. This fragmentation based on repetitive lines invites the eye to decipher and explore, but ultimately offers only fragmentary solutions. Such a sense of the unfinished, the contingent, is familiar in Greenaway's work at this time; and, indeed, it had been laboriously worked out in several professional posts.

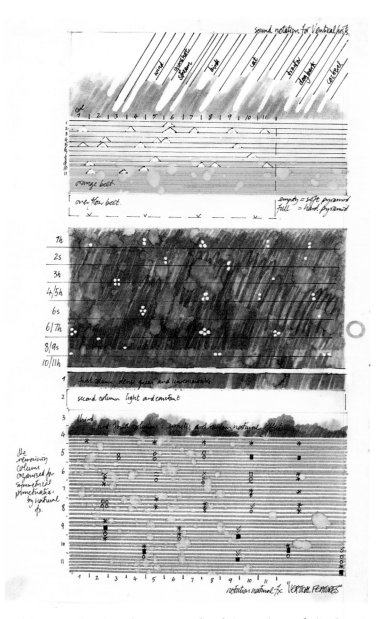

After graduating from art school in 1964 and 'trying to arrange successful painting exhibitions', Greenaway gravitated towards the darknesses of the British film industry. Taken on first as a doorkeeper at the BFI, he then found work in the distribution department (which allowed him to see hundreds of short films –'experimental, rarely seen, personal and cheaply made' – from the archive) until eventually he was employed as a 'third-assistant-editor on trial' in the broom-cupboard cutting-rooms of Soho. He began his apprenticeship here, and, having acquired raw film stock, began after hours to assemble his own films. In 1965 he was taken on by the Central Office of Information, the publicity arm of the Foreign Office, where he spent the next eleven years as an editor in the Crown Film Unit, cutting films that were designed to portray the strange intricacies of the British way of life through numbers and statistics such as 'how many sheepdogs there were in North Wales, how many Japanese restaurants in Ipswich'.[12]

> We were basically ledger clerks, organizing information on bits of paper which will be seen all round the world. The quality might have been abysmal, but the viewing figures were impressive – about one-sixth of the world's population, a figure even Spielberg might envy. Much of it was very boring but I was left on my own, with huge amounts of film to edit every week. You had to make decisions very fast. Often the shooting was less than perfect so you had to cheat, to learn ingenuity.

Greenaway's formal examination of the artifice inherent in systems of categorizing began here. In the work completed between 1965 and 1980, he imitates the structures of manifested authority such as the catalogue, the matrix, the grid, even the documentary form itself, which, by the late 1960s, had become a cliché of British cinema. However, the act of imitation serves only to mock, shedding light instead on the inherently chaotic and irrational ways in which society orders itself and the often arbitrary relationship between image and text. These early works allude to the institutions and discourses of cinema, art, literature, local history, and some aspects of the media and forms of journalism that might be considered culturally significant, or endowed with what Pierre Bourdieu has called 'cultural capital'.[13] Each representation gives rise to the next in a pattern remarkably close to Terry Eagleton's description of postmodern cultural production where 'meaning is indeterminate, plural and diffuse, a weave of codes and an inexhaustible tissue of signifiers, every image woven out of every other image, these are not so much influences as intertextual'.[14] Consequently the imagery is fragmentary and obscure to the degree that it finds its resolution in other, absent and not always determined texts.

An early short film, *Intervals* (1969; 1973), his first to gain distribution, provides an easy pointer to the impulses behind his more mature work. Over the course of seven minutes, holiday-film shots of Venice – easily distinguished from typical touristic attempts at cine-filming by their calculated composition and the omission of images of water or famous Canaletto scenes – are assembled and reassembled into varied combinations. However, the footage of Venice seems to have been shot arbitrarily, without any established notion of a soundtrack, let alone a shooting script; and the sole aural accompaniment is offered by what seems to be a Berlitz 'Teach Yourself Italian' recording. One of the credits states, 'Camera '68-69. Dubbing '73'; so typically, Greenaway was exploding expectations here – the Super 8 of the tourist – in order deftly to avoid responsibilities to narrative and, instead, revel in images that exist for their own sake. On one level, this may represent nothing more than the filmmaker's penchant for pastiching structuralist theories on such things as subject-construction in language.[15] More directly, the choice may have been designed to 'expose' the covert intentions behind the vacuous holiday shots, by way neither of explanation nor of opposition but of associative 'correspondence'. This sense that innocent façades may hide deeper significations is developed more fully in the films that follow.

In 1973, Greenaway spent a holiday in a friend's early nineteenth-century house in the Nadder Valley in Wiltshire. He was immensely moved both by the visit and the area, and they drew from him various visual responses on canvas and on screen, the first of which was *H is for House*. The tone, as before, is that of a home movie made on a bright summer's day; but on this occasion it is more personal, because Greenaway films a woman and a small girl – his wife, Carol, and daughter, Hannah – over the course of a summer's day pottering about at a house in the English countryside. Superficially, Greenaway offers a straightforward celebration of the sweet disorder of family, in a setting of dairy pasture, apple trees and large, unkempt lawns. However, the idyll is brought to a point of convergence with Greenaway's own constant concern with techniques of formal organization. *H is for House* is not merely a portrait of the beauty and ambience of architecture and *terroir* but also a quirky study of the process of naming things, the bafflingly arbitrary and confusing means by which words and objects are ascribed with meaning.

Through his daughter, Hannah, who at the time was learning

the alphabet, the film records and encounters the world through the mediation of a single character, the letter H. *H is for House* originates out of a childish list of elements connected only by the coincidence of their beginning with the same letter. The soundtrack features Hannah's voice repeating words and making mistakes; however, above and beyond this agreeable prospect, Greenaway superimposes his own rendering of a child's alphabet, except that he seems fixated on the letter "H". Hence:

> H is for Health, Happiness, Hearse, Hepatitis, Heretic, Heave, Hell, Holocaust and His Holiness . . . H is for Hat, [Hugh?], Hatchet, Hammer and Hitchcock. H is for Handicap, Handicraft, Handiwork, Handkerchief and Handle . . . H is for Cigars, Havana Cigars . . . H is for Hopelessness, Happiness, Homelessness. . . . Hesitation . . . H is for Bean, Haricot Bean and Has-Been.

Simultaneously, his daughter interrupts with her own definitions, linked to her outlook, of the other letters of the alphabet, brief extracts of Vivaldi following each of the girl's interpolations.

And at the film's third level, the voice of an ornithologist – the first of many to feature in Greenaway's early work – offers still more precise information, loosely though suggestively connected with what we see, consisting of three bizarre anecdotes relating to the points of the compass and time. Hence, a naturalist is thrown into confusion when the world starts spinning anti-clockwise; a countrywoman scans the horizon awaiting the approach of the City and is effortlessly foiled by the developers; rival sun-watchers start bickering:

> Controversy arose, the rift between those who looked east in the morning and those who looked west in the evening led to argument and abuse and ultimately to blows. Cynical observers began to look west in the morning and east in the evening and a group of satirical opticians began to look north and south in the middle of the night.

The mixture is tantalizing. Mrs Greenaway cuts the grass, a cat nudges about among some abandoned plates, a tortoiseshell butterfly flutters against a window; and set against this is the precision of Greenaway's spoken effects, the weaving of the three voices, the anecdotes winding away into absurdity.

The content of *H is for House* and, of course, its title, illustrate a concern with letters of the alphabet which returns in later films. Both *The Draughtsman's Contract* and *Z&OO* feature a child acquiring the letters of the alphabet; in the earlier film the rote learning is directed towards fruits; in the latter towards animals. Here in *H is for House* the principle is both local and universal, as the letter, purloined, isolated from its linguistic function, existing in its pure form, is deployed as a character, invested with a significance as arbitrary as any of the living, breathing figures that film habitually depicts. One may observe, in this regard, the influence on Greenaway of some of the structuralist 'underground' experimental film makers of the 1960s and late 1970s – Hollis Frampton, for example, whose *Zorns Lemma* (1970) plays a structuralist game with the letters of the alphabet. The film's opening section over an empty screen – a filmic void – consists of a woman's voice reading an ABC rhyme excerpted from a textbook; the second section is made up of one-second shots depicting single words, usually found on signs or notices, arranged in alphabetical sequence. In due course, as Frampton rehearses the alphabet, every time making use of a different set of words, each letter's space is filled by an arbitrary elemental image – the sea, fire and so forth – so that by the close of this section, Frampton has fabricated a unique pictorial alphabet, existing beyond rule or logic, each image correlated with a single letter.[16]

Another point of reference is James Joyce, whose late work *Finnegans Wake* features the characters of ALP, aka Anna Livia Plurabelle, the mother, and HCE, the father figure, the 'doomed but always ventriloquent Agitator', whose 'normative letters' betoken an endless anagrammatic play. HCE appears as the 'EternalChimeraHunter' (*Finnegans Wake*, 107.14; my capitalization), at the heart of whose character is that hesitancy – 'finally called after some his hes hecitency Hec' (*Finnegans Wake*, 119.18) – linking fabrication and irresolution, and which is invoked in *H is for House*. In a short film made in 1977, *Dear Phone*, Greenaway seems to follow Joyce's use of HCE, in that language is drawn out of the world of communication and questioned in its production. In this remarkable short film, static shots of fourteen written texts recounting various fantasies involving protagonists connected by virtue of their sharing initials H.C.– Hiro Contenti, Harold Constance, Harry Contents, etc. – and their use of the telephone are alternated with thirteen shots of red GPO telephone boxes situated in thirteen different locations, and framed in various ways. Over the texts, a narrator reads the manuscript's largely illegible discourses – brief and apparently disconnected fictions, all of which are made up out of the common themes of love, sex, money and all of which inscribe some connection, however perverse, with telecommunications. Over the phone boxes, various telephone sounds – ringing, engaged and dialling tones, the speaking clock and conversations on crossed lines – are heard.

Images of the original manuscript are juxtaposed with its supposedly transparent yet necessarily opaque realization on celluloid, in a repetition along the phone line. However, as the soundtrack is composed solely of post-synch sound effects and commentary that supposedly reinforce, yet in fact contradict, the edited pictures – telephone tones are heard only over shots of empty call-boxes and the narrator's unhesitating voice only over images of the illegible manuscript – the delivery of the sound calls into question the fixity of the image. This structural opposition raises the question of enunciation and expression which has recurred throughout Greenaway's early films; here, across the grain of the voice, the text and the visible traces of the text, the narrative drive is both present and absent.[17]

Greenaway concentrates on writing as endless rewriting. Each page, written in his own hand, is crammed with corrections and crossings-out, and excrescences in the form of marginal additions, smudges and drops of water which dissolve the ink in places. The written accounts are indecipherable without the intercession of the narrator's voice which makes them clear to the ear, and which obliterates, with its regular rhythm, the many hesitations, indirections and second thoughts that reveal themselves in the bare script. It is this tension between the filmed script and the voice-over that reads the words on the page which drives the film; because occasionally there is a disparity between what is heard and what is seen. Take the fourth text, which tells of Harrin Constanti insulting the operator. There at its end, hidden *sous rature*, blotted out by a large drop of ink, are two lines of the manuscript that are not recited aloud. Moreover, the script, the trace of the body on paper, seems to have become one of the constituent elements of the narrative itself, as if even the form of the text on the page dictated the content of each anecdote, making of each story the reflection of its written support.

Since many of the narratives call attention to the cost of communication – both the mundane fact that having a line installed is expensive, and the more abstract sense that 'phones disembody people, and destroy any physical rapport between individuals – the very title, *Dear Phone*, offers the possibility of a play on words and images. Hence, the expression 'small change' which appears in Letter 3, where, it is revealed, Harry Contentino paid his employees poorly 'and expected them to keep him in small change for his phone calls'. This phrase denotes not just the monetary wherewithal required to make a call; it also implies the small changes, the tiny but crucial modifications attendant on moving from one persona to another, one H.C. to another H.C., one fiction to another, and finally emerge out of the dangerous vertigo of minimalism; of repetition for its own sake. The film is structured about such small change; the idea is of variation, of difference, which conveys a strange dynamic to the seeming fixity of the cinematic images.

The two final texts in the film are typed out, the last without a blemish, recounting the history of the character, or pair of characters, H.C., who 'spent a long time composing his letters' which he reads over the telephone to their recipients. The ambiguity is clear: what is the content of these letters? In due course,

> he felt that he had developed telephoning to a fine art. Over the years H.C. refined his style, concentrated on form until the content of his calls atrophied and he reduced his conversations to Dear Phone and continued with a list of names and addresses read from the telephone directory. The only people who did listen to him in rapt amazement were his mother and the very rare wrong numbers H.C. sometimes dialled.

Oral communication has now become a travesty of writing; the phrase 'to a fine art', pronounced so flatly, is laden with ambiguity, and marks the very last word on the attempt at communication. This fourteenth text, inscribing on the screen the destruction of content by form, is the end of the line for those fictional personages who have hung on for the last seventeen minutes.

In this way, the conventional relationship between script, image and sound is shown to be as essentially contingent as that between subject and object in lived experience. Every early Greenaway film, but *Dear Phone* in particular, is marked by the placing of the static 'passive' image in opposition to a moving 'active' sound track; the synchronization of light with time. This is seen in *Water Wrackets*, where shots of water in all its liquid patterns and under every light are surmounted by a narrated fictional history of an unworldly conflict. Like the other Greenaway shorts of the period, this film seems to place the supremacy and privacy of the first-hand view (images of flowing water) against the subordinate and public role of language (the history of the water wrackets). Ripples on the surface of a lake may evoke action and fiction in childhood stories of past and future wars; but the precise subtlety of the film is predicated on our culturally acquired knowledge that sight is as much constituted by systems of thought as language. In other words, the essence of the water can be imagined only through the existence of the absurd history. This tension in *Water Wrackets* between seeing and knowing (fiction and structure) makes it a particularly close relation to both *A Walk Through H* and *Intervals*. However, this film marks a significant advance on the latter because image and sound no longer run along parallel and separate lines, but weave in and out of each other in arabesque figures-of-eight. Just as the images of water exist outside any real time and place (not the past one of the filming, nor the present one of the viewing, nor, finally, the future one of the reviewing), so the history of the water wracket army takes place only in abstract Time and Space. But, crucially, there are, or so the film maintains, links to be found – however arbitrary – between image and sound, time and space, past and future. When the voice-over story of the water-wracket army seems to bear least relation to the stream of watery images, a single word hooks itself to a particular shot. A 'lake' or a 'hill' appears; then, as words and images flow ineluctably on, disappears.

Hence, Greenaway's apparently playful games with image and sound conceal some pressing questions about, among other issues, the metaphysics of knowledge. In conventional documentaries (such as those he worked on at the COI), the commentary track was employed to glue together, after the fact, as in the Greenaway oeuvre, a flow of unnarrated images. However, the arbitrariness of conventional documentary's juxtaposition of sound and image can be construed as a metaphor for the contingency of the relationship between the private personality (the reality of the author) and his public persona (the fiction of the text).

The most explicit sundering of the reality of the *auteur* from the fiction of his text is attained in *The Falls*. Its initial premise is an Act of God – a Violent Unknown Event – which has struck the world, leaving behind some nineteen million survivors. But, as it would be impossible to examine every one of these strange cases of sudden demise, the voice-over – consisting of Colin Cantlie's neutral tones – explains that only ninety-two case histories will feature, names of the victims having been drawn from the last edition of the Event Standard Directory, and connected by virtue of their commencing with the letters FALL. The subtitle of this catalogue is 'An Investigation into Biography'; that official-sounding noun introducing a report on a statistical given, a report as precise as the phenomenon reported – the acronymic VUE – is hazy and mysterious.

The physical transformations undergone by the victims of VUE are described in a cold scientific manner; and yet they are manifestations of the irrational. Some have become immortal, complicating their lifestyles somewhat; others are attacked by insects; one suffers a sex change, another an alteration in skin colour. The most common transformation imparts an extraordinary ornithological knowledge to its victims, but at the same time it affects their upper body and shoulders in such a way as to suggest the transformation into a bird. The film is, as ever, filled with the names and the images of birds. Beyond this, Greenaway makes some jokes at the expense of cinematic representations of the avian world. Hitchcock's *The Birds* is invoked on several occasions; and it is possible that one of the buried sources for the film is *Psycho*: when Norman Bates entertains his future victim in his parlour, the shot includes many of his stuffed birds and when she refuses his offer of food, he says,

> Anyway, I know the expression 'eats like a bird' is really a fall fall falls falsity. Because birds really eat a tremendous lot. But I don't really know anything about birds; my hobby is stuffing things. You know, taxidermy. (33′46″)

Norman makes the connection between 'falls' and 'falsity'; and it is this nexus that Greenaway celebrates, fabricating the biographies out of various filmic *objets trouvés* (discarded COI footage, old photographs, Greenaway's collages, as well as sequences specially filmed for the project between 1975 and

1978) and giving some sense of the unique personal circumstances of the encounter with the VUE by using the staples of the documentary form – stills, documentary, live-action, interview, reportage – within an incoherent text. 'I was just interested in all the different ways that you could put pictures together,' he said later in defence of his sprawling work.

And yet in *The Falls* Greenaway's structuralist quest for coherence is seen to collapse into nothing more than a rather despairing mirror-image of his own vocation as a film editor with the COI and to the forebears of that organization, the General Post Office's and the Empire Marketing Board's film units of the 1930s and 1940s. The marks of Grierson's ideal of cinematic realism – 'an art based on photographs, in which one factor is always, or nearly always, a thing observed' – are, however, always undercut by Greenaway's amusement at the genre's status as a cultural object.[18] For example, the voice-over, which by its very nature should be delivered off camera and out of sight, enters into our field of vision on several occasions when the narrator, headphones on his ears, is filmed in the act of reading the script to which we are listening. Greenaway's statement about *The Falls* – 'it was a compendium of all the editing techniques I've learnt and also a few more I've found for myself. And also all the other forms of representation vis-à-vis the visual tradition of Europe' – might be interpreted as implying that the film-maker had finally accepted that the fragmentary forms of the world were ultimately unclassifiable. And so the only truth left to represent was his confession that, as the spurious inventor of self-consistent artefacts, he himself was a fiction, a falsity. Hence the film discourses with neither its subject-matter nor its authorial style but its audience, ninety-two random people gathered to watch a white screen; and when one of the characters, Armeror Fallstag (Biography 81), is interviewed, in a limousine after arriving at Heathrow, the person who poses the questions and points the microphone, mimicking the investigative journalist, is Greenaway himself.

In this knowingly faked game of private jokes and fascinations, the film attempts to confront the inexplicability of disasters by representing them through language. Particular discourses, such as maps, catalogues and recorded data, may be understood as tools for creating order from chaos, providing practical opportunities for making connections whenever this is socially and politically appropriate. But just as in *Vertical Features Remake*, where they are presented as bogus, so here, the whole nature of the cultural representation is called into question. How does one explain the inexplicable? How does one put it into words and then images? In Greenaway's early films, either the images insist on the ghostlike presence of an author while the narration ridicules the notion, or vice versa; and, as in Kitaj, image and commentary often seem arbitrarily related. *Dear Phone* effectively attempts a visual record of all the telephone boxes in England, at every time of day and in every kind of place, while the soundtrack relates a rare collection of eccentric phone calls. *H is for House* is a home movie (one domestic set-up is used), which has been overlaid with a haphazardly spiralling lexicon. The author's home, perhaps, represents the world: the scenes of his daily life must stand for an outside world that remains a mere concept, a language, a lexicon. For Greenaway, what is real is precisely that physical truth which cannot be represented.

Literal-minded application to the factual and the material in his discourse is one of the strongest characteristics of Greenaway's work at this time: he does not fragment the object itself, but represents an image of fragmentation by means of the radical juxtaposition of a series of different objects, often incomplete in themselves, in a manner broadly comparable with his customary juxtaposition of images. Something of even greater signficance is that each individual work explicitly occupies a place of its own between the finite and the infinite, fullness and limitation, complexity and simplicity.

After leaving Walthamstow, Greenaway became particularly interested in the Land Art movement, which, at the time, was offering a new way of considering the English landscape based on the continuous presence of the artist in the natural environment. The results take various forms, using maps, words and photographs, to present places, routes, things seen, thoughts evoked and actions performed, and sculptures assembled from natural elements such as soil, twigs, driftwood or stones, which can be physically presented in the gallery space. For instance, the work of Mark Boyle, with whom Greenaway once shared exhibition space, consists of carefully presented and framed patches of earth; while Richard Long undertakes solitary walks in some of the remotest places all over the world, carrying on what has been described as 'a philosophical dialogue between the artist and the earth'. Much of Long's work is founded on geometric patterns, straight lines, spirals, squares, crosses, parallels, grids, but most commonly the circle. The significance of such structures is that they are distinctively human, existing as the simplest means by which the artist can compose his responses to the psychological complexities of man's relationship with the landscape. Indeed, the contrast of the geometric marks of man with the chaos of the natural world produces a more acute awareness of their interconnectedness. In Long's 'A Hundred-Mile Walk', for instance, he records his awareness of some of the sounds heard on the walk, how he became aware of the presence of rivers as he approached them, pockets of sound in the gullies, and how the sound disappeared behind him as he walked on. The work concerns both the internal feelings and thoughts of the artist and the external aspects of his journey, and records all kinds of sensory and perceptual experiences including time, space, movement, sight, sound, touch, taste and illusion.

In such manifestations of Land Art, Greenaway found an easy return to nature, but one differing radically from traditional representations. His very earliest films, *Tree*, depicting an old linden growing in the concrete outside the Royal Festival Hall, and *Erosion*, shot in Ireland, participated in that ethos; in both cases the rhythms and cycles of the landscape are brought into contact with geographical, social and ethnological reality. And Greenaway himself admits to undertaking a piece of conceptual art in the Nadder valley. Reflecting his interest in maps, he marked off an area of 2 square km and, using a large-scale Ordnance Survey map, planted ball-bearings at 10-metre intervals. He found, perplexingly, that the grid lines on the map often coincided with the roof of a farm building, or passed a tree trunk or a mare. 'If, however, I'd been able to plant my ball-bearings in a landscape of wax, sand and paint, I would have realized a possible means of rendering landscape in the twentieth century.'[19] Only cinema finally offered him the means of 3rendering the landscape through art.

Although Greenaway had hinted in *Vertical Features Remake* at the reality of matter, of new-found objects being shaped into simple and powerful figures, it was *A Walk Through H*, released later in 1978, that testified most eloquently to the strangely haunting relation between the passage of time and the arrangement of space that is found so frequently in Land Art. Made just after the death of Greenaway's father, who had a passionate interest in bird-watching, the film's alternative title is 'The Reincarnation of an Ornithologist'. Its solemn narrator tells how, minutes before his death, the maps that he had spent his life collecting were brought together and placed in some kind of order by his lifelong friend and fellow ornithologist Tulse Luper. Over the course of the next forty minutes, the camera shows us, in close-up, the paths that the narrator's soul supposedly took across these ninety-two deliberately ambiguous and often misleading maps, each of which has been drawn by Greenaway; each of which evaporates into a single meaningless symbol either just before or just after the narrator reaches them. And by the journey's end we return to the point at which we started – the camera pulls back to show that these maps are merely drawings exhibited in a gallery and do not correspond to or represent the world of fantasy into which we have let ourselves be drawn. These images are not fact but artefact.

Yet with their air of incipient transformation – of journey towards disclosure – these maps are, nevertheless, cinematic. Each circumscribes a neutral, menacingly denuded space, a frame or screen where anything may appear or happen; where narrative is frozen into the stasis of gesture; and where gesture, rounding back on emptiness and silence, finally invokes uncertainty. Just as Greenaway's previous work explored the vertiginous instability of a contingent world, so these canvases portray the horror of recurrence, of the forever frozen (because ceaselessly repeated) gesture, which is embodied in the idea of the map, and which is associated for him not only with the longing for flight but with various attempts to associate it with human freedoms, no less than material flux. As he observed in 1993, 'The map is three tenses in one. It can show you where you have been, where you are and where you will be. It can always show you where you could be, where you could have been and where you might like to be'.[20] The map must be read as a symbol, both material and figurative, of the quest; as much in the sense of psychology as topography. Some of the ninety-two maps evoke the meanderings and forms of the brain; but the final image upon which the camera comes to rest is a book, which marks both the beginning and the end, symbolizing perhaps both the simultaneity of the two extremes of existence experienced by the soul at the moment of death – a kind of time at which the end of the story remains fixed in the past tense, at the very same day and hour of the departure – and the simultaneity of text and image.

The film is divided into five sections, corresponding to urban landscape, countryside, forest maze, frontier and desert; from the cities of pigeons to the wilderness of crows. Throughout, the ornithologist is accompanied by images of birds, their images traversing the screen in increasing numbers as the film proceeds, often in the form of jump-cuts. This film's pretext is the word 'flight', about whose double meaning it hovers as it recounts flying and also fleeing; that liberating freedom from responsibilities expected by the land of the living. This is a long-standing fascination, and it reached its apotheosis in Greenaway's 1993 Louvre exhibition *Le Bruit des Nuages*, when he observed:

> The impossibility of personalized flight has naturally made it a prime subject for depiction as a frozen moment in two dimensions. A mocking perversity. Flight violently contradicts those two states of being. However, I, for one, am always eager to respect the intention of all those optimistic pictorial intimations that say, 'This is how you could fly if you could fly'. They are evidence. In the English language, flight also means escape.[21]

The same impulse leads the narrator to announce at a fairly early point in the proceedings, 'I was encouraged by the sight of a bird'; but does this mean that seeing the bird he was heartened, or that he had, by this time, acquired a bird's-eye view of the world? And then, equally pressing, there is the fleeing, the race against time; against the clock certainly, against mortality even, since the maps and the itineraries dissolve midway through the journey, causing 'the anxiety of the map fading through the wasting of time'. This concern even affects the title: rather than *A Walk Through H*, 'It was rather "a run through H"'. The energy of the film emerges from the preposition 'through', which implies not only situation but also recognition.

The film, which constantly plays with word, figures, images and the relationships between each, is also an exercise in reflexivity; that kind of mannered and oblique self-regard that Greenaway developed more fully in later work. It reproduces the process of its own fabrication. When the narrator says, 'I began to run; to hurry', this signals a sudden acceleration in the sequence of shots; similarly, the progressive form, 'I was running', is expressed visually by a long rostrum tracking shot of the canvas. However, when the image of a bird perched on a branch appears, the voice says, 'If he could relax, perhaps I could do the same', and immediately, the camera imitates this relaxation by undertaking a very slow shift to another map. The space travelled, the territory strewn with obstacles, with labyrinthine paths, also corresponds to the duration of the film: thus precisely two-thirds of the way into the film we are informed that the narrator has covered two-thirds of the distance.

Greenaway is undertaking a simultaneous exploration of the process of narrative and the process of film; and it is therefore very tempting, especially in terms of this picaresque narrative sprinkled with windmills at which one might tilt, quixotically, to hear an evocation of the creation of art in the words of the walker: 'Perhaps this territory only existed in maps, in which case it was the traveller who was creating the landscape as he walked across it.' The narrator speculates that the countries exist only in the cartographers' imaginations and realizes that by altering the maps himself he can alter the shape or direction of his own experience. At one point the narrator tells us that the usual intentions of cartography were now collapsing – 'Either that or the route itself was becoming so insecure that mapping it was a foolhardy occupation.' Maps, then – conventionally, a representative tool for creating order from chaos – are inevitably presented as bogus and absurd, so that the whole nature of representation is placed in doubt. These painted 'maps' are exemplary vessels of inauthenticity, their method of abstracting nature subverting the reality of being in the landscape. They substitute a cognitive condition of 'being unknown' – an ignorance that can be remedied, at least in principle – for an inescapable phenomenological tension which Merleau-Ponty referred to as *l'être des lointains*, the ever-present allure of distant horizons. The unreachable horizon locates where the speaker is and provides an essential ground of his being and his journeying. This aspect of the experience of landscape is missing from the conventional map, indeed is negated by its rejection of the possibility of any essential incompleteness, a rejection entirely consonant with the dominant rational view of the world. In this way the map, seeking to reinforce our well-being and self-possession, falsifies our experience of landscape.

At the heart of the film is a prolonged sequence that considers the most significant map, the 'Amsterdam Map' (illus. 17), which the narrator has allegedly stolen from Van Hoyten, the keeper of owls at the Amsterdam Zoo. At this point in the film, the elements are in free association, lacking the usual relationships between picture and caption, text and illustration, diagram and label. It is impossible to divine what is significant and what is marginalia, as trails of marks lead up down and diagonally. The eye has no orientation; it can only attempt to decipher the palimpsests of strange signs and symbols, the mass of clues and forking paths in which some kind of revelation about incarnation possibly seems to be concealed. And now Greenaway forces us to think about the relationship between mapping and painting as a question of format and a matter of function: that is to say, how a map implies the absence of a positioned viewer as if the mapped world pre-dated him, even though maps as pictures and picture-like maps were both engaged in gaining knowledge of the world. But in Greenaway's film, this is produced in an age of obliquity – the land is not surveyed and, rather than a direct confrontation with nature, there exists a trust in devices, in intermediaries such as maps that represent the landscapes for us.[22]

In these isolated maps, which together comprise the film, Greenaway achieves an extraordinary visual expression of one of the prime truths of our perceptual experience: we rely on the maps because they are often all we have. Take 'Who Killed Cock Robin' (illus. 18), a map created out of several media. A letter written in German in a cursive nineteenth-century hand forms the base of the map. Above this has been placed a piece of hand-made cartridge paper on which the leaf of a blackberry bramble has been traced minutely; so minutely, in fact, that the trace of an insect is included. Such accommodation is generous, since the insect seems to have eaten its way outwards towards the edge of the leaf, growing as it goes, until it needs a fatter passage to expedite its new bulk, a passage which is traced in the collage of the map. Also included here is a third piece of paper – nothing more than a slip, in fact, appended to the picture by means of a paper clip – which contains, in Greenaway's own hand, the place and the date of the observation. It is a piece of evidence which may be treated forensically; failing that, as he suggests in his commentary, 'one day the paper clip will rust and improve the picture'; a natural process will always better an artificial one.

Once again we are thrust back on the theme of the absent creator, with its religious overtone of the *deus absconditus*. In Greenaway's abandoned Edens, the void of creation always appears at one remove, the desertion of material objects by their human artificers paralleling that of mankind by its deities, the guarantors of forms. What remains is a menacing, residual vitality, the bafflement of things deprived of function. Like maps, these landscapes represent the mystery of an absent will, a loss, and grotesquely mimic the forms that begot them, humanized in the absence of man, just as man is mockingly divinized by the absence of God, or indeed any other great architect. Thus the

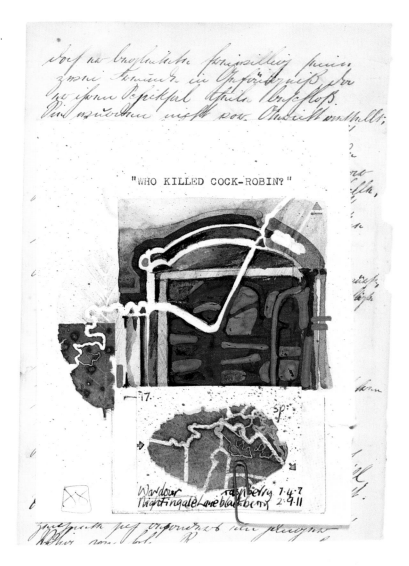

'Duchess of Berry Map', fabricated out a French engraving of the
mansard in which the notorious woman was arrested, shows the
route in the planes and angles of doors and walls, before indicating the sortie in the roof; yet our gaze remains fixed on the flat
picture plane, an entrapment, like the Duchess's, both sinister
and comic. And the 'Last Map' is created out of discarded
envelope, which seems to have been rescued from the floor after
having been stood on, such is its crumpled and grubby appearance; it is 'no more than a splashing of bird lime on the back of

an envelope, significant enough as always to the holder of the key, but a continuing mystery to the unititiated'. This marks the end of the journey; the last stop is a piece of paper destined itself to travel, to fly even, until it is torn apart by those expecting some kind of message concealed within.

So the winding path is gradually leading the viewer to a destination, for the paradox does have another salient characteristic, after all. It lays claim with great certainty to truth, but it is precisely that certainty that makes us suspect the opposite, the untruth. The play of opposites is an artificial construction, a black-and-white argument, and precisely because of that demands the most refined subtlety of thought. As a result, the paradox leads a life entirely of its own as a recherché, formal, closed statement whereby the world is reduced to two extremes: fact and artefact. Yet Greenaway knows that it is precisely this which possesses such a liberating character and implies an intellectual freedom; for paradox is the place where logic basks in creativity, so creating room for the irrational.

3 Fields of Vision

Midway through *The Draughtsman's Contract*, Mr Neville, engaged to draw a series of landscape pictures, engineers a liaison with his patroness, Mrs Herbert, whose reluctantly given sexual favours are forming the best part of their strict agreement. Turning his back to the camera, he cuts the laces of her corset with a pair of scissors, and meanwhile invites her to view one of her husband's cabinet paintings, which, he speculates, Mr Herbert acquired simply because 'he has an eye for optical theory'. The picture (illus. 19) is by the eighteenth-century German artist Januarius Zick (1730–97), and pays tribute, in crude allegorical form, to Isaac Newton's theories, which, according to the poet James Thomson, made us see that

> Even Light itself, which every thing displays,
> Shone undiscovered, till his brighter mind
> Untwisted all the shining robe of day;
> And from the whitening undistinguished blaze,
> Collecting every ray into his kind,
> To the charmed eye educed the gorgeous train
> Of parent colours
> ('To the Memory of Newton' II, 96–102)

White light is, in fact, complex and promiscuous, the phase of a metamorphosis combining several other things; and a phase which might be metamorphosed back again, as with a rainbow. Hence, Zick's picture is, partly, a paean to what Thomson elsewhere described as 'The various Twine of Light, by thee [Newton] disclos'd/From the white mingling Maze' ('Spring', 211–12).[1] A bright light breaks through the turbulent clouds into a timeless ancient scene, the focus of which is a young man – a representation of Newton – whose gestures establish him as hero and victor. He sets his right foot on the prone figure in the left foreground, who may be taken as a personification of Ignorance and Untruth. In his right hand, the conquered enemy holds a mask, symbol of deception and feigning, while about

his head snakes coil. Nearby lie his shield and his downcast torch, its flame burning bright white. Looking away, Newton, the conqueror of ignorance and untruth, points with his right hand at himself and with his left at the two bearded old men disappearing into the gloom. They are, to some extent, illuminated by the light shining on the front face of the sundial, which indicates the first hour of a new day and, by implication, the dawning of a new age. These figures may represent Euclid, the famous mathematician, and Diogenes, the cynic, who perhaps embody the most meaningful predecessors of Newton. They have, however, realized that a greater genius has now arrived, and so they willingly vacate the stage. Newton's light also falls on the childish figure, possibly Amor, in the centrally placed Temple of Virtue. The earthly goods burnt on the altar, as well as this helpless cherub, illustrate the frailty of wealth and love, which the hero, in striving after higher values, has evidently overcome.

19 Januarius Zick, *Allegory of Newton's Service to Optics*, 1785.

There is a rough and ready chiaroscuro effect here, as Zick seeks to suggest that light is both intensely changeable and a cause of change. Some lines from Thomson may be apt: 'The downward sun/Looks out, effulgent, from amid the flush/Of broken clouds, gay-shifting to his beam' ('Summer', II, 1666–8). The pleasures of looking at a scene are chancy and contingent, and synonymous with the pleasures of seeing the changes incessantly made by the passing of time and the perceiving 'I'/eye. Both the eye and nature waver; nothing can be counted upon to be constant, including the act of seeing. To observe, mentally or physically, is to experience evanescence, and the artist as central 'I'/eye must accept various transformations. In so doing, he may even see abrupt metamorphoses.

Hence, in Zick's picture there is a perplexing ambiguity about the figure in the temple, which adds a wider dimension to the allegory. Consider the manner in which Newton's spirit is reflected by the mirror above the altar at the rear of the temple. At first, the viewer is led to think it is a reflection because Newton's right hand, pointing to his heart, and the dove, hovering above his head, both appear reversed in the mirror. However, the certainty soon disappears, on reflection. The left hand of the real Newton points with palm facing downwards; whereas the corresponding right hand of the virtual Newton is outstretched palm up, in a gesture of reception rather than of indication. The real Newton seems to be looking at the old men, but, once reflected in the mirror, his head is slightly raised, and his eyes are, instead, directed towards heaven. Outside the confines of the temple, the dove with the olive branch in its beak may symbolize peace; but in the virtual image of the reflection, it may have become a symbol of divine inspiration. In the space between the figure of Newton and his reflection there is a transformation; our view of the hero has necessarily changed, and the question must be faced: how does the real measure up with the ideal?

As the voice of the Draughtsman offers his speculative commentary, the camera cuts to different aspects of this 'pictorial conceit':

There is drama, is there not, in this over-populated garden. What intrigue is here? Do you think the characters have something to tell us?. . . Madame, could you put a season to it? . . . What infidelities are portrayed here? Do you think that murder is being prepared?

It's a daring attempt by Neville to place things in perspective, to make sense of the confusing, the impermanent, the uncertain, in order to fabricate, to make what is three-dimensional life into a two-dimensional artefact. A perspective, then, is not a 'copy' of reality but an emanation of what was and still is; an evidential force, a partial narrative. Each close-up shot of the painting elicits another new question, which emerges into a continuum, in which the account of the painting begins to correspond with the plot of the film. The key elements of the film ('garden', infidelities', 'time', 'intrigue' and finally 'murder') are all present, refracted like light through a prism, or reflected as in a mirror.

'Do you see, Madame, a narrative in these apparently unrelated episodes?' asks the Draughtsman. No doubt Greenaway's swift cutting is meant to remind us that while the perusal is taking place, not only Mrs Herbert is being undone; equally, Neville – though he is unaware of it – is undoing himself. When, in the final moments of the film, he is murdered, his shirt, torn from his back, will be 'scattered about an estate, as ambiguous evidence of an obscure allegory'; and scattered within Zick's picture are images that will emerge later to indicate an alternative allegory. A lantern will be carried by Mr Noyes, when he informs Mr Talmann of the allegations against his wife; torches will be carried by the murderers and used to blind Neville; masks will be worn to conceal their identities; the fire smouldering on the plinth of the hermitage will consume Neville's thirteen drawings; and in the temple, the child of love, Amor, protected and sheltered against vicissitude, will, in due course, be engendered by the contract between Neville and Mrs Talmann.

In this pivotal scene, however, Greenaway is also allegorizing the language of cinema; of painting with light. As the rostrum camera moves, a point of view, a direction, is imposed from without (a voice off screen) and the image is directed. The close-ups allow us to see only a small section of the mysterious goings on within a garden in the same way as the fragmentation induced by the juxtaposition of several shots prevents the necessary space for a good overview. The camera takes in the content of the canvas on its own terms, so depriving the spectator of the control that might come from standing in front of a picture, free to stay there for as long as he or she likes. That question, 'Do you think the characters have something to tell us?', is posed by Neville to Mrs Herbert and captures several possibilities, from warning to conspiracy; but Greenaway is also making inquiries of the audience of the film. The general effect remains perplexing and causes us to reflect upon the gap between perception and comprehension, seeing and knowing. The question that both Zick and Greenaway ask is: Who is being directed by whom? Who is framing whom?

The Draughtsman's Contract was the first film for which Greenaway had a reasonable financial backing; it was the first time he had access to a large public; the first film for which he put together a linear narrative; and the first time that he scripted characters and their dialogue. Yet he had not turned away from the concerns of his previous works and the film carries through the basic formal pattern of his art. There was, more than ever, the need to explore the links between nature and representation as far as the individual is concerned; to make fun of rational perspectives; to measure the effect of time on space; to give some sense of the changeable beauty of the English landscape and to people it with a knowing sense of composition that only a painter could be expected to exhibit; to place into question, in the course of a narrative structure, the very credibility of that structure, and, finally, to introduce into the frames of a film some doubt about its limits.

Throughout the film, the question of frames and perspectives is considered from various angles; in particular the social, since new view-finding devices, such as a Claude glass – a small, blackened, convex mirror which could be carried round on coach journeys to make aesthetic sense of the passing landscape in the gentle light of Claude Lorraine – offered a new mobility to the viewer.[2] The framed representation was not integral to any locus (as in say Giotto's Arena Chapel or Michelangelo's Sistine ceiling): it did not cling to a signified, but could be executed anywhere. By the close of the seventeenth century, portable camera obscura, equipped with lenses and tubes to focus sharp images of objects from various distances, had been developed (illus. 20). Because of their pictorial quality, the images projected within the camera had the potential to become literal; whether used for artistic purposes, or just as visual surveys of places and objects, the pictures drew attention to the faithful recording of the world as seen by the eye of the beholder.[3] Consequently, the camera obscura 'coalesced into a dominant paradigm through which was described the status and possibilities of an observer';[4] and in Greenaway's film, this para-

20 Drawing
equipment, from
*The Draughtsman's
Contract* (1982).

digm centres on the labours of the Draughtsman who is
observed both before the easel and in the landscape, translating
what is seen into a 'scene' dependent on Newtonian optics.

Near the beginning of the *Opticks* Isaac Newton recounts how:

> In a very dark Chamber, at a round hole, about one third Part
> of an Inch, broad, made in the shut of a window, I placed a
> glass prism, whereby the Beam of the Sun's Light, which
> came in at that Hole, might be refracted upwards toward the
> opposite wall of the chamber, and there form a coloured
> image of the Sun.[5]

Since a prism is substituted for a plane lens or pinhole, the
device Newton used to develop his theories is not strictly a
camera obscura, though its structure is virtually the same: the
illustration of an exterior aspect occurs within the rectilinear
confines of a darkened space. At first sight, Newton's technique
might seem to objectify the gaze; it makes him less the observer
than the mechanic, the operator of an apparatus from whose
actual praxis he is physically separate. Hence, he seems to exist
as a disembodied witness to a mechanical and transcendental

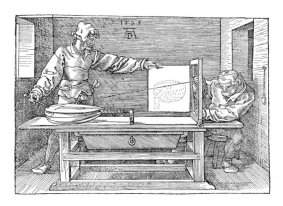

21 Albrecht Dürer,
Perspectival
apparatus, from
*Unterweisung Der
Messung*, 1525.

22 The Draughts-
man at work, from
*The Draughtsman's
Contract* (1982).

23 The Draughts-
man's grid, from
*The Draughtsman's
Contract* (1982).

representation of the objectivity of the world. And yet his presence in the camera also necessarily implies the simultaneity of
the spatial and temporal, of human subjectivity and objective
apparatus; the spectator a marginal supplementary presence
existing independent of the machinery of representation.

But 'who are these people who represent the world?' asks
Mrs Talmann of her boorish and impotent German husband.
For Greenaway, they are artists and directors. Turning his back
to the camera, Neville observes the garden through the grid of
his view-finder and so occupies a place which is equally that of
spectator and that of a director in the process of filming. A
famous engraving by Dürer (illus. 21) shows an artist pulling
strings from the object to the frame in order to achieve accurate
perspective; more conventionally, draughtsmen covered the
plane with a rectangular grid through which they looked at the
objects from a fixed point of view – sometimes with the assis-
tance of an actual eyepiece mounted in front of the picture
plane. Producing a drawing by this method was akin to captur-
ing images in a stiff net strung across the space between the
observer and the objects observed. Guided by the mechanical
system of grids and immobilized points of view, the Draughtsman landscaped in the black frame of his device; and in this

process an analogy exists with the language of cinematography, and, in particular, the way in which cinema directs the perception of the spectator by means of the realist tradition. The grid, like the camera lens, is presented as a framework for the real. But once it is so arranged, there is no escaping it. The true sense of the film commences with the establishment of this grid; with the division of the field and rearranging (or not) of reality that that implies, with the vision of the Draughtsman, his drawing by transfer of grid to paper, and so forth. To frame is to exclude, to select, to synthesize; and in representing Neville, the camera synthesizes the visions seen by the director with the images that he sets down in black and white. When Neville is occupied working on the details of the third drawing, for instance, which depicts the laundry, one image is superimposed on the next; the real and the represented occupy the same time on the screen, to the second. The cinematographic act partakes of the same desire to appropriate the landscape as Mr Neville's enterprise. We see the gloved hand at work; but inside the glove is Greenaway's hand, since the drawings were executed by him. The Draughtsman's contract exists also between audience and director. The whole narrative – the fact of the Draughtsman's finding or inventing clues to mutilation and murder, his discovery of corruption beneath the surface of the ordered English manor, or the portrait of his own corruption that surprises him within his drawings, corruption that he in fact installed by contracting to use his art as a means to sexual pleasure or perversion – draws or derives its movement from that same contract.

To 'be framed' (the *mise-en-cadre*, as Eisenstein puts it, rather than *mise-en-scène*) is to be forced into another's structure, a structure that is not of one's own making. Hence Neville, the framer, is being framed for the murder of Mr Herbert. This Draughtsman 'is definitely upright, an eye on the world, an eye that stations itself, with the easel carried from place to place, much like a tripod [for a camera]',[6] or a Claude glass. Neville's weakness lies in the fact that he clings obstinately to the simple equation of sharpness of vision with power. 'He draws what he sees', which, in practice, means an army of attendants ensuring that nothing changes from day to day. Neville demands that Mr Talmann, the person who has imposed himself into the frame, wears the same clothes the following day for the continuation of the drawing. Neville's regime is simple: 'I try very hard never to distort or dissemble', and so he is content with the choice of a single point of view. He lacks imagination to make the larger picture, and instead makes himself blind to any enlargement of his vision. He is pre-Newtonian: he sees things only in black and white and is, in effect, colour blind. He sees so much detail and yet sees nothing. With her eye fixed beadily on Neville, Mrs Talmann argues that

> painting requires a certain blindness, a partial refusal to be aware of all the options; an intelligent man will know more about what he was drawing than he will see. And in the space between knowing and seeing he will become constrained, unable to prove an idea strongly, fearing that the discerning – those he is eager to please – will find him wanting if he does not put in not only what he knows, but what they know as well.

He likes to think of himself as both an intelligent man and a painter; but her aesthetics will not allow such liberties to be taken or taken for granted.

'Your drawings are full of the most unexpected observations,' Neville is told by one of the dinner guests. 'Looking at them is akin to pursuing a complicated allegory.' These images, which the camera follows from their origins to their conclusion, are above all isolated plans which, because of their ambiguity, set up a multitude of possible interpretations that are foregrounded in the film's final sequences. It is to fabricate these images that the Draughtsman is invited to remain in place at Compton Ansty; and the juxtaposition, the 'montage', of these detailed images forms the heart of the film's intrigue. The drawings do not tell a story; instead they create a silence, while remaining vigilant for a narrative. They turn mystery into everything that is most domestic – sheets, boots, shirts – while at the same time suddenly solemnizing the human condition – birth, death, sexuality and transience. On one occasion, in a long and patient shot on a windy day, with the black-edged view-finder caught squarely in the frame, Greenaway captures the arrival of the sun, the movement of whose rays through the depth of field inflames the forms and colours, transforming the picture absolutely. It is a Newtonian effect also caught by Thomson's lines in *The Seasons*:

> A faint erroneous ray,
> Glanc'd from the imperfect surfaces of things,
> Flings half an image on the straining eye;

While wavering woods, and villages, and streams,
And rocks, and mountain-tops, that long retained
The ascending gleam, are all one swimming scene,
Uncertain if beheld.

('Summer', II. 1687–93)

As far as the film is concerned, it is a special effect, certainly, but one created naturally, and captured for the space of an instant in the rectangular frame of the shot.[7]

On the other hand, in many of the interior shots Greenaway devotes himself to the creation of chiaroscuro effects, using candles in particular. The candle makes visible the place where it is exposed, but it cannot be said that it illuminates. Nor can it be supposed that the people it illuminates realize that they are visible. In the sequence where Mr Noyes sets out to Mrs Herbert the facts of the blackmail that he has stirred up, darkness reigns within the room. The bright light of midday is not allowed in; instead it filters across the closed blinds to be consumed by the luminescence of the candles, which, like those lighting up the opening of the film, arbitrarily give out their evanescent glimmerings. When Mr Noyes clarifies himself and the plot with the phrase 'the Draughtsman's contract', a servant enters and, with her, the light of day. All that Mrs Herbert can do is to conceal herself behind her black fan.

In *The Draughtsman's Contract*, as elsewhere in Greenaway, there is a manifest desire to create compositions that, in their stasis, their colour and their arrangement of internal forms, suggest the conventions and signifying systems of representational art, and, in particular, the styles and techniques of seventeenth-century painting. In the work of such artists as van Honthorst, Rembrandt and de la Tour, chiaroscuro light reveals truths and half-truths; but the revelations exist without the knowledge of the figures portrayed, who are caught unawares at the table or in their bedchambers or in reverie. This sense of the private world invaded from without is, of course, at the heart of the film's plot, and it's captured well by Greenaway's direction. For instance, in one sequence, bathed in muddy brown light, Mrs Neville is shown having her feet washed by a servant; a candle burns in the centre of the frame (illus. 24). It is a glimpse of domestic routine; but it is also an unmistakable visual allusion to Georges de la Tour's *La Madeleine Terff* (illus. 25). The intellectual connection is simple:

24 Homage to de la Tour (i), from *The Draughtsman's Contract* (1982).

25 Georges de la Tour, *The Repentant Magdalene* (known as *Madeleine Terff*), (?)1616.

26 Homage to de la Tour (ii), from *The Draughtsman's Contract* (1982).

Mrs Neville is made to resemble a woman reflecting on and repenting her prostitution.[8] Later, when she is presented making her toilet, weeping before her daughter, she clearly finds the role she is expected to play difficult. 'So; I am grieving because Mr Herbert is away?' she asks, to which Mrs Talmann replies, 'Yes, mother.' Among the reflections of her dressing-table, a mirror permits us to see Mrs Neville's face, turned away in three-quarter profile, bathed in tears (illus. 26). The other world

27 Georges de la Tour, *The Repentant Magdalene*, known as *Madeleine Fabius*, (?)1616.

is there in the dark waters of the mirror, which stands out like a door opening on to another world; just as the green water of the estate's moats and ditches hides dark truths, including Mr Herbert's corpse. This chamber scene is clearly modelled on another of de la Tour's Magdalene canvases, known as *Madeleine Fabius*, a painting in which the Magdalen expects to see her own features but seems instead to see the world of the dead and its silence (illus. 27). Through the silence of Greenaway's scene, ordinary things strain for an extraordinary intensity. The traditional tears of the penitent do not run down her face; and she is not a repentant Venus but a mature woman whose body has been abused and who now finds herself thinking of her losses. The seductress no longer looks at us; nor does she look directly at her daughter. She looks at the reflection, which, in a sense, is no longer her own.

Elsewhere, Greenaway seeks to draw attention to the fact that his shots are so obviously posed. For example, during the evening sequence, when Neville and Talmann argue about aesthetics, the dinner table is shown in section, and then twice revealed in its entirety by a slow and evenly placed track right and then left. This technique draws attention to the constructed nature of the film's fictional space, while simultaneously criticizing the conventions of classic cinema in which mobile framing and tracking shots are given a pay-off in the form of a narratively significant action. On the level of content, the constructed nature of the social relations at Compton Ansty is also emphasized. It is precisely this tension that Greenaway is playing on when Mrs Talmann reminds Neville that their first sexual liaison is imminent. She approaches him by tacking across the area he has chosen to represent, and which he wants to be immutable and sacrosanct. As she approaches she is deliberately strewing his field of vision with items of her clothing. The effect of this stratagem is not just to render visible the eroticism that is so clearly a part of their contract; also, her methodical transgression of all his instructions and interdictions, which are heard at this point on the sound-track, is designed to suggest to him that the landscape is prone to unforeseen changes, traces of mutability, signs of life, even, which it is both presumptuous and absurd for an artist to seek to abolish. Hence her phrase, delivered directly to the camera, is resonant: 'It is time, Mr Neville.' This is not just a reference to their liaison; it also draws attention to the passing of time, which we have just experienced on screen, and to the shifting contingencies of life, which Neville's art can neither countenance nor encompass.

AGREEMENTS IN BLACK AND WHITE

It is Neville's intention to 'fix Mr Herbert's property on paper'; and Greenaway's film is fascinated by the need to fix, which lies beneath all the contractual obligations. For those who enjoy order, who value the status quo, what could be more reassuring than the terms of a contract? Everything is fixed in advance in the strange registers of the law, whose clauses, terms and codicils can legislate even for the most outrageous behaviour, if it is properly agreed in advance. All is drawn up in black and white, just as Neville's pictures are set down in the same neutral tones. For Mr Talmann, his wife's alleged misbehaviour appears in the drawings in 'black and white for all the world to peer at'. Yet the combination of black and white does not just imply a lack of colour: the resultant greyness can conceal a mannered obliquity. In the final scene, Neville is especially exercised by the fact that Noyes, though custodian of 'private agreements in black and white', seems to have lacked discretion and allowed his own ambition to colour his actions.

Greenaway's characteristic sense of verbal, as well as visual, texture is at work throughout. He told an interviewer that the title of the film was chosen with great care. 'Draughtsman' implies design – a designer of cars or planes or a person who draws the country houses of the aristocracy; or indeed the role of an artist, as when Leonardo draughted the sketch of the *Virgin of the Rocks* or his helicopter. Moreover, 'draught horses' are working animals, slow, powerful and oddly vulnerable; 'draught' is the breath of fresh air that passes under the door and causes discomfort within the household; while a 'draught' beer is delivered under pressure. There is arising from all these cases a resonance, which Greenaway intended. The film's language was controversial; it is wordy, but none of its words exists without sanction of contemporary diction. Take 'meretricious': Mrs Pierpoint is proud of her 'meretricious conduct in the company of Mr Seymour', a man of influence and power. According to the *Oxford English Dictionary*, the word had come in the puritanism of the early part of the century to denote the behaviour of a harlot; but soon its sense was widening to include the implications of artistic prostitution, of alluring by a false show of richness. Therefore, in Neville's conception, the ladder that materializes in front of the laundry is described as a 'meretricious vertical'. 'Stratagem', meaning cunning, is another word that is applied to various personages and situations. Again, it has roots in the Renaissance but comes to prominence in dramatic representations of marital intrigues. Greenaway frequently makes clear the film's indebtedness to the dramas that were being staged in London at the time of the film's setting, such as Farquhar's *The Beaux's Stratagem* (1707). The film's very title too recalls the circumstances of other Restoration comedies, where the terms of the contract – between spouses, between artist and patron or between prostitute and client – recur in terms of the body and the material.

Neville's attitude to nature is 'strictly material', and he sees it as his purpose to 'manufacture' twelve drawings. Creativity, it seems, is irrelevant; all that matters is labour. Greenaway, who was responsible for them, said:

> I remember with some irritation the time it took to produce them . . . but it was necessary to give them this laborious feeling of a conscientious striving after truth, which was the basis of the Draughtsman's pride . . . These are laborious drawings of a man capable of making a living by painting, but without

any opportunity of being remembered for posterity. How could a man of such vanity, wearing such clothes, hope to leave a lasting trace?

Greenaway presents a snapshot of a social dynamic. He sets the film in 1694, the year of the establishment of the Bank of England, and money is dwelt upon throughout. It preponderates in the opening sequence, where the members of the company are present 'merely to express confidence in one another's money' as manifested in property, 'for what is a man without property and foresight'. The estate manager, Noyes, who intones these words over the dead body of Neville, is ambitious, and has linked up with another outsider, Mrs Pierpoint, a woman of Italian extraction, to work out a 'symmetrical stratagem' that might provide 'the satisfaction that our betters might be seriously discomfited' and perhaps even to furnish the 'two parterres and a grove of orange trees', which earlier he had told her she was worth.

At first glance, Neville is murdered because a 'paid servant . . . bound by a contract' has penetrated and violated the class system, in the person of Mrs Herbert. 'Would you be so good as to kneel?', he asks politely before pushing her, face down, on to a cushion and mounting her from behind. The language is of great propriety but the action is scandalous as a noble woman is humiliated, physically and socially, by a professional artisan in her husband's garden. The shot is extraordinary; the black dome of the parasol fills the frame, keeping out prying eyes. The other scenes presenting the consummation of the contract are awkward, not least because Mrs Herbert is anatomized. In one shot we see only her back; in another, a leg; the corporeal exclusivity is carefully designed. In contrast to her mother, Mrs Talmann consistently maintains a position of superiority. She is frequently shot from below, which explains her position in the social space, relative to Neville. For instance, in the bath-house assignation, she informs him that only he will undress; and, from her position perched on a chair, she can see both outside and inside. In this stratagem, she is the omniscient mistress.

The social order seems strict and centred on the order of name; but Greenaway's film suggests that lying beneath is the contingency of game, of *jouissance*, that legal distinction between public name and private property. What exists behind the façades of country houses, and what stands before them, are the 'meretricious ladders' that allow social mobility. The truth – at least one version of it – emerges in the long interview between Mr and Mrs Talmann when he accuses his wife of siding with 'a tenant farmer's son'; Mrs Talmann informs him that she is the granddaughter of 'an army victualler'. What seems fixed – the composition of English society – is, in fact, in a state of flux. Compton Ansty, too, is itself about to undergo massive change, the 'harsh geometry' of the garden softened, in order to introduce a new ease to the complexion of the estate. The Dutch landscape gardener, Van Hoyten, will 'make a dam and flood the lower field' with an ornamental lake. These developments perturb Neville, since he realizes they threaten to carry his pictures and his reputation away, and so he asks, 'Do you intend to join Ansty to the sea?' The reply reminds him that it was he who opened the Dutchman's eyes to the formal possibilities of the landscape.

The wider historical aspect is important here, which is unusual for Greenaway. *The Draughtsman's Contract*, the opening titles state, is set in August 1694, six years after the Glorious Revolution that saw the Catholic sovereign banished, to be replaced by the Dutch king, William of Orange, who reintroduced Protestant values to England. Talmann has assumed guardianship of Augustus after his mother became a Catholic: the action of the film, Greenaway once explained, was set at a time of such mixing of nations and families. The old Jacobite and Catholic population saw itself expelled with the arrival of foreigners, principally Dutch and Germans, and to make reference to that event he draws attention to the tongues of Talmann, the governess of little Augustus and Van Hoyten. Their foreign origins strike the ear, to the extent that the words are sometimes rendered untranslated on screen.

But just as behind the fixity of the English monarchy lay the turbulence of faction, so lying at the centre of the film is the issue of issue – the very legitimacy of the ruling classes, which amounts to their 'patrimony or the lack of it'. Talmann sneers that 'The English are not blessed with the most appropriate fecundity at the moment. They can raise colonies but not heirs to the throne'; yet this German, whose presence looks forward to the Hanoverian succession, is impotent. The larger point is simple. Beneath all the ornate social and political structures lies the body, in its base, changeable, unpredictable form; and bodily functions and failures, none of which can be legislated for or against. The body exists as the stake of the contract, the instrument of pleasure, assuring both the power and the survival of the contracting parties. Hence, the stratagem to employ Neville: 'Why not enjoy our patronage?' There, pleasure and service are mentioned in the same breath; but through their conjunction there eventually emerges a possibility of an heir to inherit the estate which Neville had succeeded in mastering on paper. 'We are thriving,' says Mrs Talmann to him on his return from service with the Duke of Lauderdale. 'In our need of an heir, you may very well have served us well,' says Mrs Herbert to him in the orangerie. In both instances, the first person is more likely to be conspiratorially plural than stoically singular.

Although filmed at Groombridge Place, in Kent, *The Draughtsman's Contract* is set in an area of Wiltshire that had always been so fascinating to Greenaway: the Nadder Valley. The idea for the film came from the story of a young artist employed by Lady Hamilton to provide as a gift for Lord Nelson twelve drawings of Fonthill, a folly constructed there by William Beckford in the late eighteenth century. Near Fonthill and Fovant, whose delightful church is mentioned in the opening minutes of the film, is Wilton House, the seat of the greatest patrons of the seventeenth century, whose family name is, coincidentally, Herbert. In showing 'the curriculum for the execution of the drawings' of Mr Herbert's estate, Greenaway's film exhibits a taxonomy of patronage; but it shows the full implications of executing works of art to commission. There is a fascinating exchange between Neville and Mrs Talmann:

> MRS TALMANN: Away from the house, Mr Neville, I, I feel I grow smaller in significance.
> MR NEVILLE: Madame, what signifies does not grow smaller for me.
> MRS TALMANN: Your significance, Mr Neville, is attributable to both innocence and arrogance in equal parts.
> MR NEVILLE: Er. . . you can handle both with impunity, Mrs Talmann. But you will find that they are not symmetrical, you will find that one weighs heavier than the other. Which do you think is the heavier, Mrs Talmann ?
> MRS TALMANN: Your innocence, Mr Neville, is always sinister, so I will say that the right one is the heaviest.

Mrs Talmann feels diminished away from her property, and Neville seems to agree that the true signifier in their association

28 Homage to Gainsborough, from *The Draughtsman's Contract* (1982).

29 Thomas Gainsborough, *Probably a Self-Portrait with his Wife Margaret*, 1746.

is the estate itself. The tone is typical of the kind of mannered obliquity that characterizes so much of their conversation; but most striking here is the visual confirmation of the complex relationship between patron and artist. They converse seated on a bench, under a tree; the park stretches away behind them (illus. 28). The visual reference is unmistakable. Greenaway is alluding to Gainsborough, to the elegant early canvas, now in the Louvre, of the artist and his wife (illus. 29). The man, who has set aside a book in a pale grey cover, perhaps a sentimental novel, is motioning to the woman with a gesture of the hand, and she, dressed in a finely painted pale pink dress, is looking out at the viewer; part of a temple building – perhaps consecrated to Hymen – similar in design to that in Zick's later painting, is seen in the background. However, in Greenaway's version of Gainsborough, a view-finder takes the place of this building; the ubiquitous frame is as binding as any contract between husband and wife or artist and patron.[9]

The film opens with the story of the Duke de Courcey, who invites his water mechanic to the top of an elaborate cascade and asks him if he could build such a marvel for anyone else. The man, after offering various thanks and pleasantries, finally admits that with sufficient patronage he probably could, at which point the Duke pushes him in the small of the back, 'and the wretched man plummeted to watery death'. The point is clear: patronage that begins as support in the execution of a work of art can end simply with the execution of an artist. The water mechanic and the Draughtsman are both overwhelmed by watery deaths.

Alone before the statue of the horseman, executing his thirteenth drawing, Neville tells Talmann 'I am finished'. He is not referring to his draughtsmanship, but to himself, for he is about to be executed, in a sequence whose extraordinarily severe formality is reminiscent of *The Blinding of Samson* by Rembrandt. In the moments before the attack, all the figures are immobile, divided between the darkness in which they appear and the gleam of light that partially illuminates them (illus. 30). Looming out of the shadows, touched by a glimmer of light, they are making an incomprehensible, suspended social gesture: drawing up a final contract whose terms circumscribe the life and death of Neville. These bodies, seen from afar underneath a statue, thereby gain the stature of idols; the very limited number of colours with which they are endowed enhances their appearance. The structure of these shots, and of the bodies that fill them, is an enormous framework that intentionally impinges on the limits of the surface, which is divided by big patches of very solid, black-and-white tints. The volumes enclosed by the darkness and the attitudes induced by immobility are almost stiff, and tend to become geometrical. The extraordinary monochromy is due to the gleams of light from

torch and lantern. In this way, as Rembrandt knew, the most humble bodies can sometimes become monuments, *objets d'art*, and make one think of the very representation of the divine in art. The details die: the shade devours Neville off-camera and eventually he is thrown into the moat. Everything becomes increasingly solemn and increasingly simple. Night simplifies; the single source of light, which consumes his drawings, unifies the garden.

As a lost innocence that is recreated through representation, the garden in *The Draughtsman's Contract* is the site of desire, but also a spiritual recreation of what was lost in the Fall. Clearly, the metaphoric reference point of the garden of Compton Ansty is the idea of paradise, the state of innocence before the fall of man. It is also the site of childhood, of both precultural bliss and of acculturation. Augustus, the young orphan, is forcibly taught the German alphabet by his governess ('a is for apricot; m ist für Marille; z ist für Zitrone; a ist für Ananas; p is for pineapple') and made to wear vast wigs 'that made him look like a dwarf under a white rug'; yet despite the cultivation, he is natural enough still to see what adults choose to ignore, and sees magic in an English garden – a moving statue – where others see only property or reputation. In a clear reference to the origins of another of Isaac Newton's theories, one of the scenes depicts an apple falling around Neville's easel; the Draughtsman picks one up but, rather than pondering it, he throws it at the obelisk, where it breaks up into tiny pieces.

In this film, fruit is rarely associated with knowledge as innocent as an alphabet or a theory of gravity or optics; instead, it is linked with another sort of knowledge – carnal – which describes a falling away from ignorant bliss into experience, from civilization into savagery. But beyond this, the pastoral worlds of, say, Andrew Marvell's gardens lead only to ruin:

> What wond'rous Life in this I lead
> Ripe Apples drop about my head;
> The Luscious Clusters of the Vine
> Upon my mouth do crush their Wine;
> The Nectarean and the curious Peach
> Into my hands themselves do reach;
> Stumbling on Melons, as I pass,
> Insnar'd with flowers, I fall on grass.
>
> ('The Garden')

The sources of pleasure, so often at the centre of conversation and anecdote, are as ambivalent as Marvell's 'fall on grass', as the fruits of the garden are the metaphors behind which language takes refuge in order to evoke desire and the sexual act. Noyes informs Mrs Pierpoint that he 'would well favour you myself above two parterres and a drive of orange trees', and, as he fondles her breasts, clothed in the finest Italian fabric, he observes the real value of fruit: 'oranges smell so sweet; they are so invigorating'. Neville echoes Noyes's words when he mounts Mrs Herbert and tells her, 'limes can smell so sweet, especially when they are allowed to bloom without hindrance', which suggests, appropriately enough, that cultivation can only go so far. The ambivalence of tone is sounded from the first frames of the film, which show an aristocratic mouth chewing on a plum, to the last, where a living statue gorges on the flesh of a pineapple. In all these cases, the fruit represents the female, profiled behind all sorts of botanical metaphors and associated inevitably with humiliation and frustration. The first sexual encounter between the two signatories is brutal and ruthless, as Neville transforms Mrs Herbert into a fruit tree. Marvell wanted to convert all eroticism into 'a Green thought in a green Shade', but Neville goes a stage further, and grafts a discussion of the state of fruit trees in the garden on to his exploration of his patron's upper body: 'The trees have been poorly cared for; the angle between the branches and the main trunk is too steep, but the original work is good. And what of the pears? Are they presentable?' These two last questions, voiced just before he kisses her breasts, depend very simply upon the sort of bawdy *double entendre* so familiar in Restoration comedy. Later, while addressing horticultural issues to Mrs Herbert, Neville enjoys 'the maturing delights of her country garden'. Like Hamlet's quibbling on 'country matters', the language here is fallen, ineluctably double. Words appear as traps, or conceal double meanings, and, sundering body from spirit, they divide nature and art.

When Neville returns to Compton Ansty after his sojourn with the Duke of Lauderdale, autumn is approaching; the leaves are reddening, the atmosphere is smoky with bonfires and mists. He has brought with him three pomegranates – a gift from the Duke's garden – and presents them to Mrs Talmann who is walking with her Dutch landscaper in the park. Though these fruits have been 'reared in English soil and under an English sun', their survival has depended upon unnatural means: 'one hundred panes of glass and half a year's supply of artificial heat'. The next scene sees Neville taking tea in an oak-panelled room with Mrs Herbert, who invites him to dine with her 'and when we are ready, I will show you, along with my gardener Mr Porringer, what we at Ansty are capable of cultivating. It will be by way of returning your gift in kind.' Bright white light streams in through the window; it is countered by the reddish glow radiated by the wood burning in the grate (illus. 31). Once more, the visual allusion opens up new perspectives, since Greenaway has designed his scene on a painting completed by Hogarth late in his career, *Picquet, or Virtue in Danger* (or *The Lady's Last Stake*) (illus. 32). The subject, the artist, was 'a virtuous married lady that had lost all at cards to a young officer, wavering at his suit whether she should part with her honour or no to regain the loss which was offered to her'.[10] So much of the painting to which Greenaway is alluding has a bearing on the textures of his film: statues support the grate; the clock registers 4.55, so time is getting short, as the shadows lengthen; and above the clock is a Cupid with a scythe. The Old Master canvas over the fireplace depicts a penitent Magdalen in the desert; while the firescreen is decorated with a small Dutch still-

31 Homage to
Hogarth, from *The
Draughtsman's
Contract* (1982).

32 Hogarth, *The
Lady's Last Stake*,
1758–9.

life of various fruits, including a pineapple and pomegranates.[11]

These fruits taste strongly of artifice and so do those present-ed by Neville, because they are associated with the story of Persephone, as recounted by Mrs Herbert in the orangerie in the minutes after the final sexual encounter with the draughts-man. In the myth, Persephone is raped and carried off by Pluto into Hades. Her mother, Ceres, 'the goddess of fields, of gar-dens, of orchards', searches, but her quest makes the world bar-ren. When she finally locates Persephone, Hades refuses to release her daughter, who has 'eaten seven graines of a Pome-grannet (a fatal liquorishness, which retains her in Hell; as the Apple thrust Evah out of Paradice, whereunto it is held to have a relation)'.[12] A contract is struck and Persephone is restored to Ceres and, with her, fertility and fruitfulness to the world – but only for half of each year. The pomegranate, then, within its bloody juice contains both life and death, summer and winter. Unwittingly, we have first heard of the fruit much earlier in the film when the German governess tells Augustus the circum-stances of the myth in a little scene that is inserted between the first sexual liaison with Mrs Herbert and its aftermath, where we witness the patroness vomiting in her bedchamber. The implication is that, in response to her continued patronage, he has acted in a way that precludes paternity; and so she is spit-ting out Neville's seed from her mouth.

Though the climactic scene in the orangerie lasts over six minutes, only three shots comprise the sequence. The first is of the lovers lying in a post-coital state; in the disposition of their pose, the couple recall Botticelli's *Venus and Mars*. The next shot, in which Mrs Neville elaborates on the pomegranate's signifi-cance, remains fixed and one now sees the two women acting together in the field of vision in order to frame their victim. While the mother washes the blood-red juice from her hands, her daughter approaches and observes that 'Fruit from the hot-house . . . is seldom fertile'. Like a prisoner, Neville is impotent, caught between the two women, who exit the frame on either side of him and leave him alone on his knees like a condemned man. The shot switches as, still on his knees, he turns towards his judges whose faces are not very clearly visible as a result of the back-light coming from the garden. It seems to blind the draughtsman, as it did the figures in Zick's painting. All that is left for Neville is to be literally blinded, as, for him at least, arti-fice becomes life.

The extraordinary parallel between the opening shot of the film and the final one is equally revealing of the tension between art and life, appearance and reality. The film begins with the image of a face with lips outlined in red, whose make-up forms a veritable mask of death; and it closes on a shot of a Dionysian figure, whose greedy mouth recalls the red of life under the bronze paint – the nature beneath artifice – leaping down from the plinth on to the lawn in order to devour the juicy pulp of the pineapple, another hothouse fruit. Perhaps its flesh is rotten; or perhaps art can never appreciate the natural, but the living statue spits out the flesh in a highly theatrical gesture. Through this figure, Greenaway brings together nature and artifice, for the stone man is emblem of the director's stylistic excesses throughout *The Draughtsman's Contract*. 'My film is about excess: excess in the language, excess in the landscape, which is much too green – we used special green filters – there is no historical realism in the costumes, the women's hair-styles are exaggerated in their height, the costumes are extreme. I wanted to make a very artificial film'.[13] For this reason, the camera pauses several times on this statue, and, at the hinge point of the film, when Neville is working on the sixth drawing on the sixth day, breaks away from the frame of the view-finder to light on a sign of life within the garden where one least expects it. The statue is 'composing' himself and arranges his genitals before perching on a pedestal, in a pose of his own choice. As the camera rolls about this bronze figure, we see that, with his fingers pointing to the sky, he forms the figure 'three', signalling to us in the wink of an eye that this is the third time he has appeared on screen. With his right arm outstretched, he resembles in his pose that of the reflected image in the canvas by Januarius Zick; but here, there is no mirror in sight, only Green-away's camera, out of sight.

4 Medical Experiments and Art Theory

A Zed and Two Noughts is the first of a series of Greenaway's films of the middle to late 1980s that examines the relationship between beginning and ending, origin and extinction; and the convergence of these two elements is stage-managed brilliantly by the opening sequence, which commences in the strange artificial light cast by the title – three enormous letters inscribed in fluorescent blue on a dark screen. After this, the first image of the film superimposes itself on the title, three letters – ZOO – of precisely the same dimension, typographical design and colour as those in the credits, and occupying exactly the same place in the frame. This time, however, the letters are a blue neon sign standing out against a nocturnal background and are reflected back by a puddle of water on the tarmac. Then out of the inky blackness of the scene emerge in stark red letters the words 'A Zed and Two Noughts'. In this move from letter to word, from single character to the fullness of phrase, there emerges the desire to transform the sign into a narrative, to flesh out the story of this dark zoological garden and transform it into a myth.

Once the image of ZOO has left the screen, the frame is immediately enclosed by vertical lines and depicts a cage on the other side of which a tiger paces round in solitary confinement. The script describes the exact shades of this imprisonment:

> The relentless pacing of the tiger in its cramped cage has worn away the paint layers at the back wall of the cage: the top surface of turquoise, the undercoat of white and the successive layers of colouring down to the pink plaster and the red friable brick.[1]

On the floor of the cage lies the decapitated head of a zebra, on which the camera now settles, before turning to accommodate the observer of the scene, a young blond-haired man – Oliver Deuce – sitting with a stopwatch in his hand counting off the number of lengths the tiger paces. The result is 676; that is, 26 squared. In another part of zoo, a young man remarkably similar to the first – only his brown hair distinguishes him – stands in front of a cage containing a one-legged gorilla. Again, as the primate hops about in his prison, the screen is filled with the vertical lines of bars; and all the while, beyond the pen, Oswald Deuce records the movement on a motor-driven camera with synchronous flashlight. The juxtaposition of these two activities – timing and photographing – is, of course, at the heart of any cinematic narrative. But in the opening moments, before even the credits are at an end, Greenaway has both provided an idiosyncratic image of the relationship between an image and the means by which it is recorded in time, and has drawn attention to the means by which narrative is pieced together out of small, isolated shots or frames.

Outside the zoo's gates, directly underneath a large, artificially lit Esso hoarding featuring the famous corporate image of a tiger running free, a bizarre traffic accident has taken place: a mute swan has collided with a large white car – a Ford Mercury, registration number NID 26 B/W, driven by a woman wearing white feathers named Alba Bewick – causing it to crash on a zebra crossing and strike the striped Belisha beacon. Throughout Z&OO, there is a deliberate catalogue of the various ways to light a set, and this scene of extraordinary carnage presents Greenaway and his cinematographer Sacha Vierny with the first of many opportunities to explore the artifice of light: of daylight, dawn-light, twilight, candlelight, firelight, moonlight, starlight, searchlight, of light reflected from water and through Venetian blinds, of cathode tube, arc lamp, neon lamp, projector beam, car headlamps, fog-lamps, among many others. And Vierny – who had secured his reputation in the early 1960s for his work on other films, among them Resnais's *L'Année dernière à Marienbad* – clearly relished the challenges offered him.[2] Hence, in the late evening light, several different artificial light sources illuminate the scene of the crash outside the zoo: a harsh orange ambulance flashlight, the red light of a police car, the blue light of the acetylene cutters, and a large arc light erected to aid the the work of the emergency services, precisely the kind of equipment which might be used to illuminate a film-set. The camera lingers over the carnage, descends and approaches the stricken vehicle, and then – its way now lit by the still working headlights of the car – tracks through the broken windscreen and discovers the unmarked corpses of the two female victims of the accident, lit now by the sparks and flashes given off by the cutting equipment that is being deployed to free their trapped bodies.

In the next shot Greenaway plays with the cinematic short-hand of the newspaper headline, so often used to give information compactly in the course of film narrative. But here he dissolves effortlessly from an event that is filmed in colour, to one that is fixed in monochrome certainties of newsprint; from the motion of cinema to the stasis of a black-and-white still photograph. Hence, two women – in fact, the wives of the zoologists Oswald and Oliver – have become the news, bled of their colour and their lives and deaths contained in a journalistic headline, 'SWAN CRASH, TWO DIE', as absurd as the event which it reports.

In the following days Oswald spends his time cutting up hundreds of copies of newspaper accounts of the accident that caused his wife's death, in the hope that a surrealist game of collage, the cutting up and reassembling of text, will make more sense to him than the straightforward report does. Oliver, for his part, picks up the pieces of glass and places them in his handkerchief, weeping in the silence amid the red and white ribbons underneath the Esso poster that, lit from below, are blowing in the wind. In an operating theatre, bathed in green light, the surgeon, Van Meegeren, having finished amputating the leg of Alba, the driver of the car, now kisses her breasts and moves towards the window; at once the operating theatre is bathed in sunlight. Then the other widower, Oswald, is shown concealed in the semi-darkness of his laboratory; objects are momentarily illuminated by flashes that permit them to be photographed by the banks of cameras ranged around the studio. There are other light sources here and there: a bluish heat lamp over a tray of seedlings, a red developing light over an aquarium of water weed. The tracking shot continues and eventually discovers Oswald, his head in his hands, weeping in the darkness.

At the burial of their wives the two brothers have a conversation about decomposition whose tenor is simultaneously scientific, theological and ironic; and, after following them as they return to lay flowers at the scene of the accident – where now the Esso tiger is in the process of being obliterated to make space for something new – Greenaway introduces the documentary aesthetic so familiar from his early films. But here the difference is that the voice – that of David Attenborough in his famous BBC natural history series *Life on Earth* – is as real as the subject about which it discourses or, at least, as real as any film can be when quoted by another. When the voice intones,'very slowly, even the progress of life forms, changing and evolving in a long continuous proces', the camera directs its gaze directly at the Esso hoarding where some workmen are just in the process of papering over the last section of the tiger, so that we are now confronted with a newly blank white screen inside the cinematic screen. Greenaway's frame, then, reveals another frame, hitherto occupied by a representation of a striped animal; and from now on, this blank space will become the symbolic structure on to which the artificial visual world, which the Deuce twins intend to direct, will be projected.

The implications of the sequence that now follows may serve to enrich the suggestion, for Greenaway exhibits images from Attenborough's documentary, accompanied by a barely audible voice-over. The screen of the documentary and Greenaway's film converge on a desert landscape, under a rising sun, about which the voice observes, 'The conditions for the origin of life on earth can never be reproduced again.' The next shot is of a film projector in the centre of the screen, directed at us and throwing its light at us. Greenaway is attempting to turn things around; the documentary spectacle now takes place off-screen, and the shot takes in the figure of Oliver sitting in the gloom. The image no longer implies some sacrosanct single perspective, an eye around which all representation is organized; instead the gaze of the spectator is dazzled by the glare of the projector, in whose beams are carried a scientific discourse on the evolution of the species, designating us, the audience, as specimens to be observed. The voice states:

> It's comparatively easy to understand how one species gave way to another, but perhaps more difficult to understand the evolutionary leap necessary to bridge the most sophisticated of the apes with man, to contemplate how life has created itself apparently out of nothing.

At this point, on that word, 'nothing', and all that it circumscribes – a circle, an O for Oblivion, a nought – the prologue to *Z&OO* comes to an end. It is so carefully achieved, for in the title of this film, just as in the play text, nought has the last word, as all the twins' attempts to divine the mysterious movement from origin to end come to nought in the damp field in L'Escargot.

'Das Wesen des Kinos is die Bewegung' claimed George Lukacs in 1913.[3] In *Z&OO*, however, the movement from origin to end, or alpha to omega, or A to Z is arrested and curtailed by both the cage and the camera. The film has its beginnings in Biography no. 28 of *The Falls*, with the figure of Cash Fallaxy, the circumstances of whose life 'have been reconstructed from meagre evidence found in an overturned blue saloon car, registration number NID 301'.[4] The report speculates that 'It is not impossible that the driver of the car had been the victim of birdstroke. A swan, maybe two swans, had smashed, or been smashed, into the windscreen.' This does not just sound contrived but also highly suspicious, since the modulation from active to passive – 'had smashed', or 'been smashed' – suggests a strange kind of 'accident' wherein an assailant might hurl a bird into the path of a speeding car; while the shift from birdstrike to 'birdstroke' – something akin to sunstroke – implies that a physiological interpretation of Fallaxy's accident might be needed.

For Greenaway, the official premise of the film was straightforward enough:

> How do animal behaviourists think about their subject – how do they relate their anxieties with their studies? The greatest loss I could imagine would be the death of my wife. So kill the twins' wives in a car-crash – the most possible and yet gratuitous of events. Grief-stricken, the twins try to use what they know best – natural history – to comprehend the event. To complete the circle, the crash is caused by an animal – a swan. We now have the beginnings of a plot to explore many things: the absence of meaning in gratuitous death; is death predetermined?; how do religion and science deal with the problem; is Genesis or Darwin the most likely myth; what other myth-systems try and answer the question?[5]

In the first place, the twins turn to Darwinian theories of evolution, as filtered through *Life On Earth*, the extracts from this eight-part documentary providing so much of the skeletal structure of the film. In fact, at times the two discourses, that of the BBC documentary and that of the film's fiction, even become one, as Greenaway lifts Attenborough's images into his film. Filling the screen are images of volcanic eruptions; microorganisms under the microscope; transparent amoebae; all kinds of reptiles that evoke prehistoric fauna; troops of zebras, monkeys and gorillas; and then, finally, come shots of groups of aboriginees with painted faces, feathers in the hair and armed with spears, over which Attenborough's voice intones: 'The most difficult step to comprehend in the theory of natural selection is the enormous leap from the higher ape . . . to man.' This, the final quotation from the documentary film in Greenaway's fiction is well and truly sceptical, implying, in the final analysis, that the theory of evolution is nothing more than a myth. It can explain only so much, and certainly not the questions that Greenaway poses in his introduction: 'Are animals like car crashes – acts of God or mere accidents – bizarre, tragic, farcical, plotted nowadays into a scenario by an ingenious storyteller, Mr C. Darwin?'[6]

Darwin suggested that humans had evolved accidentally, that biological forms were infinitely plastic, conforming to no *a priori* logical or conceptual categories. Consequently, notions of the fixity of living form, for example, of unity, uniformity, homogeneity, constituted fictions that correspond to an older Aristotelian philosophy of nature. 'According to Aristotle, neither accidental properties nor monsters allowed of explanation and hence were not the proper subject matter of science. . . . On the modern view of science, it is precisely the "accidents" and "monsters" that call for explanation. It was Darwin's attention to so-called accidental variations that led to his theory of evolution, and it in turn demolished the Aristotelian distinction between essential and accidental characteristics.'[7] Darwin argued that no normative representations exist in nature and that, indeed, it speaks most loudly and eloquently through its more abnormal forms, through its excesses and anomalies, its accidents such as 'rogue' plants, black sheep and white rabbits, old hens that 'assumed the plumage, voice, spurs and warlike disposition of the cock' and capons that brooded eggs and brought up chicks, the human monstrosities such as the hirsute Crawfurds or the even more unfortunate Lamberts with their 'porcupine-like excrescences'.[8]

In his art, Greenaway has frequently dwelt on such grotesquerie, either social or physical. *Priapic Frogs* is a sequence of illustrations to a 'hypothetical adventure involving Regent's Park Zoo in the 1860s, which reputedly had a roped-off animal house called "The Obscene Animals Enclosure". It was the tem-

porary home of certain exotic species sent from Africa to London.'⁹ This tall story, in turn, emerges in *Z&OO* in Venus de
Milo's narrative when she claims that one of the animals contained within the compound 'was a toad, or at least it had the
body of a toad'; and the pen-and-ink drawings themselves
emerge when Felipe Arc-en-Ciel gives here by way of thanking
her for introducing him to Alba. In a drawing such as *Animal
Game* (illus. 33), completed a few years after the making of
Z&OO, Greenaway examined the implications of hybridity. Two
bizarre animals, part pig, part dolphin, 'inspect a gentleman
player's remains on a gaming-field laid out with marking posts,
perhaps an allusion to Victorian certainties regarding the playing field. But this is a game where 'death seems to be the stake
and the protagonists inhuman and incalculable'. And on the
question of the incalculable creature, 'What about mermaids,
centaurs, the Sphinx, the Minotaur, werewolves, vampires, and
that proliferating zoo of contemporary hybrids?'¹⁰ Yet Darwin's
theory of the mutability of species did strike at the normative
thinking that regarded monsters only as deviations from Platonic or ideal form. In a universe where the hybrid is perceived as a

'living mosaic work, in which the eye cannot distinguish the discordant elements',[11] the fabulous monsters of mythology become conceivably no more than hybrids with their discordances exaggerated by selective reversions over vast periods of time.

Greenaway's interest in the life and work of Darwin is long-standing; and in some respects there are points of contact between the two. The scientist's obsession with collecting, which began in early childhood and which he believed to be innate, evolved in adulthood into the habit of collecting arcane facts 'on a wholesale scale' and without any theory. This notorious mania for totalization and completeness in the face of the infinitude delayed the publication of *The Origin of the Species* for two decades.[12] Just as *The Falls* appears as an ironic abstract of a greater work, a synecdoche, whose parts must stand for the whole theory of the VUE, so Darwin regarded the *Origin* as a compendium of such superfluous documentation that he admitted 'very few would have had the patience to read it'.[13] In a sense, Darwin (like Greenaway) was rescued when he was distracted from the idea of an inventory or taxonomy – which would have simplified the Book of Nature, turning it into a mere dictionary of living forms – and concentrated instead on the fragments, obliquities, paradoxes and anomalies. In other words, they both came to regard phenomena as a network of relations, as a text, rather than as a statistical table. The frame enclosed a palimpsest, a surface of alternate inscriptions, erasures, traces, superimpositions and blanks, which taken together betokened various histories – of shifting circumstances and their impact on physical form, of proclivities satisfied and then abandoned, of needs emergent and forsaken, of instincts waxing and waning, and of evanescent affinities and departures.

Greenaway's fascination with Darwin culminated in 1992 with the television film he made, a series of tableaux on the scientist's life and theories. His conclusion is worth quoting at length:

Darwin's evolutionary theories have dramatically obliged us to look at our animal origins and our physical selves with new eyes. Our ideas of corporeality and sexuality have to be adjusted with new sympathies. Now that we are no more or no less than a naked ape, our connections with our animal heritage make us severely doubt notions of there being any purpose to our existence other than that we can ascribe to animals, and since Darwin's theory suggests the individual is the insignificant servicer of the species then apparently the necessity to reproduce is our only pertinent function. Our programmed sexuality is the prime motivation of our existence. Each individual is only a suitcase for carrying and passing on the genetical code. Post-Darwin, it is not easy to successfully make any other human action, or behaviour, or achievement significant. In the light of this fact, we have been obliged to re-examine notions of the greatest sensitivity, to reconsider such dearly-held concepts as conscience, spirit and the soul, concepts which we pride ourselves on possessing to make us a superior animal, capable of communicating with even greater forms of intelligence, mortal or immortal.

If we have not been able to ascribe our animal ancestors with these characteristics, how can we conceivably invent these characteristics for ourselves? The aims and ambitions that man has held important for so long, indeed which most of the last 2,000 years of Western civilization has been built upon, no longer have the same significance. There can be no validation for good and evil, no fixed moral code, no sacrosanct states of moral consciousness; there are no longer the same goals of moral perfection; progress has seen so many dead ends, cul de sacs, and abortive developments, especially in the highly developed species. Man could be described as a highly developed species.

Darwin has given man such a short communicable history and such a long uncommunicable prologue that looking back is no comfort either, because evolution appears so directionless, and so apparently purposeless. Darwin has finally put man irredeemably out on his own.

. . . Darwin has given us a freedom that no social or religious programme has ever given us, for, if man is on his own, then all the checks we relied on to excuse or explain our own shortcomings and mediocrities have been removed. We are, at least, now free for what we want to be.[14]

And yet so many still rely on the 'checks', so that the freedom to be 'what we want to be' may necessarily be more illusory than real. The method the twins adopt to deal with their grief consists, equally, of fixing the 'connections with our animal heritage' through reproduction, and inscribing them within the very frame of the screen. These 'highly developed' photographic practices serve to capture first in still and then in moving images the inert objects attendant upon their grief, following approximately the various stages of Darwinian evolution.

Perversely, mischievously, however, the first subject of the experimentation is not animal but vegetable: a glossy green apple taken from a fruitbowl on the bedside table of Alba Bewick, the woman who assumes the role both of tempter and nourisher to the twins. This is the apple of Eden, a piece bitten from it and its flesh exposed by the time-lapse photographic equipment, providing a sequence of flash shots accumulated over a period of days, the first such sequence to form part of the body of the film. And it comes to seem, paradoxically, that it is the very experimentation that accelerates the decay. The white flesh blackens, melts and shrinks away; a stain forms and seems to devour it; withered and holed, it collapses like a piece of desiccated tissue. The accompanying dialogue enriches the symbolic import of this. His eyes fixed on the screen where this record of decay is being projected, Oswald addresses Venus de Milo, the prostitute who has been attempting to console him by telling him stories. While the shot of the decomposed apple appears on screen on the sound-track, Oswald's voice observes: 'Oliver says it starts with the stomach, the liver, the pancreas, the spleen.' To test this theory, vegetable must become animal. Consequently, the second specimen observed in decomposition is a saucer of prawns, ironically recalling a still-life. Next, it's the turn of two angel fish, facing each other, their eyes disappearing, the sockets whitening and deliquescing, and their bodies shrinking as a result of the putrefaction. A small crocodile, the next in the chain of evolution, melts at great speed before our eyes, by the same procedure of montage and acceleration as before; and then, by way of sweet revenge, the brothers acquire a swan on which to experiment. The sixth object to be observed is a Dalmatian, which in the opening moments of the film is seen obstinately refusing to walk past the zoo, but which ends up, nevertheless, crushed on the zebra crossing, and finally the one-legged gorilla, whose decay makes a fascinating spectacle, tagged with red and blue ribbons. To complete this investigation of the Darwinian myth of origin, one experiment still needs to be done; and this closes the film.

Darwin's myth required extinction, first of the individual

organism and then, eventually, of the species. But there are alternatives. Northrop Frye has identified the strange inclination of myths to 'stick together and build up bigger structures. We have creation myths, fall and flood myths, metamorphosis and dying god myths, divine marriage and hero ancestry myths, etiological myths, apocalyptic myths.'[15] As far as Greenaway is concerned, 'The classical humanist myths have all the stereotypes of every story ever told.' Felipe Arc-en-Ciel admits that, 'If I had the money to own a zoo, I would stock it with mythological animals.' Hence, this one is staffed by the equivalents of the characters from Mount Olympus. Venus de Milo is the zoo prostitute, the gatekeeper is a lightly disguised Mercury who wears the zoo colours – a silver hat with wings – the symbol and colour of Mercury. Pluto, god of the Underworld, is the Keeper of Reptiles who makes an alternative animal collection of black-and-white animals because there is no colour in Hell.

Outside the gates, amid the wreckage of the car crash, emerges another myth, the narrative of Leda, who gave birth to the heavenly twins, Castor and Pollux, after being raped by Jupiter in the guise of a swan. On the scene, a policeman converses with a disembodied voice emerging from his walkie-talkie, which asks some big questions, among the 402 posed in this film:

> A swan? What sort of swan? Leda? Who's Leda? Is she the injured woman? Laid by whom? By Jupiter? What was the cause of death? A female swan! How do you know it was female? Eggs! Egg-bound! Was it wild? Perhaps it was a wild goose! Did it come from the zoo?

Greenaway later wrote about the Leda myth when he included a drawing by Michelangelo in an exhibition at the Louvre (illus. 34). He described it as 'A dynastic move. "If I cannot fly myself then my offspring shall." But alas, it did not turn out that way. Leda's four offspring were all human, though born of eggs. What can you expect, for the swan was Jupiter and gods make mortals in their own image?'[16] A more Darwinian explanation might be that the natural prerogative will always overcome the social ambition; the species will continue, whatever the cost to the individual. After sketching the mythical background, Greenaway describes the texture and composition of the drawing: 'The darkest part of this drawing is at the point of anatomical consummation and the twist of the Leda body makes no

34 Italian school,
after Michelangelo,
Leda and the Swan,
16th century.

compromise on its intent and on our concentration. This is a copulation on a bolstered bed with a swan. The swan's neck and head snugly share the same line as Leda's belly and breast. Beak and lips meet in an ornithological kiss.' What is most extraordinary here is the coincidence that this Leda, like Alba, is lacking a leg; her limb seems almost vestigial, fading away into shadows in the midst of her encounter with the swan.

To complicate matters still further, the car in which the two women die is a Ford Mercury, whose two front *wings* are visible in a long tracking shot which runs the length of the smashed vehicle. As for the number plate of the car, NID 26 B/W, well in evidence in the same shot, this too confirms the conjunction of the feathered woman, Alba Bewick, and the myth of Leda and the swan. Hence, NID is *noeud*, a nest; the number 26 is used in various ways as a structuring device, either denoting the letters of the alphabet or, more arcanely and controversially, figuring the extant canvases of Vermeer; and the black-and-white (BW) stripes on animals' clothes and bodies give the film much of its visual rhythm. As Stephen Heath notes: 'The body in films is also moments, intensities, outside a single constant unity of the body as a whole, the property of some *one*; films are full of fragments, bits of bodies, gestures, desirable traces, fetish points'.[17] And the fetish point here is the stripe, which becomes a veritable framing principle. Consider the bars of the cage, which, in turn, contains the stripes of the zebra (illus. 35) or the tiger; the

35 Zebra stripes, from *A Zed and Two Noughts* (1985).

red and white stripes of the ribbons that cordon off the scene of the fatal accident or the striations of light reflected from water or through the Venetian blinds that play across the walls in so many scenes. However, this motif of stripes also becomes a veritable narrative device. Venus de Milo is always seen dressed in black and Alba Bewick in white; however, the latter reveals to Oscar and Alba's daughter, Beta, that she prefers black-and-white striped knickers. The completeness in Alba's life comes with the arrival of the legless Felipe Arc-en-Ciel, his name implying all the coloured bands of the rainbow, which, thanks to Newton, are known to come from the diffraction of a single source of white light. His presence prompts Alba's resolution to banish the black-and-white dichotomies from her life – the twinned but ultimately sundered Deuce brothers. Having taken them as lovers, she will, naturally, give birth to their twins – Castor and Pollux ; but, against the brothers' claims to natural paternity, she contrives to have her children brought up after her death by her masculine twin, Felipe Arc-en-Ciel, who, though lacking legs, nevertheless makes her feel complete. Through the use of a surrogate, even the natural can be thwarted by the artificial.

'Why do we have to have two of everything?' The answer

comes: 'Symmetry is all.' And it is to satisfy the fearful require-
ment of symmetry that the second limb of Alba needs to
be removed. Yet Greenaway raises an important question
throughout: is symmetry a manifestation of the natural or of the
artificial?

> *A Zed and Two Noughts* began with a fascination with twin-
> ship. Being a twin is perhaps the nearest you can come to
> meeting yourself. Many world mythologies share a theory
> that we are born as twins and in most cases the second twin
> dies in the womb, leaving us incomplete, always looking for
> the lost half. We compensate by trying hard all our lives to
> pair with a stranger. Our bodies constantly remind us of this
> duality – this two-ness – nostrils, feet, breasts, testicles,
> ovaries.

The motif of twins has always fascinated Greenaway, and
they feature earlier in his work: one thinks of the symmetrical
characters who populate *The Falls* and *The Draughtsman's Contract*. Symmetry seems to be the template for so many of the
shots; the image is ceaselessly divided and redoubled on itself.
Midway through *Z&OO*, in one of the rare sequences that take
place in daylight rather than artificial light, Greenaway undertakes a subtle speculation in order to exploit the idea of the double. Making use both of water and a mirrored image, Oswald
immerses a mirror in a tank and uses it to reflect the angel fish
symmetrically back on itself. However, this action resonates not
with nature but artifice; and as Greenaway admitted, 'I was creating a rich and detailed world full of literal and metaphorical
and referential meaning that is totally artificial but mirrors our
own.' In one scene, the twins visit the surgery of Dr Van
Meegeren, a connoisseur of Vermeer, and sit, their legs crossed
and pointing away from each other, under reproductions of *The
Astronomer* and *The Geographer*, 'two paintings of what could be
the same man or identical twins'.[18] To emphasize the semblance
of twinship, the image on the left, *The Astronomer*, has been
reversed so that the figure in it points right, towards its more
worldly counterpart.

Earlier the two brothers take Alba's daughter, Beta, for an ice-
cream in an attempt to demonstrate to the child the extent of
their twinship. Their replies to her questions alternate with a
perfect regularity: first Oswald speaks, and then Oliver, until
the conclusion, 'You see, between us, we know everything',

36 Twins in bed,
from *A Zed and Two
Noughts* (1985).

which they attempt to prove to the little girl. The phrase is partially repeated by Oswald ('between us we do') as Greenaway stresses how perfectly poised is that preposition 'between', both joining and dividing, and yet also suggesting a certain self-sufficiency, since it also contains an echo of 'twin'. So they now speak for each other; moreover, the physical traits that once distinguished them have disappeared little by little. In the final scenes Oliver's hair darkens to match that of his brother and is parted to match, and to cement their similarity they even commission from the seamstress Venus de Milo a black-and-white suit with two sleeves and three legs into which they can both fit at the same time.

Eventually, their extraordinary 'secret' emerges: they were once Siamese twins, and were separated when young, though the scars of division remain still on their bodies. They have hidden their origins so as not to become exhibits in a human zoo. In the sequence where, in bed with Alba (illus. 36), they reveal their past, she suggests, 'Now, how about changing sides?' to which Oswald replies, 'I'm happy on the left. I exactly know my place'; but here twinship ushers in questions of schizophrenia. For example, dressed in their double suit, their backs to the audience and seated on a bench in front of a screen, Oswald and

37 The double suit,
from *A Zed and Two
Noughts* (1985).

Oliver witness the decay of the zebra; and, as in Godard's *Les Carabiniers*, the image is also projected on to them (illus. 37). Their eyes fixed on this scene of putrefaction, Oliver now asks his brother, 'Do you think Oliver was a Siamese twin?' to which Oswald replies with another question, 'What happened to his brother?' Whereas Alba has progressed from being a whole body, to a one-legged body, to a body without legs, to a corpse, so the twins regress from being distinct persons, to being brothers, to being twins, to being Siamese twins – to all intents and purposes, a single person – before they die. The surgeon, Van Meegeren, observes that 'Animals on the whole are designed with a view to symmetry. One of decay's first characteristics is to spoil that symmetry.' Certainly, as Darwin had suggested, individual bodies are relatively symmetrical; but Greenaway's film questions whether, outside the cages of artifice, the ordering in social form of more than a single body ever can be symmetrical. Hence the scenes in Alba's boudoir, with the twins lying left and right in tableaux of perfect mirror-image symmetry. But, frozen into stasis, these figures imply that symmetry can never be the preserve of the animate; only the inanimate, the inert, the artificial.

Consider again the implications of title. Oswald and Oliver are the two Os on the staff of the zoo, the two noughts of the title *Z&OO* and also the graphical representation of a symmetry that comes to nought in the final sequences of the film. Beyond this, laid on the grid on which they die, they form a figure that goes beyond numbering. Oswald and Oliver have undertaken experiments on seven specimens in order to evolve to an eighth stage in the Darwinian sequence – that closest to us – and place themselves in the frame as the final object of scientific scrutiny. So, in quest of finite answers about the infinite, they lay themselves down in a minutely calibrated frame; but here Greenaway's visualization wants us to realize that in mathematical and in optical notation infinity manifests itself as '∞'. Perhaps an eight laid on its side or, alternatively, two noughts side by side.

What, finally, is the difference between *A Zed and Two Noughts* and ZOO? Of course, the word 'zoo' itself is a diminution; and as a prefix it means spontaneous movement.[19] Here it represents the shift of word into its letters, a sort of decomposition into constituent parts, a revelation of its bony skeleton underneath the flesh, the skull beneath the skin. And so consider the scene towards the end of the film when Milo goes into the zebra enclosure; the letters that form the neon sign are seen from behind and therefore ought to be back-to-front. Of course, the two Os are unaffected by the reversal, but the symmetrical Z, which *should* be reversed, instead can be read as normal. Hence, 'ZOO' becomes 'OOZ'. The implications might be that the order of the letters has been artificially reversed, and we are seeing the end and looking back to the beginning; hence, 'OOZ' may be coming to signify the primeval ooze from which life on earth originates. On these stark letters, Greenaway builds his theories against the possibility of resolving even the simplest questions about our origins and destinations; the various games with letters and numbers suggests the sheer arbitrariness of things. The truth is that, as Alba observes after the accident, 'Another set of things could produce something completely different.'

ZOO-PRAXIS

It was such a sense of arbitrary possibility that drove the work of Eadweard Muybridge, one of the pioneers of the moving image. In 1880, this English-born photographer began to develop the 'zoopraxiscope', which would eventually enable him to project his images at speed to simulate the appearance of continuous motion.[20] Since 1832, the zoetrope had marked the limit of moving pictures. Invented as a popular scientific toy, this so-called 'wheel of life' resembled a lampshade with vertical slits, but was in fact a revolving drum with a strip of sequence pictures mounted around the inside. Each picture faced a slot cut out in the opposite side of the drum and, when it was revolved, the pictures were seen briefly one after the other, giving a crude illusion of movement.[21] Muybridge's more sophisticated device consisted of a lamp house and lens of a normal projection lantern, but, instead of a slide tray, there was a mechanism whereby a glass disc containing images could be fixed vertically and rotated with a handle. The effect was a loop of action; and with it he published photo sequences to illustrate his studies of animal locomotion, considered as a marvel of Victorian electro-mechanical skill. The *Philadelphia Times* described the technique: 'The photographs are taken by three batteries of cameras, with twelve lenses to each battery. These batteries are placed at right angles to each other . . . and are all focused on one subject. When the model or object under consideration is photographed, thirty-six negatives are obtained . . . [representing] different stages of muscular action from the three different points of view . . . In this way every inch of man's or beast's progress can be photographed, no matter what the speed.'[22]

Just as in the twins' laboratory, motion was broken down into a series of fractionally intervalled snapshots. But whereas Muybridge's subjects were humans performing a variety of athletic and everyday actions – a naked man running or throwing a javelin or descending a staircase, a naked woman picking up a jug or a cloth or climbing into bed – and each sequence revealed the constituent instants of these deeds, the twins' experiments on dead bodies only show the movement of decay. As Greenaway admitted:

> It's meant to be a pre-cinema quote as well – Muybridge quoted as proto-cineaste, pre-cineaste, moving the still picture into the moving picture, relative to what the two natural historians Oliver and Oswald were doing in the film with their stop-motion photography.[23]

Yet in each case, what sort of picture of the world emerges? If a sense of movement was intended, then the instantaneous photographs do not provide this. Though the images might be animated, *in extremis*, they are nothing less than an inventory of postures; yet they possess their own singular psychology.

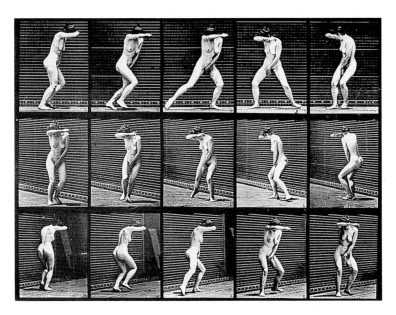

38 Eadweard Muybridge, 'Turning Around in Surprise and Running Away', from *Animal Locomotion*, 1887.

Action here is not a matter of doing something; instead it is a matter of going through the motions (illus. 38). In this respect, the grief-stricken twins are themselves Muybridgean subjects for Greenaway's camera. There are no purposes, only functions. The actions of the body – and its decay – are demonstrated, and every step of a movement is made to look as significant or insignificant as every other step. This lends Oliver and Oswald a pathos and helplessness, as they vivisect, and then are vivisected, anatomized into temporal fragments. This is the heart of the film; though they are indisputably taken from life, we know that life isn't quite like that: in other words, their work is scientific artifice. Although movement in Muybridge is effectively caught in a framework of purpose – a grid – in order to allow spectators to understand fully what is happening, his technique will work only on some very definite, established, predictable action. Greenaway guessed, no doubt, that if you subjected the twins' grief – something both uncertain and unique – to this technique, a strange and quite meaningless sequence of events would emerge.

It is hardly surprising then that at a lecture in London, Greenaway described Muybridge's legacy as:

a project that mocks human effort . . . It's as an unfinished and unfinishable catalogue of anecdotal ephemera that I like it the best – twenty-seven pictures from three angles of a naked woman throwing cold water over her naked female companion, forty-four pictures from four angles of a naked Muybridge walking a short plank, twenty-four pictures from three angles of an obese woman lifting her stomach off the ground. It's a telling example of all those highly equivocal human attempts – from Newton to Linnaeus, Messerschmitt to Darwin and every historian and scholar you can think of – to record, order and try to make sense of the variety of chaos.

Yet Greenaway frequently borrows from the photographer. Footage from Muybridge is used in the 1990 video film *A TV Dante*, using the photo sequences to illustrate the movement of Everyman, and, more elaborately following the theological necessity that Christ was God remade as man, making use of stock from the strip, *Man Walking Downstairs* to suggest Christ walking down into Hell.[24] But even though his name is not mentioned in the script, it is in *Z&OO* that Muybridge figures most directly. Indeed, the starting point of the film seems to have been drawn from an episode in the photographer's career.

In August 1885 Muybridge removed his zoopraxiscope to the Philadelphia Zoological Gardens. On the first day he photographed pigeons and then went on to set down the movements of crow, hawk and finally an owl. In subsequent sessions these were followed by studies of cockatoo, vulture, eagle, ostrich, stork and finally swan. Soon Muybridge succeeded in recording animals as diverse as mule, horse, ass, ox, pig, goat, deer, antelope, giraffe, cat, elephant, camel, baboon, kangaroo, dog, rhinoceros, tiger and lion. The carnivores presented special problems, since they could not be removed from their cages, and entering their pens was also out of the question. Consequently, the lion had to be photographed through the bars of his cage; but the shadows cast by the bars transformed his appearance and made him resemble a tiger or even a zebra.[25] Under the aegis of motion, one species became another; a double take.

The double image created here is oddly complemented by Greenaway's own artistic praxis, since in many sequences of the film he too was borrowing from the singular work of Francis Bacon. In an interview, the film-maker explained his design in *Z&OO*:

> the intention was to make a double-take quote – quoting Francis Bacon quoting Muybridge's Animal Locomotion studies – with the animal specimens – this time not alive but locomoting with the movements of decay – presented on the meticulously squared-up backgrounds.[26]

He is alluding to the fact that in his work of the early 1950s Bacon was heavily indebted to the locomotion studies, describing them as 'raw statements of motion',[27] using them to articulate figures in movement, revelling in the cool atmosphere of neutrality in which these sequences are presented. Nicolas and Elena Calas have argued that 'Bacon is probably the first artist to consistently use blurring to suggest mobility. He seems to proceed from the assumption that the model moved while the picture was being taken'; but this effect would not have existed had Bacon not seen Muybridge's work.[28]

The indebtedness is best seen in the five paintings of dogs Bacon executed between 1952 and 1955, all of which depict movement by means of reproductions of the blurred photo-

graphic image, in this case frames taken from Muybridge's photographic study of the mastiff, entitled 'Dread Walking', carried
out in the Philadelphia Zoo in 1885. Several of the shots in this
sequence are indistinct – the dog's head is out of focus and partially in shadow as he walks away from the light source – and
the overall effect is of a fleeting motion too swift to be fixed on
film. In *Dog* (1952) (illus. 39), the upper part of the canvas
is stained uniformly black, while the lower part consists of a
linear grid circumscribed by a hexagonal geometrical shape,
bounded in neon red. The impression produced by juxtaposing
flesh and grid is bizarre: the red fleck of its tongue looks bloody
against the ground, and interrupts the rapid strokes of white
tan and grey pigment that describe and yet almost dissolve the
animal's head and body.

In 1955 Francis Bacon described painting as 'a method of
opening up areas of feeling rather than merely an illustration of
an object . . . A picture should be a re-creation of an event rather
than an illustration of an object; but there is no tension in the
picture unless there is the struggle with the object. I would like
my pictures to look as if a human being had passed between

them, like a snail, leaving a trail of the human presence and memory trace of past events as the snail leaves its slime.'[29] Such a trail emerges in Greenaway's *Z&OO*, and not just when the snails crawl across the bodies of the twins in the dying seconds. The sense of re-creation emerges when the Dalmatian is filmed on the grid, and a month of decay is compressed into twenty seconds of time-lapse footage. For, as the maggots attack, the dog suddenly appears out of that movement and seems almost to acquire an uncontrolled sense of existence, even though it will be consumed by motion in the next instant. Yet the moment is sufficient to lay bare the confusion between life and death, motion and stasis, at the heart of the film.

As well as offering a point of connection with Bacon, Muybridge's work also looks back to the Dutch master, for in his sequences 'one rediscovers a particular talent of Vermeer, who attempted to capture the absolute fixity of the moment: the fraction of a fraction of a second', the point at which life is frozen almost to stasis.[30] In his introduction to *Z&OO*, Greenaway claimed that the 'overall visual – master – of ceremonies of the film was to be Vermeer – adroit and prophetic manipulator of the essentials of cinema – the split-second of action, and drama revealed by light'. He continues:

> It cannot be proved that Vermeer's *Milkmaid* is a painting representing one twenty-fourth of a second of seventeenth-century time, exposed at f8, but the direction of the light is certain: always from the left of frame, coming from a source four and a half feet off the ground. The intention to preserve this discipline rigorously in *Z&OO* was as often as not eroded by the vagaries of locations and the free-range habits of the animals, but the spirit was preserved.[31]

As he admits, allusion to Vermeer in the film through 'composition, gestures and picture detail' is continual and perverse. Alba claims that she resembles the *Lady standing at the Virginal* 'because you never see her legs – she's not trapped really – she's strapped and stitched to her music stool'. Later, when she's fitted out with a prosthesis, Alba wears a dress, an exact replica of that worn by the model in both *The Concert* and *The Music Lesson*. Heavily pregnant, Alba reads a letter by the light of the window. The composition is similar to Vermeer's *Woman in Blue Reading a Letter*, which may have featured the painter's pregnant wife, Catharina. Van Meegeren creeps up behind her and

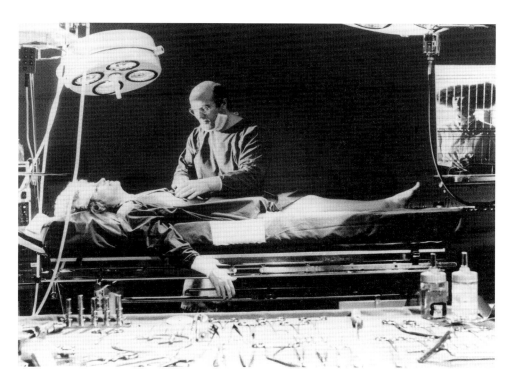

40 Van Meegeren,
from *A Zed and Two
Noughts* (1985).

startles her, and presents her with a gift: a framed reproduction
of the very painting she has unwittingly imitated.

Van Meegeren is the key figure. Allegedly the nephew of
Vermeer's master faker – the man who successfully convinced
Europe (and Goebbels) that there were certainly more than
twenty-six authenticated Vermeers in existence – he 'wants to
be a painter – in fact, the Dutch painter Vermeer, no less'.[32] His
surgery looks like an empty set for a Vermeer painting, replete
with 'globes, maps and leather chairs', his wife has been
renamed Caterina Bolnes in honour of Vermeer's spouse, and in
various *tableaux vivants* based on the canvases he frames her
among the props, subordinating her to the overall design. This
is a familiar intention in the world of *Z&OO* (illus. 40).

Near the end of *Z&OO*, the Deuce brothers suggest that Alba,
now terminally ill, bequeath her body to their researches, so
that they can film her decomposition. Oswald satisfies her that
only the camera will be watching, to which she responds,
'What's the use of watching me? My body's only half here.'
'Then you'll fit better into the film frame,' replies Oliver, to
which Alba responds emphatically, 'God, I should have known.

115

Maybe you've always been in league with Van Meegeren. A fine epitaph: here lies a body cut down to fit the picture.' It's a characteristically black joke, with a killing pun on 'cut down' to suggest the body needs to be well-hung before the reframing can take place; but by this means, Greenaway is yet again ironizing the function of representational techniques, both in the sphere of artistic creation and in the extent to which they impinge on our apprehension of the world. His joke raises the crucial question of representational determinism. In painting, as in photography, the frame should be constructed to fit the picture; but, of course, as soon as that ordering of priorities is recast to accommodate the framing process as a primary part of any act of composition, it becomes clear that the act of cutting is deeply implicated in decisions of what is and what is not to be recorded and represented, displayed in film.[33]

It is especially significant that Van Meegeren's profession is surgeon, for ultimately in *Z&OO* Greenaway seems to have in mind Walter Benjamin's 'The Work of Art in the Age of Mechanical Reproduction' (1936), which establishes a distinction between the painter and the cinematographer, a dichotomy based on the difference in their respective relations to reality, here imaged as relations to the human body. 'The magician heals a sick person by the laying on of hands,' Benjamin writes, whereas

> the surgeon cuts into the patient's body . . . Magician and surgeon compare to painter and cameraman. The painter maintains in his work a natural distance from reality, the cameraman penetrates deeply into its web. There is a tremendous difference between the pictures they obtain. That of the painter is a total one, that of the cameraman consists of multiple fragments which are assembled under a new law.[34]

A painter such as Vermeer, then, might undertake practices and illusions that are distanced from (and can have no real effect upon) reality, portrayed here as a sick body. On the other hand, by cutting deeply in order to amputate, by approaching reality with an incisively critical lens, as it were, the cameraman, Van Meegeren, can solve the fragmentation inherent in the cinematic medium by intensifiying it and, paradoxically, creating what Benjamin describes as 'an aspect of reality which is free of all equipment', a reality 'cured' and in some sense redeemed again. The cost, however, is high for the individual, as Alba acknowledges when she observes, 'I'm an excuse for medical experiments and art theory. Look, I'm stitched and sewn to the music stool.'

In his direction of *Z&OO*, his cutting and stitching of word and image, his dressing some sets with framed reproductions of actual Vermeer paintings, his producing the feel and composition of other Vermeer paintings or combinations of paintings in his own shots, and his asking Sacha Vierny to mimic Vermeer's lighting effects by lighting each tableau from the left with a source about four and a half feet from the ground, perhaps Greenaway, too, acts like a Van Meegeren.

Consequently, the reproduction of the 'Allegory of Painting' in Van Meegeren's surgery constitutes the central image of this extraordinary film.[35] The brief but crucial scene emerges immediately after a close-up of a zebra's hide, which fills the screen with vertical stripes. In the script, the *mis-en-scène* reads:

> Slowly zoom out from the zebra stripes of a slashed costume Van Meegeren is wearing that is copied from the 'Allegory of Painting' by Vermeer, to reveal a total image that is copied from the same painting, where Catarina Bolnes is posed naked, with her red hat on and holding a book and a trumpet. Van Meegeren is photographing her. He takes flashlight pictures reminiscent of Oswald Deuce's time-lapse flash camera (illus. 41).

In Vermeer, the model and the artist are face to face; the painter has turned his back on us, and is anonymous, faceless. Clio, the Muse of History, stands motionless before him; or rather, the young woman who impersonates her holds herself still in the awkward pose which demands that she carry a unwieldy trumpet and a heavy book in front of her (illus. 42). Above her head, the sunlight glints off the polished surface of the brass chandelier and washes over a contemporary Dutch map of the Netherlands by Visscher, catching its pleats and creases.[36] This should give us pause, since there is a potent sense of the illusionistic character of the image; an illusionism founded on a firm basis of perspective and optical rules.[37] The large tapestry on the left of the painting – simulating the protective curtains that the Dutch often placed over their pictures – has been pulled aside, its colours, textures and folds overlapping with the extreme left corner of the map. This curtain suggests nothing less than the space of a stage; the drapery a proscenium

cloth, the half-finished canvas a play within a play, the painter a *mise-en-scène*, the model an actress.

The heart of the painting is this relationship between nature and artifice; more precisely, the discrepancy between them, as a laurel wreath of three dimensions is recorded, and reordered in two. Vermeer has painted the garland on Clio's brow in obvious and considerable depth; however, the painter at his easel, commencing the reproduction from the top, can effect only a flat image, without shading and chiaroscuro. Vermeer represents the contingencies of his art with consummate poise, but he cannot sustain his paradox of abundance. On one hand, he continues to reconstruct dimensioned space in mimicry and dissimulation; on the other, he acknowledges the flattened space that any artistic endeavour implies. And at this point in the debate, Greenaway turns the concerns of the painting into photography. Van Meegeren, bending over his camera like a painter at his canvas, photographs his model, Catarina Bolnes, who, in turn, holds the trumpet and a book containing a reproduction of Vermeer's original – in both cases, music and literature in the service of art. His wife wears a large-brimmed red hat in homage to Vermeer's *Girl with a Red Hat*; however, it is not a convincing attempt to mimic the figure on the canvas since, apart from the hat, Catarina is completely naked. Nevertheless, this extra allusion is significant, since Greenaway has in mind one of Vermeer's most intimate paintings, which depicts a young woman sitting on a bench behind the chair on which she rests her arm (illus. 43). At first glance, it may seem that her hat is a flaring assertion of self, and the light that models her face endows her with psychological contour; but once again Vermeer has made use of the distancing effect of the camera obscura.[38] Those lions' heads on the end of the bench are formed by and may only be seen through unresolved lenses; they cannot be formed and may not be seen by the naked eye. Vermeer deliberately undercuts the instrument of perception. He does not use the camera now (as he had formerly) to purge the eyes of preconception and to clarify unaided vision. Instead, he uses it to create images that cannot otherwise be seen, to confound unaided vision. The blurred lions' heads – the dissolution of *their* focus and attention – balance his sitter's entrapment in the world that is too much with her. The rings of captivity the lions wear have never been so visible. And on closer inspection, she too seems uncomfortable trapped in that narrow space – and

43 Vermeer, *Girl With a Red Hat*, c. 1665.

her hat shields her eyes from the shock of recognition that both of us are in the same exile. Greenaway realizes that, like Van Meegeren's wife, Vermeer's figure has also been cast into the cramped cage of disinheritance. It is as if that ill-defined tapestry behind her had closed off the sacred interior of the *Art of Painting* from which she and the artist are now excluded; as if the richness of that hanging textile were an intimation of the riches lost to them. At this point, Greenaway's film breaks the tensions present in both pictures: the model drops the trombone and the book and walks out of the frame, accusing Van Meegeren of having an affair with Alba Bewick. The illusion of the art of painting has been shattered by the cinematic frame.

5 Mechanical Reproduction

FLESH AND STONE

Vermeer's *Art of Painting* provided the thematic nexus of *A Zed and Two Noughts*. In Greenaway's next feature, *The Belly of an Architect*, the central image is the equally famous *Flagellation of Christ* by Piero della Francesca (illus. 44). The work of the artist had featured previously in *The Falls*, when in Biography no. 30 Coppice Fallbatteo focused his 'exploration of the significance of birds in European painting' on the Montefeltro Altarpiece, known more commonly as 'the "Egg-Painting"; in which the Virgin, surrounded by saints, sits on a throne holding the Christ Child. Above the Virgin's head, suspended on a fine cord, hangs a white egg':

> Coppice knew everything there was to know about this painting: its conception, its mathematics, the mineral constituents of its colours, the hagiography of its saints, its value in lire, dollars, gold and osprey feathers. The centre of all this fascination was of course the suspended egg. To Coppice it became the very symbol of the Violent Unknown Event, and the one wholly perplexing feature for which he had no definitive explanation.[1]

44 Piero Della Francesca, *The Flagellation of Christ*, 1455–60.

121

Such perplexity is common enough among critics of Piero's work; and it is perhaps for this reason that Greenaway makes use of another of the artist's paintings in *The Belly of an Architect*. Yet the *Flagellation* is never reproduced in the film, existing instead spectrally, beyond the frame and beyond the mysterious figures who dominate its design.

The film poses three narratives – of work, birth and death – and opens with a train crossing from France to Italy, through Ventimiglia. In a sleeping carriage, Stourley Kracklite, a 54-year-old American architect, and his wife, Louisa, are making love – she conceiving, as it turns out, just as they enter the country in which her father was born. Kracklite is travelling to Rome in order to organize an exhibition in tribute to the eighteenth-century French visionary architect, Etienne-Louis Boullée, whom he has idolized for many years, and who will become yet more important to him as the film (along with Kracklite's life) runs its course. The narrative follows the American over the ensuing nine months, during which time his belly and that of his wife gradually change – his growing with an aggressive malignant cancer, hers swelling with pregnancy. Their marriage disintegrates and, as Kracklite dies slowly, Louisa embarks on an affair with one of his young Italian colleagues. Eventually, the architect jumps to his death from the Vittorio Emanuele II monument – where the exhibition is about to open – his leap causing Louisa to give birth in the company of the exhibition's Italian organizers, Io and Caspasian Speckler.

One of the film's most harrowing sequences comes when Kracklite, having been told that his cancer is terminal, drinks too much and loses control at an open-air restaurant. Baring his belly at a female diner, he invites her to touch it, as a way of grounding his condition (illus. 45). Perhaps we are meant at this point to think of Silenus, the fat old man who, having overimbibed, has lost his way. In 1992, as part of his Louvre exhibition on flight, Greenaway included a representation of the satyr by the early sixteenth century Veronese artist Galeazzo Mondella, in which – echoing Stourley Kracklite at the alfresco dinner – Silenus is both dead drunk and a dead weight (illus. 46). Greenaway comments:

Of course, this podgy lump of human meat is more than a Silenus, he's an allegorical personification of fatness, plumpness, the rotund, his body an inflatable series of ball-like vol-

45 Drunken
Kracklite, from *The
Belly of an Architect*
(1987).

46 Galeazzo
Mondella, *The
Cortège of Silenus*,
c. 1500.

123

umes – breasts and belly and head with a double chin. He is like an adult baby, like a maturing version of that child we see in the background. An inflated ballooning comes to mind, and balloons have been known to fly. But such a phenomenon does not come to pass, for these fleshy balloons are not going to be airborne. But if these arrow-eared fauns manage to lift this lump of inebriated meat at least a few inches from the ground, it's a hopeful sign. Silenus probably does not care himself. Alcohol can always be relied upon to make its own flights of fancy.[2]

However, it is not just that gravity is represented by a fat man, almost too heavy to lift; fatness also coexists with babyhood, just as the enlargement of Kracklite's belly coincides with that of his pregnant wife. However, the flight of fancy that the drunken architect creates in this harrowing scene is to see himself not so much as Silenus but as Christ, for, after being rebuffed by the restaurant staff and upturning several tables, he cries out, 'Jesus Christ himself would have died of stomach cancer if you people had not crucified him first.'

This, Greenaway has claimed, quietly alludes to the situation depicted in Piero della Francesca's *Flagellation*:

> The murdered Christ is Kracklite, the hero, the sacrificial victim of the film. Three enigmatic figures converse at the foreground of the frame – in the film, these are three members of the Italian intellectual mafia. The three characters have their fun by means of an ironic death sentence which they pass on Kracklite when they first meet him, and make him believe that like Boullée he is a victim of stomach cancer. Later, drunk and panicstricken, he cries, 'Jesus Christ himself would have died of stomach cancer if you people had not crucified him first.' We were not intending to make reference to the painting's context; instead, with the contempt for him and the sentence of death, we wanted to make use of the entire form and content of Piero's painting.[3]

Hence, on the left side of Piero's painting – the sinister aspect, seemingly – the representation of the architecture shows a masterful grasp of perspective; the design of the Corinthian capitals, with their acanthus leaves, bas-relief friezes and volutes, is supremely delicate. But the most singular effect of all is the disposition of the various forces of light and colour. John White, in his seminal account of the relationship between illusionism and linear perspective, has suggested:

> Strong lighting, or strong colour, consistently applied, are another means of emphasizing depth and solidity . . . sharply contrasted lighting distinguishes the various planes and their spatial relationships even more clearly than the linear pattern with its insistence on sharp angles. In the same way, strong light on a rounded form stresses its solidity by the smooth transition from an intense highlight to a deep shadow. Only if the forms become complicated, and the lighting arbitrary, is the effect destroyed, and replaced by a dazzling surface vibration.[4]

Through the complication of its formal design, Piero's painting is simply 'dazzling'. Outlining the limits of the architectural shapes, while at the same time illuminating the central compartment of the coffered ceiling, the light bounces off the white architrave of the temple and slides down along the fluting of the columns to ignite the frontal border of the black-and-white floor. Yet here it is softened in a chromatic mix designed to enliven the figures of Christ and his tormenters, modulating the shadows and defining the pink and black clothing and hat of the man who observes at the left, before finally dispersing into darkness on the edge of the frame.

It may be that these aspects – colours washed out as if by the passage of time against the classical architecture, and the intense perspectival distancing – render remote, eternal and baffling the episode depicted; and if this is the case, then the right half of the work perhaps is meant to represent instead the contingent reality of the present heavily impinging on the panel. Philip Guston writes that 'the picture is sliced almost in half, yet both parts act on each other, repel and attract, absorb and enlarge one another'.[5] The three robust figures who dominate the right foreground, heavy in the fabric of their garments, the contemporary architectural forms and the cool blue of the sky all speak of the point to which history had brought humankind and the Church.[6] They are inscrutable; and there is no trace of any emotion appropriate to the event in the faces or bodies of this mysterious trio in the foreground, nor of those who are carrying out the flagellation. Such impermeability, their mute hardness, causes us to ask questions about their physical composition. They lack flesh and blood, certainly;

perhaps, instead, they are compounded out of substances similar to those of the exquisite architecture that frames them, of the friezes and ceilings and floors and columns, all of which seem executed in *pietre dure*. The figure in the hat with his back to us wears a robe the colour and texture of white marble; and on the evidence of this panel, one is almost inclined to think that Piero was not interested in human beings as living, acting, sentient creatures. For him they seem, on the contrary, inert, three-dimensional objects – statues, even – which he might have gladly substituted with arches, pilasters, capitals, cornices and even walls. Indeed, it is only in his depiction of the distinctive architectural lines that Piero betrays something resembling lyrical feeling. He paints what he cannot ever hope to realize: like the architect, Kracklite, Piero follows a dream of pure artifice worthy of his mind and his heart, and where his soul can feel itself at home.

Why, then, is this work of art never shown in the film, only vaguely alluded to in Greenaway's later exegesis? He perhaps offers a clue when he makes the following observation about the difficulties of reproducing an artist's work in the medium of film:

> If you look carefully at della Francesca, who has an obsessive and complicated concern for perspective, he's probably using some dozen different perspective systems in one image. Unless you deliberately built the set with false perspectives, you cannot compete. But false perspectives only work from a given fixed point, so the chances of taking the della Francesca as a starting point to develop and move into other cinematic concerns is not so profitable.[7]

Once again, the stasis of paint brushes up against the kinetic energies of film. The illusionistic reproduction that the medium of paint offers is far less expensive in material and creative terms than that which film might be able to offer. The difference is that in film, as was suggested in *Z&OO*, bodies cannot be rescaled and cropped in order to fit the geometrical equations of the perspectivist; the self cannot be deformed or twisted into new shapes just for the sake of the illusion. Painters can easily cheat, but the camera does not lie; not unless it is made to. Perhaps Piero's false perspectives represent both of these alternatives, especially in light of the sculptural figures; and perhaps they also point simply to the fine artist's effort to reproduce, to

47 Terminal prognosis, from *The Belly of an Architect* (1987).

bring the three-dimensional body into a two-dimensional mode of representation.

Sculpture, in particular, is invested with such a metaphorical charge and carries with it the kind of corporeality that obsesses Kracklite and Greenaway. It forms part of the cinematic discourse, which, in many shots, strives for the effect of abolishing the frontier between living people and representations carved in stone. For instance, Kracklite turns his head towards the photographer Flavia at the Piazza Navone, presenting to the camera a profile oddly similar to that of the bearded face of one of the allegorical figures in Bernini's statue of the *Four Rivers*. A comparable use of Roman statuary occurs when Kracklite's doctor, walking with his patient through the cloister of the hospital, pronounces the terminal prognosis (illus. 47). As the pair move glacially down the corridor's length, the perspective is one that could be derived from Piero. The colonnade – wide with high ceilings and a stone floor – opens on to a sunlit courtyard, the birds sing in the bright blue air and a small fountain trickles into a bowl; and all along the right-hand side of the corridor is a line of Roman busts on plinths or pedestals. As they pass the stones, the doctor gives a brief account of each emperor's fame and infamy:

Galba . . . a miserable sort of man . . . bisexual . . . fancied mature slaves, especially if they had been a little mutilated . . . all his freed men had no fingers on the left hands . . . he's dead – died screaming . . . in a cellar.
(They walk on. They stop again.)
Titus . . . he started well . . . soon became greedy . . . disembowelled on the Tiber steps . . . he's dead, died screaming . . .
(They walk on.)
Hadrian . . . as you know, an architect of note . . . put a lot of faith in stones . . . died peacefully . . . planning a Temple to Wisdom . . . still . . . (Shrugs) . . . he's dead . . . Nero . . . best not to talk about him – burnt Rome, caused untold misery . . . deserved to die; died screaming in a summerhouse.
(They come to an unnamed bust and the doctor stops.)
Unknown . . . no name . . . he looks serene enough, let's suppose he was you . . . same fleshy face . . . what happened to him? How did he die?[8]

Through these fragmentary representations of Roman emperors, Kracklite's future is brought to a point of convergence with a historical perspective; he is petrified into a more reassuringly solid time than his own future. Standing in front of each bust, the doctor repeats 'died screaming' in order to remind the architect that these blocks of stone were once bodies, vulnerable and human; and then at the end of the promenade, in front of the final statue, the connection between flesh and stone is made, finally and visually. The doctor stands on the left of the screen, the bust occupies the centre, while on the right is Kracklite, his back to the wall and his body cut off mid-torso by the cinematic frame. In this position he faces outwards, his head slightly raised; but his gaze is as absent as those on the faces of the bust or on the bearded Christ in Piero's *Flagellation*.

Roman art, in the form of fragments and ruins, here provides a fitting and terrible symbol of the breaking-down of the fabric of Kracklite's body. The apotheosis of this occurs late in the film, in the monumental interior of the Capitoline Museum, where the architect is charged after his drunken behaviour a few hours earlier. His human frame – large enough, in itself – is contrasted with the vastness of the bits and pieces of statues that are on display here. The artistic allusion soon becomes clear. In 1778 Henry Fuseli visited Rome and there sketched himself placing his right hand on a huge fragment of a sculpted foot, and,

48 John Henry Fuseli, *The Artist Moved by the Grandeur of Antique Fragments,* c. 1778–80.

dwarfed by a massive stony hand, placing his left hand on his head in despair (illus. 48). *The Artist Moved by the Grandeur of Antique Fragments* is a work that now, apparently, 'tends to appear comic, [and] reveals the shortcomings of his art'.[9] This is too simple, however, for Fuseli was not just affected by the heroic scale of the remnants; all too pressing, too, must have been the problem of conveying the physicality of such body parts on canvas or paper. When in Rome the only possible solution was, as ever, to follow the ancients and set up an awesome juxtaposition of human with divine, body with statue.

This is precisely Greenaway's plan in the scene in the Capitoline Museum. When Kracklite is interrogated by a policeman, the architect's increasingly fragmentary mortal identity is contrasted with the broken *objets d'art* that surround him. Framed in a long shot, he is situated exactly under the navel of a massive partly damaged torso (illus. 49). Two bellies are now visible in this carefully composed framing: that of the smashed statue and that of Kracklite himself, now partly obscured by the head of the man who is questioning him. The optical illusion is such that this head forms a dark space, a cleft in the belly of the architect who stands still before him. The visual suggestion seems to be that the belly of flesh no longer exists but has been worn away by cancer; however, the belly of stone above resists any such erosion. The finger that points upwards to heaven, as

in Fuseli, now assumes an ironic dimension: in that direction,
but for the grace of art, go we all. At the heart of this interrogation scene, the language, like the statues that surround the
architect, is fragmented, amputated, reduced to a cold juxtaposition of isolated words deprived of their syntax. The policeman
who interrogates him exists only in outline – as in Piero's
Flagellation, he is a faceless bureaucrat, little more than a voice
which intones neutrally, 'Name. Address. Married. Age next
birthday. Occupation.' All that seems to matter here are personal details; the points that ground an individual in subjectivity
and responsibility but which, nevertheless, will guarantee his
obscurity once he dies. Then the interrogation closes on an
exchange whose significance is far in excess of this sequence,
and which leaves a wry smile on the lips of the architect:

> POLICEMAN: That's all, thank you. You may go.
> KRACKLITE: You mean that's really all?
> POLICEMAN: What else could there be?

'You may go' is not simply a dismissal from the presence of the
policeman; it is also a release from the pain and responsibilites
of mortality. However, Kracklite's surprised question suggests
that he expects rather more from life.

49 Torso interview,
from *The Belly of an
Architect* (1987).

A just reply to the policeman's question might be an 'art' that secures reputation and memorializes human achievement into eternity. The possibility of achieving this ideal lies at the heart of the film, as Greenaway admitted: 'As Devil's advocate, it begged to ask the question, was a form of immortality at all possible through art and manmade creation?' Such bias against artificial forms, working in and around a film whose aesthetic sense is so highly developed, hardly masks an appeal to some prior and recoverable nature: natural pleasure, natural procreativity, natural drives. At one point, responding to his views on the perdurability of art, Louisa says to her husband bitterly: 'Everything's possible for Art. I mean, look at our marriage. Art first, Kracklite second, the rest a long way down the line.' As Greenaway accepts:

> Despite putting forward evidence of man's ability occasionally to create possible items of lasting value – like the buildings of Rome – the immortality question was asked with some desperation and certainly much vanity. It could surely only be answered with an equivocal response, for the architect commits suicide to avoid a painful and only too mortal demise, but also to make way for his child – whose birth cries end the film – the child who is perhaps his successor in the creation stakes but certainly his natural successor in the Darwinian stakes.[10]

In his elegant introduction to the screenplay, he mentions the 'architectural heritage of two and a half thousand years' which sets 'Kracklite's nine-month predicament into perspective' by underlining 'the ephemerality of one foreign individual striving for significance in an eternal city'.[11] That phrase 'into perspective' resonates against our awareness of Piero's forms, and perhaps those of Hadrian's Pantheon. He continues: 'architecture is the least perishable of the arts and the most public. Architects (perhaps like film-makers) are supposed to be accountable to art, to finance, to the specialist critic, to the man in the street and perhaps to posterity.' Kracklite, however, has hitherto chosen not just to disregard the immense weight of the classical past by presuming his importance as an architect in the present; he has also disdained the responsibility of the present and any liability for the future. Instead he works, or rather broods, on some ideal realm called art; on the Enlightenment architect Boullée, whose works exist only on paper, and who claimed that 'the architect should study the theory of volumes and analyze them, at the same time seeking to understand their properties, the powers they have on our senses, their similarities to the human organism'.[12]

The proposal of Boullée for a cenotaph dedicated to the memory of Isaac Newton is perhaps the most important expression of the trust the leading figures of the Enlightenment maintained in their power to transform physical spaces into intellectual concepts. His designs for the building depict a structure that would have set out a physical theory in great detail (illus. 50); indeed, Boullée from the outset had 'conceived the idea of enveloping [Newton] in [his] own discovery' that the earth had originally been perfectly spherical before it had become flattened through rotation.[13] Therefore, the main chamber, with the sarcophagus at its base, is a perfect sphere, and all the supporting architectural forms are its geometrical derivatives – cylinders, segments, quadrants and so on, while externally, the perfection of the ball is maintained by means of curves cut into the lower cylinder. In some respects, Boullée was borrowing from Hadrian's Pantheon, whose construction is ruled by symmetry of three parts: a circular floor, a cylindrical wall and the dome, into which was cut an *oculus*, a circular opening to admit light. Richard Sennett has written eloquently of the illumination within the building:

> On sunny summer days, a lightshaft searches the interior, moving from the edge of the dome, down the cylinder on to the floor and then up the cylinder again, as the sun outside moves into its orbit; on cloudy days, the light becomes a gray fog tinted by the concrete of the shell. At night the building mass vanishes; through the opening at the top of the dome a circle of stars looms out of the darkness.[14]

By making use of an equally novel system of lighting, the interior of Boullée's building would imply a firmament: 'The lighting of this monument, which should resemble that on a clear night, is provided by the planets and the stars that decorate the vault of the sky.' To achieve this effect, Boullée planned that the planetarium's dome be pierced by 'funnel-like openings', so that 'The daylight outside filters through these aper-

50 Etienne Louis Boullée, *Project for a Cenotaph to Sir Isaac Newton*, 1784.

51 Etienne Louis Boullée, *Interior View by Night*, 1784.

tures into the gloom of the interior and outlines all the objects in the vault with bright, sparkling light'.[15] According to the detailed designs he drew, the viewer would have entered the building from an outside passage far below the sphere, then walked up steps to enter at the very base of the chamber; having caught sight of the heavens, he would descend a flight of steps and emerge at the other side of the building (illus. 51).

Hadrian's Pantheon (which, even though he had never visited it, Boullée took as the starting point for his planetarium) almost aggressively orientated the spectator within its structure, placing him in a context of five rows of deeply sunk panels, or *lacunaria*, twenty-eight in each row. However, looking up into the artificial heavens, the viewer in Boullée's planetarium would have no sense of his or her own place on earth. There are no internal designs to locate the body. 'We see only a continuous surface which has neither beginning nor end,' he wrote of the dome, 'and the more we look at it, the larger it appears.'[16] Furthermore, in Boullée's sectional drawings for Newton's Tomb, the human beings are nearly invisible within the immensity of the sphere: the interior sphere is thirty-six times higher than the mere human specks drawn at the base. As in the heavens outside, unbounded space inside is to become an experience in itself. To Boullée, this may have been exhilarating; but others may just have felt imprisoned by Newton's theories of light and gravity.

Greenaway attempted to catch the sense of constraint when he discussed Redon's *Le Boulet (dit Le Prisonnier)* (illus. 52) under the heading 'A Centre of Gravity', and wrote eloquently of the relationship between the boulet and Boullée:

> As a bold and unequivocal instructive, we start with a simple volume that will never fly. It is the first imperative. Gravity as a ball underground. At the bottom of the hill. A heavy full stop realized as a volume. The end of a sentence that we have not yet written. A re-imploded black hole made whole. And it is as shiny as a cannonball . . . which, of course, under suitable conditions, will fly, though the bore in the barrel of the gun to take this missile would suggest a barrel of inordinate

52 Redon, *Le Boulet (dit Le Prisonnier)*, 1886.

53 Redon, *La Boule*, c. 1878.

length and a massive power of propulsion. A cannon devised by Boullée, Etienne-Louis Boullée, master of the heavy mass, guardian of gravitational spirit.

. . . The ball is set against a column in a dark space. Is the dark space night or is it a secret and an underground cell? If it's underground, then flight is even farther away. The drawing is called 'The Prisoner'. Is this philosopher chained to this ball? Is this ball the familiar ball of the ball-and-chain that tells in shorthand that a man is a prisoner in so many caricatures and cartoons? If this potential flying philosopher is chained to this ball, then there is no chance he can fly. No. The philosopher is free to come and go. The ball is the prisoner.[17]

And the ball, the globe, imprisons us too, since, as Newton proved, the measured force of gravity is a combination of the gravitational force due to the pull of the earth on the object and the opposing centrifugal force generated by the earth's rotation. In fact, the sphere is the very last word, as Greenaway suggested in his discussion of another drawing of a ball by Redon (illus. 53), which he included in his Louvre exhibition:

And finally the dead weight, the full stop, the gravity sphere again . . . Just a ball with a shadow, of unknown size, because there is no reference for size. A heaviness and a next-to-nothingness, the earth and an atom all in one. The reflected light of its smooth surface is contained and acknowledged within its own shadow. And a mocking highlight reflects what? The light of the sun?[18]

Or the light of Newtonian enlightenment?

On his first night in Rome, a meal is given in Kracklite's honour in front of the Pantheon, the monument that acts as a motif throughout the film, vaunting its perfection and the success with which it arranges architectural volume despite the pull of gravity. At one point during the dinner, the conversation turns towards the evidence of Newton's theory that 'appears in every Englishman's pocket'. As Byron puts it in *Don Juan*:

> Man fell with apples, and with apples rose,
> If this be true; for we must deem the mode
> In which Sir Isaac Newton could disclose
> Through the then unpaved stars the turnpike road,
> A thing to counterbalance human woes. (Canto X, Stanza 1).

At the time that the film was made, in 1986, the English £1 note – guaranteed to counterbalance human woes – bore the image of Sir Isaac Newton, and the illustration of the apple blossom that adorned the upper part of the note was an allusion to the physicist's gravitational theory. It turns up in the remains of the cake – itself a replica of the Boullée monument dedicated to Newton – smashed open at the close of the meal. Out of circulation through most of the film, the note returns only when Kracklite offers it in error to the guard to gain access to the top storey of the Vittorio Emanuele monument; and, in the last moments, we see the note again. The architect has jumped and fallen on to the slope of the huge Boullée model of the truncated pyramid and broken his neck; finally his corpse has come to rest on the roof of Caspasian's car. A close-up shows the pound note still clasped in his hand; and the cause of death – Newtonian gravity – is revealed. A tracking–reversing crane-shot now begins, as the camera continues to move away and eventually settles on the eight-year-old boy seated on a stone bench playing with his gyroscope. The camera moves in to the toy and concentrates on its axis, which is growing more and more diagonal, until the tiny device that can temporarily withstand gravity also collapses.

Throughout, Kracklite increasingly identifies himself with Boullée, who, he is led to believe, also died of stomach cancer. On Friday 19 July 1985 he writes to the French architect:

> Dear Etienne-Louis,
> The colours of Rome are the colours of human flesh and hair
> – for the most part warm – orange, orange-red, browns; and

warm whites – cream – often warm black. No blue and only
the darkest of greens – an exaggerated point of view? What
colours would your buildings be? I have grown so used to
your drawings being in black-and-white – it's difficult for me
to see them in any colour.
Yours,
Stourley Kracklite[19]

Colour is but another means of ordering, another cryptologi-
cal system, along with numbers and letters, the hues working
with and against one another so that the city can be read as
colour-coded. In particular, Greenaway felt that the warm tones
of Rome's buildings were too suggestive of a healthy human
body, and so Sacha Vierny was instructed to tone down as far as
possible. 'With orange filters in the camera, the green and blue
of the natural world in this film was purposefully reduced to
emphasize the environment of a manmade city.'[20] When green
does appear it implies artifice and decay. The English banknote
is green; and when Kracklite uses the photocopier his face is
repeatedly illuminated by a livid artificial light.

In the three photocopying scenes – in which Kracklite xerox-
es the belly of a postcard reproduction of Augustus, the stomach of a figure by Piranesi who might pass for Boullée and the
abdomen of Bronzino's Andrea Doria as Neptune – the question of colour returns as the machine throws out orange, green
and white lights that contrast with the emerging monochrome
copies:

> He selects a button and the machine starts – adding orange
> and white lights to the green. Twelve large, enlarged, photo-
> copied stomachs of Augustus roll out of the machine's
> mouth; with painful, mechanical noises – halfway between
> coughing, choking and screaming – the machine 'gives birth'
> to twelve stomachs. When the machine stops, Kracklite picks
> up an enlargement and examines it. The enlargements are
> damp and a little shiny. He lifts his shirt and feels for his
> stomach. He takes an enlarged photograph of the Augustus
> 'belly' from the machine and looks down at his own belly. He
> identifies his stomach with the stomach of Augustus and
> feels the pain as though it's Augustus who is suffering.[21]

Greenaway's 'gives birth', so carefully ironized by the quotation marks, draws attention to the idea of artistic reproductions.

After enlarging a detail from a postcard of Augustus, he xerox-
es it repeatedly, enlarging the belly of the sculpture, subjecting
it, in fact, to a process of multiple instant reproduction that
both sustains and yet – as it is mechanical – undermines the
metaphor of pregnancy. Once he has finished the copying, he
clutches the image to his own belly and then examines himself
in a mirror, setting up a complex series of relations between the
real image and the copy. This scene is the starting point for the
wilderness of mirrors: between the reality of Kracklite's belly
stands the photocopied image of a photographic image of a
sculpted form of the trunk of the long-dead Augustus. By placing the image against his own trunk, Kracklite both draws
attention to the contingency of this paper reproduction and
attempts to bring it back into contact with his body.

Despite the colourful functioning of the xerox machine, it
reproduces only the black-and-white image of the two-dimensional copy; and in this way Greenaway's film becomes, or produces, an image more akin to writing than to cinema. A
particularly distinctive pattern of green and orange light is
transformed into the flatness of the xerox, which in turn
becomes the basis for a discrete sequence of travels through
Kracklite's obsession. Hence, the photocopy amounts to a
change of medium, a paradigmatic shift from cinema to text; a
reversion to the black-and-white reproductions of Neville in
The Draughtsman's Contract and the zebra stripes of *Z&OO*. The
xeroxed sheet represents a statue of a dead emperor, being
made to represent the suffering of an infirm architect, the cancer in the belly, the death in the heart of the Eternal City. These
graphics soon overwhelm his hotel room, covering the floor,
along with books on Boullée and models of the Newton memo-
rial, until the whole room is filled with the proliferation of that
first copy of Augustus's torso (illus. 54). And if the shift to photocopy is not sufficiently explicit a move to a printed image produced by the machine, then Kracklite will underline the idea as
he draws on each of the copies, sketching intestines on them, in
the way that a doctor might draw the location of a shadow on
an X-ray. Kracklite implies yet another intimate correspondence
between the detail of Augustus's sculpted abdomen and his
own body, between art and life; and simultaneously, Greenaway produces designs on behalf of the architect in which
Augustus's belly is filled with multicoloured round forms that
could be small stones, poisoned figs or foetuses.

54 Hotel copies, from *The Belly of an Architect* (1987).

The conflict between colour and monochrome systems of representation is codified in the scene when Flavia, having persuaded Kracklite to pose as Andrea Doria, after Bronzino, says, 'I don't know how to paint, but I know how to take photographs.' A few moments later, Kracklite, left alone as she fixes a roll of film in the darkroom, wanders around her studio in a bathrobe. Here several representational systems are set against one another. Her coffee tables, for instance, are strewn with fragments of Roman statuary – heads, primarily; and in the inner sanctum he discovers a little exposition of his life in snapshots, an exhibition covering the walls, retracing and remaking his and his wife's lives over the previous months (illus. 56). Accompanied by Wim Mertens's reflective piece, 'The Struggle for Pleasure', the narrative commences in long tracking shots from left to right over the collage that, at first glance, seems to contain publicity stills from the film itself. However, all the shots reproduced on photographic paper have been secretly taken, and recall Kracklite's various indiscretions, repeating his actions and fixing forever those seemingly evanescent situations that have been passed over by the *mise-en-scène* of the film. Here the three-dimensionality of the sculptural body parts is set against the two-dimensional images, which record, among other intimacies, Louisa's pregnant belly and liaisons between her and Flavia's brother. This montage – whose progress is marked by a red ribbon, the kind of line seen laid across the maps of *A Walk Through H* – appears increasingly familiar, as its linear progression redoubles the narrative of the film itself. The camera's long travelling shot, as it unifies the images, begins to undermine their status as photographs and they begin to evoke the mounted quality of film, suggesting once more a continuity between the projects of photography and cinema. The first shot in the sequence represents the cake shaped in the form of a Boullée dome, a reminder that the first evening the architect spent in Rome marked the beginning of the end of all that mattered to him. At the other end of the syntagmatic chain the ribbon passes through a composite picture of Kracklite's head surmounting a separate image of Augustus's torso, and then drops away as it reaches a plaque on which is printed 'Etienne Louis Boullée 1728–99'.

At this point Flavia re-enters, having just finished developing a roll of film featuring shots of the bellies of sculptures in the Piazza Navona. She hangs the red ribbon around Kracklite's neck as though it were a rope and pulls him behind a translucent white blind, which blocks out the daylight and which suggests nothing so much as a cinema screen and thus an entry into the representational space of film (illus. 57). Previously, at the Piazza Navona, seizing Kracklite's camera, she had made an unambiguous link between two types of reproduction when she said, 'Come to my studio. I'll process while you take a shower, and we'll see which of the two comes out of the bath the more developed.' Flavia begins to make love to him, and their bodies become abstract shapes in the bright white light. This is followed by a very abrupt cut to a camera on a tripod, which blocks our view of the couple now copulating on a couch. The technical paraphernalia of cinema is interfering with our view of the character; the possibility of voyeurism is this time compromised and will be curtailed a few seconds later by the arrival of Caspasian in the studio (illus. 58).

Just after dawn on Thursday 20 August 1985 Kracklite climbs the stairs to his apartment. Hearing the sound of laughter coming from within, he takes a chair and sits in the corridor transfixed before a keyhole – that most ubiquitous of voyeuristic frames – through which he sees Caspasian romping around the chamber with Louisa, making animal noises and at one point

55 Agnolo
Bronzino, *A Young
Woman with her
Little Boy*, 1540.

clasping a large phallic model of Boullée's design for a light-house between his legs. All the time, a child watches Kracklite watching and then crying; and, in due course, the child's moth-er arrives and places her hand on her son's shoulder (illus. 59). The pairs seem familiar; and the image is another visual allu-sion to Bronzino, to his portrait of an unknown woman and her child (illus. 55). But the deep linear perspective derives from Piero della Francesca's *Madonna*. The sequence is a complex *mise-en-scène* of visuality, a highly configured spectacle of sight lines;[22] but it is also where truth breaks out, as the bright light of a Roman day seeps through the cracks in shutters and through the keyhole into the eye of Kracklite, whose name now begins to have a larger significance. The child speaks:

CHILD (*in English*): What are you crying for?
KRACKLITE (*without moving his body but looking at the child*): There's a draught in the keyhole and it's making my eyes water.
WOMAN (*her voice just audible from the room behind the child, in Italian*): What's the man crying for?
CHILD (*in Italian*): He's got a draught in his eyes.

56 Flavia's mural, from *The Belly of an Architect* (1987).

57 The white screen, from *The Belly of an Architect* (1987).

58 Caspasian's entry, from *The Belly of an Architect* (1987).

59 Woman and child, from *The Belly of an Architect* (1987).

That word 'draught' reminds us of its connotations in a previous Greenaway film; here the word implies a cold blast of air, but also the tyranny of the draughtsman's frame. Kracklite's view of what remains of his marriage is now dependent upon the aperture that stands between him and the truth of his life. For Kracklite at least, the scene ends a few moments later in accident, when the chair collapses and he is pitched to the floor heavily, his pratfall prefiguring the final fall. The child helps him up, and in return Kracklite gives him the gyroscope, which, as much as any apple, is a monument to Isaac Newton's theories of gravitation. Spinning at speed in the final moments of the film, it creates a virtual dome, like the one Boullée designed but never built, before becoming increasingly unstable and collapsing just before the credits roll.[23]

CHILDREN'S GAMES

The Belly of an Architect ends with the death of the architect, who falls to the earth just as his child is born; a neat illustration of Darwinian succession. Most of Greenaway's films have examined the social and biological function of children, and in 1988, after the making of *Drowning by Numbers*, he admitted that in the course of his four major feature films a child had been growing older and 'becoming more difficult to ignore'. In *The Draughtsman's Contract*, the child is six and is forcibly taught the German alphabet by his German governess. At play, he likes to draw with chalk on a blackboard, but is soon 'reprimanded for any ideas he might have about becoming a painter'. Despite this, 'the boy was sensitive to what adults chose to ignore and saw magic in an English garden where others saw only money and property'. In *Z&OO*, the child is a year older and has changed sex to become Alba Bewick's daughter – a well-mannered little girl, Beta, named after the second letter of the Greek alphabet. She is wise beyond her years and – with an early understanding of sexual games – she easily tricks adults into ridiculing themselves by showing their underwear, or lack of it. Most of this child's play consists of her gathering creatures to exhibit in her own private zoo; she will put spiders and flies together on the grounds that they share the same colour. In *The Belly of an Architect*, the child has grown older still, and is now an eight-year-old Roman boy – 'handsome, pampered a little and possessing a truly Stoic attitude to death – especially that of

144

his father'. He watches Kracklite's fall and, unlike the older Roman males, such as Caspasian, he is responsible for the one unselfish action in the film: the exchange of an orange (a healthy symbol in a film about sickness possibly caused by poisoned fruit) for a gyroscope (a simple educational toy used to illustrate the centrifugal force that keeps the planets and the stars circulating in the heavens).[24]

This proposition is well appreciated in the game of the child who introduces the next film, *Drowning by Numbers*, described by Greenaway as 'a children's tale for adults'. It opens with a young girl in an extravagant crinoline dress and a full face of make-up, counting off the stars in the night sky as she skips and dances on the edge of the sea. The house in front of which she plays is illuminated intermittently by the beam from an invisible lighthouse – a beam designed to save men from drowning – while an enormous body of a bird, possibly an albatross, is suspended from a wooden post (illus. 60). Behind her a massive shadow looms, while inside an upstairs room her mother is on the game: 'She says she wishes she'd been Nell Gwyn, because she'd liked to have serviced Charles II.'[25] This young girl jumps the rope, never losing her breath or her place, calling out to the night sky the names of the stars, until she reaches the hundredth on the list: Electra, the daughter of Agamemnon, who helped her brother to avenge their father's death at the hands of their mother, Clytemnestra. In Freudian psychotherapy, the daughter's name is given to the complex in girls or women that stems from an attachment to their father involving unconscious rivalry with their mother. As Greenaway's drawing *The Skipping Girl* (illus. 61) explicitly demonstrates, the girl is 'menaced by sex'; for out of the stormy skies whirring around the brewery chimneys, water towers and lighthouses – a reminder of the hurricane that struck southern England during the making of the film in October 1987 – there seems to be emerging over her something rather more than a phallic symbol. It is the phallus itself.

In *Drowning by Numbers*, it seems the child's duties in previous films as artless wit and wise joker have been occupied by not just one but two children; and they have grown to an age – thirteen – when childhood innocence is giving way to complex experience. The other child, Smut, is the emancipated son of Madgett, a coroner, and is consequently well versed in the ways of death. His favourite hobby is to count corpses; he and his father refer to this as 'The Great Death Game'. He fires off rockets

60 Girl and shadow, from *Drowning by Numbers* (1988).

at the death spot and paints the spot either red or yellow depending on the day of the week death occurred; the place is then marked with a stake, the time and place of death inscribed on a map, and the scene recorded on Polaroids. Beyond the rules of these games, Greenaway intended that the activities of this boy and the girl should comment on and parallel the activities of their elders. The girl – 'like a beautiful moth caught in the spotlight of the lighthouse' – attracts the attention of Smut, the intrepid young male so childish in appearance ('short trousers, dull clothes, spectacles, a little stooped') who persistently approaches her, romantically hopeful, arriving on his childish bike, 'addressing her with garbled stories culled from his Sunday school classes and his perusal of books on Art'.[26] Although he is exactly the same age as the girl – thirteen, unlucky for some – it is no surprise that the girl exceeds in sophistication and is indifferently contemptuous. Much of what Smut says has to be corrected by superior authority, which in the girl's case is her errant mother and the Bible – both being incontrovertible and matchless sources of information and advice:

GIRL: (*with complete innocence*) Are you circumcized?

147

62 Formal considerations, from *Drowning by Numbers* (1988).

SMUT: What's that?

GIRL: A piece of your willie is cut off. It's in the Bible. (*She taps a thick Bible beside her chair.*) My mother . . . (*indicating with her head the room above*) . . . says it's better that way.

SMUT: Oh.[27]

Of course, this is no ordinary little girl, but one existing out of her age and out of her original depth of field. There are formal considerations (illus. 62): the house is flat-fronted with regular symmetrical windows and a small, triangular-roofed shallow porch, whose front door is arched. On either side are two bay trees, each clipped into the shape of a sphere on a long trunk. The girl sits in the centre of the frame, the arched hoop of her skirt and braided hair making a series of parallel arcs of a circle to correspond with the arch at the top of the door frame; and when Smut visits, the wheels of his bicycle form two open circles against the parallel horizontals of the house's façade. Greenaway explains the compositional issues:

Hoops and arcs and right angles and strict horizontals and strict verticals and equilateral triangles and parallel lines – all arranged in a shallow stage space. The elements are small, discreet, familiar and domestic in scale. They are reminiscent of the shapes and the scale of a child's set of building bricks – the traditional shapes of which, despite variations in materials, have persisted from the nineteenth century until now – then in painted wood, now in coloured plastic.[28]

It may allude to a child's toy, a doll's house, even; but in its familiarity, this formal composition is also intended to remind the viewer of another, rather more sophisticated scene:

> Her costume belongs to the seventeenth century, a monstrous encumbrance that must have required complicated manoevring to enter a doorway, walk against the wind, turn sharply, sit at a table, walk with a crowd. It is a costume that quotes the Spanish Infanta, the Inquisition, Velázquez.[29]

She is a child out of Velázquez, then; and, as such, she brings to the structure of the film all the difficulties and preoccupations of *Las Meninas* (illus. 63), where the organization of perspectives and 'planes of reality' is so central to the interpretive game.[30] The scene takes place in Velázquez's studio in the Royal Apartment, a room hung with forty paintings after Rubens, including copies of *Apollo and Midas* and the *Fable of Arachne* by Maso. Yet amid the picture frames, the window frames along the right-hand side which draw the linear perspective and the door frame in which a figure pauses, we are able to catch sight of something in the mirror on the back wall, which exists, as it were, beyond the rules. The author of this fascination is glimpsed looking out upon us, painting our response. The compositional organization is more complex than that of a mere painting within a painting, so numerous are the possible central

63 Detail from Diego Velázquez, *Las Meninas*, 1656.

149

focuses of the work, for is the Infanta, or Philip, or Velázquez, the true protagonist? Or is it – as Ortega y Gasset has suggested – the central space itself? *Las Meninas*, then, not only contains riddling and delectable play on conventional perspective and the normal 'distance' between artist and viewer, but also reaches out beyond the frame in an ironical and engaging fashion to put the viewer in the picture about the royal family.

Velázquez delicately sustains the central ambivalence, and in precisely this way – through the dexterous play upon different perspectives, striving to maintain the central oscillation of reference to himself, as theatrical mage, as creative intellect and as his own shadowed persona – Greenaway in *Drowning by Numbers* performs a similar feat in a cinematic context. These works, in their self-conscious complexity and flair of execution, are vanities of their creators' art. The power of Velázquez's brush is amply demonstrated in the painting; and similarly Greenaway's film celebrates the power to create images out of artificial light. 'Many of the scenes are shot in the orange light of dawn or sunset . . . shot at night – a night for the most part quietly benevolent . . . but occasionally erupting into enigmatic and ambiguous malevolence.'[31] Both works display the magic of illusion and the power of the artist to organize it in an entrancing way; in both cases, we see from behind the easel of the painter and encounter the baseless and insubstantial materials on which both paint their arbitrary fictions.

When the skipping girl enumerates stars by name up to a hundred she indicates the point of the film. In answer to Cissie's question 'Why did you stop?' she says, 'A hundred is enough. Once you have counted one hundred, all other hundreds are the same.'[32] In this film – just another game – the numbering scheme supposedly organizing the action is as arbitrary and contingent as any child's play. Greenaway admits: 'There are strong memories of childhood games, counting rituals, fantasies from illustrated children's books and from childhood imagination'; given such childishness, any principle of order will be destined for replacement amid a weary acceptance of futility, just as the tidal current bears all away, and the child is father to the next generation.[33] Through the indifference of these games, Greenaway seeks to ruin any possible comfort in whatever organizing principles the human imagination could possibly design. Here two such systems drive the film along: one is is the narrative of the three women – all of whom are called Cissie Colpitts – murder-

ing their husbands; the other is a numerical sequence, 1 to 100. This series is inscribed, in increasingly daring ways, into the very fabric of the film's images, either in the form of set decoration (figures are painted on the rumps of cows, living and dead, on bees, on swimsuits and bathing caps, on bare bodies, or merely inscribed in letters and notebooks) or at the level of the dialogue itself. Number 1 appears in the first scene after the main title – boldly white on a tree that was set upright after the ravages of the Hurricane; 98 figures later, from the same tree, or possibly another, Smut hangs himself with the rope of the skipping girl. Around his neck is a notebook on which is inscribed 99, his last recorded writing and evidence of his contribution and knowledge of the number count (illus. 64). Perhaps after all it was he who engineered the whole business.[34] Greenaway explains:

> The narrative represents the freewill choices made by the characters and the implacable number count represents the limits of free choice. However we feel we can exercise freewill – there are severe limitations. The boundaries are inevitably marked. A film is an artificial construction decided upon by the film-maker's use of time – the numbers represent the ticking away of the frames, the seconds, the minutes, the allotted

65 Pieter Bruegel, *Children's Games*, 1560.

time for the narrative to take place. When you reach fifty in the number count, you know you are halfway through the narrative; when you are in the nineties, you know the story has not far to go and when you reach one hundred, narrative and number count arrive neatly at a photo-finish. The film – this artificial construct – is at an end. The game is finished.[35]

The final number, 100, is painted on the prow of the boat in which the non-swimmer, Madgett, is abandoned in the last image of the film. 'When your number comes around. . .' Madgett, the master game-player who devises complicated rules and regulations, knows this truth better than most.

On an easel beside his bed stands a large reproduction of Bruegel's painting, *Children's Games* (illus. 65), no doubt a useful reference manual for Madgett at moments of flagging invention. Greenaway describes the painting: 'More than a hundred children flood the canvas and each child is involved in a game'; his verb here is significant, and his eye is drawn inexorably to the hidden currents in the panel: 'On the far left periphery of the painting is a river and in the river . . .?'[36] At the time Bruegel was painting, children's games were equated with an easy, thoughtless and sometimes foolish activity, so he may have wished to illustrate thoughtlessness. Yet visual clues signal the importance of specific games, as well as the relationship of one game to another. The setting is one of extraordinary perspectival clarity, 'and was undoubtedly influenced by Italian city views of

the type that had started with Piero della Francesca': a complicated network of figure groups, set out in diagonals and horizontals, is placed within a massive playground, bordered by
the architectural elements.[37] Especially conspicuous near the
prominent building on the left (which contributes a sharp diagonal continued by the fence behind it) are the boy with the mask
and the two girls throwing dice (using old sheep bones); further
up, another group playing blind man's buff stands between
building and fence. As played in Flanders, the girl, blinded with
a hood, tagged a boy, who in turn became her mock bride-
groom; the game, therefore, was a type of courtship game, and
this in turn links this group with the bridal procession, the bride
(in red) marking the focal point of Bruegel's panel.

All these children's games funnel down on to issues of marital rites and, as Sandra Hindman has noted, 'The treatment of
marriage in *Children's Games* takes its place in a pervasive six-
teenth-century literary tradition that viewed marriage as foolish because it both encouraged lust and led inevitably to the
domination of the man by the woman.'[38] Certainly, Bruegel
seems to imply that just as marriage is a sure sequel to
courtship, so birth follows marriage, as is suggested by the bap-
tismal procession in the left foreground approaching the building in single file, led by a midwife carrying a swaddled baby.
The baptism presumably will occur at the mock altar in the
building on the left, presided over by the doll dressed as a cler-
gyman; while yet another stage in family life is detailed on the
floor of this room where two girls playing with dolls mimic the
actions of their mothers. But in order to gain entrance to this
place, the procession must pass by the girls playing dice. The
moral here is simple and has a strong bearing on Greenaway's
film. As the capriciousness of chance determines the outcome in
knucklebones, as well as marriage, so other games, such as
blind man's buff, have equally unpredictable conclusions and
may prefigure the haphazard selection of a mate in the game of
life. Human reason cannot control the course of play, or of love.

As the numbers reckon up, Madgett – whose name suggests
both the magic of, say, Prospero and the maggots seen in putrefying bodies, the twin criteria of imaginative construction (culture) and ceaseless decay (nature) between which he has
struggled to mediate through the film – begins to tire of game
playing. As a last gesture, he offers a tug of war to settle 'good
and evil'. Depending on the outcome, he will serve either

nature's life force or culture's law and decorum. However there is no final decision, for at the crucial moment Smut pulls out of the game. He has been informed that his putative lover, the skipping girl, following his advice and ignoring her mother's, had ventured out into the street to skip on the safest day of the week and had been killed by a hit-and-run driver. As punishment to himself for his bad advice to her, Smut leaves to play 'The Endgame':

> The object of this garne is to dare to fall with a noose around your neck from a place sufficiently off the ground such that a fall will hang you. The object of the game is to punish those who have caused great unhappiness by their selfIsh actions. This is the best game of all because the winner is also the loser and the judge's decision is always final.[39]

Smut's foot slips and, in a flurry of leaves, he falls and breaks his neck. 'Games can be very dangerous', as Madgett observes.

PAINTING BY NUMBERS

Vernon Gras has suggested that issues of reproduction lie at the heart of Greenaway's work. In general terms, he claims that 'women protagonists . . . always represent nature's reproductive, renewing force; men protagonists either engage in the futile cultural effort to order nature's changing ways or interfere in this civilizing and spiritualizing process by exploiting it commercially'.[40] *Drowning by Numbers* is the story of three women – grandmother, daughter and granddaughter, all called Cissie Colpitts, 'three generations of solidarity taking action against marital dissatisfaction' – all of whom drown their husbands (respectively Jake, a lecher and a drunk; Hardy, an overweight slob; and Bellamy, who is sloppy with contraceptives and boorish) and bribe Madgett, before drowning him too. Each woman is, in effect, a mechanical reproduction of the previous generation; and so when Cissie 3 becomes pregnant, it is probable that she will give birth to Cissie 4, an 'artificial miracle'.

Consequently in the very title of this film, it is Greenaway's intention to lay out the means by which the 'artificial miracle' of reproduction takes place.

> Hidden – not too deeply – in the title of the film *Drowning by Numbers* is the activity of 'Painting by Numbers'. An outline

154

drawing – often of some complexity – is mapped out in a series of numbered areas on a piece of prepared cheap canvas – each number corresponding to a colour. When correctly filled in – colour by colour – a picture emerges that looks accomplished enough. The line-drawing often reproduced a famous painting . . . The whole activity is a sort of fakery, a sleight of hand, a cheat, a way of appearing to do something difficult and accomplished by an easy route. Just like making a film.[41]

Mechanically reproducing the world by drawing it as it is seen through the frame of a viewfinder was a central motif of *The Draughtsman's Contract*; and in *Z&OO*, in the twins' attempt to photograph revelations about human existence in the decay of various animal carcasses. In *The Belly of An Architect*, Kracklite becomes obsessed with the photographed and xeroxed image of the abdomen, in order to make sense of his own stomach illness; while Flavia spends most of her time punctiliously recording the breakdown of the hero's private life and pins the resulting photos to her studio wall. The motif is developed further here as Smut has a Polaroid camera, which allows him to make nearly instantaneous reproductions of the world in two dimensions. But just as in *The Draughtsman's Contract*, where Neville's drawings collected together were incriminating, so Smut's mechanical reproductions – Polaroids of a half-naked boy jumping from his bedroom window, of Nancy and the Bognor brothers in their bathing suits, Bellamy apparently lying dead in the winding-sheet, various figures ambiguously dressed at Bellamy's wedding party and, most disturbing of all, Smut himself, with his body covered with coloured tape for Madgett's demonstration of fatal cricketing accidents – seem to create evidence of a child abuser. Furthermore, mechanical reproduction can be dangerous; and especially when what is imitated is the substance of art.

Smut, chastened by his ignorance of circumcision, presents his father with a glossy reproduction of the Rubens painting *Samson and Delilah* (illus. 66) and, developing an instinctual sense of its significance, he asks the right questions of this nocturnal scene of sex and violence, which may have a counterpart in his own life in childhood fantasy about happenings in the parents' bedroom. Excluded from his primary consciousness, Smut's speculations may find their way back through a paint-

ing, Samson and Delilah serving as substitutes for the participants in the primal scene. Feelings that neither Rubens nor
those who respond to his work can consciously acknowledge
are thus communicated through art. 'Art is a conventionally
accepted reality in which, thanks to artistic illusion, symbols
and substitutes are able to provoke real emotions. Thus art constitutes a region halfway between a reality which frustrates
wishes and the wish-fulfilling world of the imagination – a
region in which, as it were, primitive man's strivings for
omnipotence are still in full force.'[42]

Delilah is clothed but her breasts are bared; and it is through
this detail that Rubens calls attention both to the oral component in Samson's involvement with her and also to the complex
of erotic and hostile feelings initiated by the infantile oral
attachment of son to mother, a dependence which may under-
lie men's hostility towards women and concomitant fear of
them. In a sense, the fears as well as the positive feelings engendered by this attachment are never fully outgrown and
inevitably play a part in the adult man's relations with women.
Hence, in the trysting field, Cissie 3, by now pregnant, invites
Madgett to kiss her nipples, to which he asks, 'Will I taste any-

thing?' Rubens's Samson, bearded and coiffured just like Madgett, deprived of his strength, the pride of his masculinity, is the ready image of the victim of such a dependent mother/son relationship. Delilah's extended left hand now rests – tenderly, it seems – on Samson's shoulder as he sleeps with his head on his right hand cradled in her lap. Her bemused expression and the light touch of her hand on his bare shoulder reveal her erotic attachment even at the moment of her betrayal. Waiting soldiers look on through a door in the right background of Rubens's painting, just as in *Drowning by Numbers* the police are ready to pounce on Madgett on suspicion of child sexual abuse. The older woman who stands behind Delilah holds a candle, as does Cissie 1. A man leans forward to cut Samson's hair; clearly, we are meant to think of Cissie 2, whose husband, Hardy, takes comfort in insisting that she cut his hair with scissors. With some apparent misgivings she complies, and so accustomed is she to cutting her husband's hair that she snips the hair on his bloated corpse. Greenaway discusses the painting in *Fear of Drowning*:

> Samson is the conventional demonstration of man's vulnerability to woman. The Rubens painting, with considerable overt sensuousness, depicts the moment of the infamous Samson haircut – emasculation with the snip of a pair of scissors. Some may consider that circumcision is an act of licensed symbolic castration – an act of emasculation lightly disguised under a range of justifications and pursued by interests variously vested in sexual temperance, sexual exhibitionism, caste membership and patriarchal control. Maybe also masochism and self-mutilation – it was after all that [sic] Samson who, through lechery, aided of course by the perfidy of women, brought about his own downfall.[43]

All the Colpitts women are present, then, in Rubens's canvas; and Madgett is Samson. Smut continues the identification. Eventually, he takes scissors to his genitals and mutilates himself, all the while clutching his reproduction of Rubens. Later, he informs the girl that 'I've done what you asked me to do . . . circumcized myself – do you want to look?' Her answer is ambivalent, but neverthless contains possibilities for the future: 'No, thank you – not today.'[44] A few seconds later, however, this young mechanical reproduction of Velázquez's Infanta is dead: 'an automaton doll knocked down to serve the symmetry of the plot'.[45]

6 The Book Depository

THE PLEASURES OF THE TEXT

Michael is a gentle soul who dines out most evenings at the Hollandais restaurant and spends his nights in a book depository, 'a large – very large – dusty hall of books with high vaulted ceilings', a place whose shapes and colours evoke the plenty and the culture of the Dutch Golden Age:

> The colour is brown – various browns from almost cream to almost black. Overall the colour is predominantly a Rembrandt golden brown with touches of orange – a warm inviting space despite its huge size. Deep chiaroscuro – dramatic dark spaces and bright highlights on pale brown polished wood. There are stacks and stacks of books – ranged on tall bookcases whose upper shelves can only be reached by ten-foot-high wooden banistered ladders on wheels.[1]

In his spare time Michael is cataloguing French history: 'Louis XV', 'Versailles' and 'The French Revolution' are among the headings that he has inscribed on his bookcases to organize the contents of the depository. Georgina, the lover whom he has brought back to his residence for the first time, asks him, nonplussed, 'What good are all these books to you? You can't eat them. How can they make you happy?' And she continues, 'If you had to make a choice between me and your books, which would you choose?' Michael avoids a direct answer and, before plumping for Georgina's thighs, responds, 'Print and flesh are both equally attractive.'[2]

The choice between print and flesh, the book and the body, is one which many of Greenaway's projects over the last decade have set out in explicit detail. He observed in 1996: 'It may be that there are two simulations in life that can be, sooner or later, guaranteed to excite and please – sex and text, flesh and literature. Perhaps it is a commendable ambition to try to bring both these two simulations together, so close together in fact that they can be considered, at least for a time – perhaps for the length of a film – as inseparable.' And certainly, his films have sought to present the kinds of actions that might be undertaken under the influence of a book and, further, the harm books might do to lives.

Greenaway and Tom Phillips chose Canto v of the *Inferno* as the inaugural section for their *TV Dante* project, the video version of *La Divina Commedia*. This may have been because it features the harrowing story of Paolo and Francesca, two Florentines related by marriage, who one day read 'per diletto' ('for delight'; line 127), the story of Lancelot and Guinevere, 'enjoying' the text for its own sake, until their 'literal knowledge' of it ineluctably becomes their 'carnal knowledge' of each other. As the lovers gaze on the book the moment of their reading inevitably fades into the bygone moment about which they read; and for the instant of their kiss, the illusion of the past vanishes as they become one with the glow of desire of the legendary figures, and imagine themselves with Queen Guinevere and Lancelot. Their deference to the fiction is absolute, not conditional; but the book has rhythms of its own, which slowly possess the lovers and give rise to the disturbing, unspoken demands of their own natural bodies. The forces of word and nature act across the space between them – a space empty of moral measure or control. Francesca's narrative registers precisely this:

> Noi leggiavamo un giorno per diletto
>   di Lancialotto come amor lo strinse;
>   soli eravamo e sanza alcun sospetto.
> Per più fiate li occhi ci sospinse
>   quella lettura, e scolorocci il viso;
>   ma solo un punto fu quel che ci vinse.
> Quando leggemmo il disïato riso
>   esser basciato da cotanto amante,
>   questi, che mai da me non fia diviso,
> la bocca mi basciò tutto tremante.
>   Galeotto fu 'I libro e chi lo scrisse:
>   quel giorno più non vi leggemmo avante.

[One day, by way of pastime, we read of Lancelot, how love constrained him; we were alone, suspecting nothing. Several times that reading urged our eyes to meet and took the colour from our faces, but one moment alone it was that overcame us. When we read how the longed-for smile was kissed by so great a lover, this one, who never shall be parted from me, kissed my mouth all trembling. A Gallehault was the book and he who wrote it; that day we read no farther in it.]

In the sophisticated but revealing phrase 'il disïato riso' ('longed-for smile') and in the climactic emphasis on the 'bocca tutto tremante' ('my mouth all trembling'), her words seem to emphasize the parts of the body; while her phrase 'quel giorno . . .' sounds suggestive, charged with the implication that they turned to the book again on other days and relived the original passion. When it comes to the visual presentation of the convergence of flesh and print, Greenaway abandons the gimmicks that precede this section – talking heads and newsreel footage – and concentrates instead on two naked people, the abashed, unspeaking Paolo and the protesting Francesca, and two words. The first is 'Love', and in the moment of its utterance it emerges out of and then recedes into flames which fill the screen; and the second is 'Eve', the inexorable but generally unspoken half-rhyme of love, which effectively aligns the behaviour of Francesca with Adam's wife.

Yet Greenaway also realizes that the true conclusion of *Inferno* Canto v is the wordlessness that prevails as Dante swoons at its end. In Francesca's case, the dangers to the flesh of books have been fully explored. Her 'fault' lies not in simple sensuality but rather in allowing other narratives to dominate her body – disguising the raw reality of passion and shielding her from the questions that the flesh of Paolo would have led her to ask, had she looked steadily enough upon it. Dante was perhaps attempting a dramatization of Saint Paul's remark, 'the letter killeth: but the spirit quickeneth' (2 *Corinthians* 3:6), for, in its recounting of the story of adulterers reading a story of adultery, Canto v reflects such a quickening caused by one of the 'texts of pleasure' in which, as Roland Barthes puts it, 'everything comes about': 'Pleasure in pieces; language in pieces; culture in pieces. Such texts are perverse in that they are outside any imaginable finality.'[3] On the one hand, what could be more final than the circle of the lustful in the *Inferno*? But, on the other, what could be less final than this extraordinary television version?

In *Prospero's Books*, too, finality remains beyond the imagination, and everything comes about from the conjunction of flesh and print. Based on *The Tempest*, Greenaway's film takes Shakespeare's suggestion that the quondam Duke of Milan preferred

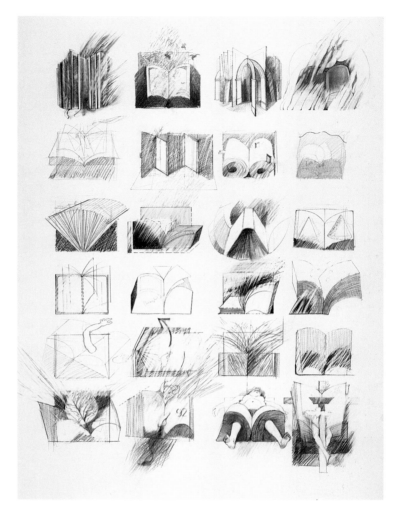

his library to his duties, his philosophical subjects to his political subjects, and presents a partial view of the life of a Renaissance text. And in particular, the life inhering in those books – Greenaway imagines twenty-four in all – 'furnish'd' by the charity of 'a noble Neapolitan, Gonzalo', and miraculously not washed out of the 'rotten carcass of a butt, not rigged,/Nor tackle, sail, nor mast' in which Prospero and Miranda are consigned by the usurper, Antonio. 'These books', Greenaway suggests, 'enabled Prospero to find his way across the oceans, to combat the malignancies of Sycorax, to colonize the island, to free Ariel, to educate and entertain Miranda and to summon tempests and bring his enemies to heel' (illus. 67).[4] Among the 'volumes' that the old Duke claims to 'prize above my duke-dom' are texts whose spines are strong enough to contain the human body. The *Vesalius Anatomy of Birth*, for instance, is full of 'drawings of the workings of the human body, which, when the pages open, move and throb and bleed'; while *A Book of Motion* describes 'how the eye changes its shape when looking at great distances, how hairs grow in a beard, why the heart flutters and the lungs inflate involuntarily and how laughter changes the face'. However, such a body of knowledge places great strains on this volume, since 'it is always bursting open of its own volition'; consequently, it needs to be 'bound around with two leather straps buckled tightly at the spine. At night, it drums against the bookcase shelf and has to be held down with a brass weight.' In an embellishment to Shakespeare's text, Greenaway suggests that Caliban has stolen an especially desir-able book from Prospero's library, *The Autobiographies of Pasiphae and Semiramis*, which, with its account of the life of the wife who is serviced by a white bull and gives birth to a mon-ster, and of that of the queen of Babylon who erects the Hang-ing Gardens, amounts to a veritable pornography.

> It is a blackened and thumbed volume whose illustrations leave small ambiguity as to the book's content. The book is bound in black calfskin with damaged lead covers. The pages are grey-green and scattered with a sludge green powder, curled black hairs and stains of blood and other substances. The slightest taint of steam or smoke rises from the pages when the book is opened, and it is always warm – like the lit-tle heat apparent in drying plaster or in flat stones after the sun has set. The pages leave acidic stains on the fingers and it is advisable to wear gloves when reading the volume.

This sexually explicit narrative of past loves still carries the traces, the warmth and even the bodily fluids of the lovers it so amply contains. Is it any wonder that Caliban attempts to rape Miranda, since it is this corrosive pillow book that the illiterate tinder collector is condemned to hold as a punishment for the rest of his life?[5]

The idea of an intimate boudoir record connecting body and text was further developed in Greenaway's 1996 film *The Pillow Book*, a contemporary story set in Kyoto and Hong Kong at the very end of the twentieth century, which pays direct homage to the Japanese *Pillow Book* written at the close of the tenth century.

This original was penned by Sei Shonagon, a female member of the imperial court during the Heian period (794–1185), and was a collection of reminiscences, lists, literary quotes and amorous adventures. The original *Pillow Book*'s style and content must have struck a deep chord with Greenaway, since it linked text and sex; the same conjunction permeates his own version, in which a young Japanese woman, Nagiko, derives the most intense carnal pleasure from having her body written upon. Her childhood birthdays in Kyoto are celebrated in a highly ritualized manner: her father, an impoverished writer and expert calligrapher, writes a sensuous birthday greeting on her tiny face with a brush and ink, while her aunt reads passages from the Sei Shonagon classic. The substance of these two actions, writing and reading, body and text, provides the substance of her life, driving the narrative of the film in the direction of fetish and oedipal complexity as also in the direction of pleasure principles.

In *Le Plaisir du Texte*, Barthes famously takes the body as a metaphor for the text, and then points out that we have more than body:

> Apparently Arab scholars, when speaking of the text, use this admirable expression, *the certain body*. What body? We have several of them; the body of anatomists and physiologists, the one science sees or discusses: this is the text of grammarians, critics, commentators, philologists (the pheno-text). But we also have a body of bliss consisting solely of erotic relations, utterly distinct from the first body: it is another contour, another nomination; thus with the text: it is no more than the open list of the fires of language (those living fires, intermittent lights, wandering features strewn in the text like seeds and which for us advantageously replace the 'semina aeternitatis', the 'zopyra', the common notions, the fundamental assumptions of ancient philosophy). Does the text have human form, is it a figure, an anagram of the body? Yes, but of our erotic body. The pleasure of the text is irreducible to physiological need.[6]

The fetish is text written on the body of a lover; a simple representation of the desire to use flesh as a writing surface, to use human skin as paper, to consider that the body should be treated as a book to be written on, to make explicit the cliché, 'I can read you like a book'. But, as Barthes suggests, the erotic body

(of the text) is not so much a structure, but rather the always unfinished list of the explosions of language that might produce *jouissance*. Pleasure manifests itself in a manner whose effects are unpredictable because they elude the imaginary; in other words, the body's ideas are not synonymous with the person's own.

There is a significant sequence early on in Greenaway's film, when, having escaped a loveless and brutal marriage in Kyoto and now working as a model in Hong Kong, Nagiko is depicted in her candlelit apartment alone with a middle-aged Japanese man who is writing 'with a brush, with pale yellow-brown ink' on her naked back and around her waist (illus. 68). He is copying passages from *The Pillow Book* of Sei Shonagon onto her body; she, rocking with pleasure from side to side, is, in turn, reading from another copy of the same book, and recites the following lines in Japanese: 'Writing is an ordinary enough occupation – yet how precious it is. If writing did not exist, what terrible depressions we should suffer.' But Nagiko is depressed, since she misses her father's special touch; for an Oedipal complexity is naturally guaranteed when the texts are written by him on the skin of his daughter. However, once the daughter becomes a woman, the desire to have men write text on her

68 Flesh and text, from *The Pillow Book* (1995).

body is so obsessive that she searches out a series of calligrapher-lovers, none of whom really satisfies her until she meets an English writer and translator, Jerome.

He suggests that she should write on his body (rather than vice versa) and a period of sexual fulfilment is achieved. But complications set in when Jerome, wishing to further her writing ambitions, presents his naked body, calligraphed by Nagiko, to her father's old publisher. Areas of his body carry different messages. On his throat a gorgeous introduction is inscribed: 'I want to describe the Body as a Book/A Book as a Body/And this Body and this Book/Will be the first Volume'; on his ribcage 'the book is in the torso', which creates the opportunity for a familiar pun on 'red' and 'read':

Seat of the heart
That pumps the ink
That is always red
Before it is black.[7]

The belly is inscribed with 'a publishing house in continual flux'; and here it is a question of 'Future and Past sharing the same thoroughfare./Book and body always showing their evolutionary history'. Finally, on Jerome's penis and scrotum is written:

I am the very necessary
Coda
The tail-piece,
the ever-reproducing
Epilogue.
The last dangling paragraph
that is the reason
for the next book's
sprouting.

The publisher, no doubt impressed with the skill of the brush-work, becomes Jerome's gay lover. But soon Jerome and Nagiko become jealous of each other, she of his involvement with the publisher, he because she impatiently writes on the bodies of other men. In a bid to win her back, Jerome fakes his own suicide, which results in his death. Naturally enough Nagiko grieves for him; more perversely, perhaps, she writes a handsome erotic poem on his corpse and buries him. The publisher exhumes Jerome's body and flays the skin from the corpse to make a precious pillow book of her marvellous text. Nagiko is horrified, and Greenaway's film culminates in her scheme to persuade the publisher to relinquish the book of her dead lover's skin. She produces for him twelve more books (half the number in *Prospero's Books*, but the same number of artefacts that Neville succeeds in producing in *The Draughtsman's Contract*) written on the skin of various handsome young men, the last of whom becomes the publisher's executioner. In due course, the pillow book made out of Jerome is returned to Nagiko and she lays it to rest in the soil of a bonsai tree.

Jerome's mother claims to have named her son after his father's confessor, 'a Jesuit in Singapore – a little red man who ate a lot of raw food before it became fashionable'.[8] But Jerome's name has a larger significance, especially given the fact that, just like the saint after whom he is named, he is a professional translator who invites Nagiko to 'Treat me like the page of a book. Your book.'[9] As a young man, St Jerome (c. AD 342–420) was an eager student of pagan literature. He then had a vision and retreated to the desert to repent, later applying his massive erudition to pious uses, making a Latin translation of the Bible, the Vulgate, which was still in use in the twentieth century.[10] A Doctor of the Church, he also became a symbol of the solitary religious life and a popular subject of Renaissance painting, appearing often with his traditional attributes – red cardinal's hat, book and a tame lion for a companion. Jerome presented a problem to painters, since his career offered few opportunities for creating a sympathetic figure: his record as a scourge of heretics and a champion of virginity was notorious; he performed no famous miracles or works of charity; nor did he suffer any spectacular martyrdom. Nevertheless, in him Greenaway sees a figure who habitually places book before body. Consequently, in the film, after the English translator's death, the publisher is seen idly flicking through a CD-ROM of various paintings; and the camera catches various depictions of St Jerome, by, among others, da Messina and de La Tour, appearing in quick succession across the screen of his Macintosh.

As part of the 1990 exhibition *The Physical Self* at the Museum Boymans–van Beuningen in Rotterdam, Greenaway included a small installation on the subject of Jerome (illus. 69). Dominating the section – and flanked by two smaller representations of the saint by Terbrugghen and Maes – was an early van Dyck picture of Jerome, possibly once owned by Rubens (illus. 70). It shows the slightly emaciated saint sitting facing us with his legs

69 St Jerome
installation at *The
Physical Self*,
Rotterdam, 1990.

70 Van Dyck, *St
Jerome*, (?)1626.

crossed at his ankles. A great mass of flowing drapery encloses his legs and lower torso; on the ground on the left is a sleeping lion and on the right a disorderly pile of papers and books. Behind him, and nestling against his right shoulder, is a young putto who stares at the viewer while proffering a quill to the old man; 'undoubtedly a physical child first and only an angel by inference'.[11] A tree grows from a rocky outcrop which runs up the left side of the painting, its foliage framing the open landscape that forms the background of the right side of the picture. Greenaway comments:

> The pictorial attributes identify the subject – books, a text, a pen, a wilderness landscape, a sleeping lion, the red robe that presages the office of cardinal, the implication of a thought suspended, and the angel – though that is an iconographical extra. Other images of Jerome might include a skull. All these iconographic clues are there ostensibly to support a religious familiarity, which, no doubt, the pious would comprehend, and through them be reminded of the example of St Jerome as a model of religious wisdom and sanctity.[12]

That sanctity meant putting the book, the Word, before the body. Hence, while this serene and dignified image includes several elements of idealization, such as the strong shoulders and the unbent posture, it does not shrink from presenting the inevitable signs of age – the wrinkled flesh, the pronounced veins, the enfeebled pectoral muscles, the grey hair. It has made an elderly unclothed body a pertinent and positive subject for depiction.

In his commentary on the van Dyck, Greenaway observes (almost incidentally) that the body of Jerome – Prospero – is contrasted with the young body of an angel – Ariel – thus connecting the painting with the film on which he was working at the time, *Prospero's Books*. As he has freely admitted, various paintings of Jerome, a scholarly, book-bound sage in exile, extending his wisdom, were source-images for the initial appearance of Prospero, 'a secular equivalent of St Jerome'. Hence, the representation of the usurped Duke of Milan in his library (illus. 71) is based on Antonella's writing room in his picture of St Jerome; a cosy wooden carrel erected within a Gothic construction, which may be a church or a palace (illus. 72). Greenaway captures well the extraordinary lighting effects Antonella achieves, casting sharp or diffused shadows,

71 The study, from *Prospero's Books* (1991).

72 Antonella da Messina, *St Jerome in his Study*, c. 1475.

bouncing beams off different surfaces and illuminating the distant landscape beyond the windows in the lower corners, and the distant cloudless sky above. And, of course, in the dead centre of Antonella's painting is the book itself, and above it, Jerome in the act of turning over a new leaf. In contrast to this architectural security, Greenaway suggests that Georges de la Tour's image (illus. 73) 'offers a very mortal image for Prospero stripped and humbled before a book'. Certainly, this picture (c. 1625) testifies to the minute attention paid by the artist to the textures of cloth and the contours and hollows of flesh and bone. The hat, a beautifully turned piece of scarlet millinery, is set against the sagging tissue-paper skin and knobbly joints, its bloody tassles hanging above, and visually echoing, a knotted and bloodied rope whip. It is a peerless image of the saint, alone in an indoor cell, a spatial void inhabited only by pebbles, with spindly shadows cast by an acutely old man, still at his devotions. His face is calm, and both his daily flagellation and his life's work are nearly complete; he is almost on his last legs. The book lies on the floor; it appears to be balanced precariously on its spine until we see that bearing it up is a skull. The eye is

170

drawn inexorably to this *memento mori*; but the larger picture shows us a man placing himself before the book and living his mortal life by it.

CONSPICUOUS CONSUMPTION

The choice that Greenaway tries to articulate, then, is always between flesh and print; but if the wrong choice is made, for whatever reason, then the body may need to become a text, or words may have to be eaten. In such cases, Greenaway ensures that the metaphor – making a book of the body, seeing the body as a book – becomes a grisly and shocking reality. Hence, in the closing section of *The Cook, the Thief, his Wife and her Lover*, Georgina, the wife of Spica, the Thief, will find the corpse of her Lover, Michael, in the darkened book depository. Some hours earlier, Spica has force-fed Michael the pages of the *History of the French Revolution* by Pascal Astruc-Latelle (illus. 75). At first glance, the image of a mouth stuffed with bloodied pages might seem to be an allusion to one of Dürer's most bizarre and explicit woodcuts (illus. 74), where St John devours the book that will secure his faith: 'Take it and eat; it will be bitter to your stomach,

74 Albrecht Dürer, 'St John Devours the Book', from *Revelation of St John*, 1498.

171

but sweet as honey in your mouth' (*Revelations* 10:8). But the leaves have been rammed down Michael's throat with the handle of a wooden spoon, in revenge for having goosed Spica's wife, becoming a bizarre act of *gavage*, which might bring about an enlarged *foie* but not an augmented *foi*. It is an act of pathological cruelty, its scenic arrangement modelled, unsurprisingly, on Rembrandt's *Anatomy Lesson of Dr Joan Deyman* (illus. 76), painted in 1656, which also appears in *Prospero's Books*. In it, the position of the corpse, shown lying directly facing the spectator, amounts to a bold foreshortening, akin to Mantegna; but this has been done to avoid having to offer any visual account of the removal of the stomach and intestine – what Ezra Pound might

75 Stuffing Michael, from *The Cook, The Thief, His Wife and her Lover* (1989).

76 Rembrandt, *Anatomy Lesson of Dr Joan Deyman*, 1656.

call 'the brown meat of Rembrandt' – and in their place is only an undifferentiated red mass.[13] This, translated to Michael, becomes a stain on his chest, which can only mean life is about to become *nature morte*.

The combination of this image with Rembrandt's brings together, finally and terribly, the twin poles of the film: nature and culture, body and mind, restaurant and library. Michael is the first to admit that the book depository's kitchen and toilet facilities are a bit 'primitive', and no doubt that is why he eats out so regularly; but from the vantage point of this 'dusty hall of books', a kind of ivory tower, the lack of facilities is balanced by 'an extraordinary view'. Yet a diet of culture is insufficient; one cannot live on books, and Michael dies when he is fed with them. Deny consumption and defecation and you deny two of the three most basic rhythms of life; the third, of course, is well known to the lovers, Michael and Georgina.

On the other hand, Spica the Thief has no sense of culture other than that prefaced by enterprise. Because his is a world dominated by false accounting, Spica thinks Michael could only be a bookkeeper; someone capable of appreciating a joke about cooking the books. So he picks up Richard's volume and suggests it be 'grilled with some mashed peas'. In several interviews, Greenaway has drawn attention to the political impetus behind the film. He told Gavin Smith that Spica represents 'a man who knows the price of everything and the value of nothing' and that the film conveys 'my anger and passion about the current British political situation'. He was even more explicit when he stated:

> *The Cook, the Thief, his Wife and her Lover* is a passionate angry dissertation for me on the rich vulgarian Philistine anti-intellectual stance of the present cultural situation in Great Britain . . . There's a lull in the film where Spica says to the lover who is reading, 'Does this book make money?' That line really sums up this theme. In England now there seems to be only one currency, as indeed one might say about the whole capitalist world.[14]

Spica is operating a protection racket, squeezing money out of businesses in the area; but the restaurant that he patronizes is no ordinary establishment. It is 'Le Hollandais'. Its back wall is covered with a reproduction of the *Banquet of the Officers of the Haarlem Militia Company of St George, 1616* by Frans Hals

77 Frans Hals, *Banquet of the Officers of the Haarlem Militia Company*, 1616.

(illus. 77), 'the first monumental landmark of the great age of Dutch painting . . . [which] exults in the healthy optimism and strength that helped build the new republic'.[15] This pictorial quotation fulfils several roles. For one thing, in its depiction of these amateur archers of Haarlem it represents the burgeoning bourgeoisie as a class, and Albert, for all his money and pretensions to 'class', cannot escape his bourgeois bloodlines and habits. For another thing, Hals himself represents both Spica and what Spica might have been, had he been successful in his attempts to purchase class. Moreover, the feasting Haarlem *corps de garde* give an impression of secure masculine power which is not without parallel in Spica's world; one representation of conspicuous consumption gazes on the other, just as the diners at one table in a restaurant might cast knowing glances at those on the next (illus. 79).

Yet the central painterly fascination in Greenaway's film is not with Hals's work, but lies instead more generally with representations of inanimate objects, bereft of narrative context, representations that nevertheless combine the illusion of vitality and the reality of inertia; representations that came to be known in the Dutch Republic as *stil-leven*.[16] In 1988, giving an account of *Drowning by Numbers*, a film which features 'Dutch morality metaphors' – reminders of transience in the form of the bursting bubbles on the pink soap, or a ground beetle soon to die stranded on its back – Greenaway discussed how the genre broke its strict bounds altogether and came to depict corpses:

the Dutch were adroit at painting dead meat – plucked or unplucked, butchered or merely just slaughtered. Some painters of the art were such slow practitioners that their subjects deteriorated before their eyes – flowers faded, fruit decayed, vegetables decomposed, meat rotted – prophetic activity when the painting was commissioned to be a moral reminder of time passing – an ironic still-life would self-reflexively include the mould and the fungus.[17]

Hence, in *The Cook, the Thief*, two vans loaded with produce arrive in the opening moments, courtesy of Albert Spica: 'racks of red and white meat and tiers of blue and white fish; pigs' heads, trotters, bulls' tongues, offal, kidneys, tripe; squid, clams, herring, flatfish, lobsters, prawns. The rich, colourful boldly-lit raw food is examined with both enthusiasm and nausea.' In these stunning ensembles 'reminiscent of Dutch seventeenth-century painting' there is an attempt, in particular, to alert us to Rembrandt's *Slaughtered Ox* (illus. 78); and, with regard to the fish, to the work of the master of the piscine still-life, Abraham van Beyeren. Such a style of painting placed high demands on the physical integrity of its subject-matter; ripeness was all, but inevitably decay would follow *ad nauseam*. And so, by the midpoint of Greenaway's film, the two vans are filled with flies and the once-solid contents have deliquesced.

78 Rembrandt, *Slaughtered Ox*, 1655.

When the doors are opened, 'the inside of the [fish] van is a gruesome mess of rot and decay – liquid rot, maggots and flies – including the deeply rotted bodies of two large dogs'.[18] Consequently, *nature morte* must somehow arrest the stages of putrefaction by freezing life into stasis; but refrigeration by means of paint was an expensive process, possibly costing more than the products to be preserved. Hence, it was the art itself rather than the subject-matter that was advertising its opulence, its luxury, its conspicuous consumption of time and money.[19]

In particular, the spectacular work of Jan Davidsz. de Heem, in which the depicted objects arouse a marvel second only to that evoked by his rendering of them, provides a point of departure for many of the more ornate table displays created for the benefit of Spica's party. De Heem, who was born in Utrecht, moved to Antwerp in 1636 because 'there one could have rare fruit of all kinds, large plums, peaches, cherries, oranges, lemons, grapes and others in fine condition and state of ripeness to draw from life'.[20] The distinction of his *pronkstilleven* lies in the lavish brightness of the colours and the extraordinary attention to detail, both in the fruits and the swathes of opulent fabric that so often frame his canvases. Take his *Still Life with a Parrot* (illus. 80),[21] a triumph of illusionism in its render-

79 The dining room, from *The Cook, The Thief, His Wife and her Lover* (1989).

176

80 Jan Davidsz. de Heem, *Still Life with Parrots*, 1648.

ing of textures and light effects, used to present a rich conglomeration of objects in an encyclopaedic fashion. It features objects representing the elements: the birds of the air, in the form of the macaw; the oysters and shells; the fruits of the earth; and the metal vessels that required heat for their fabrication. Yet, as recent critics have suggested, it is difficult to read such images of *pronk* without recalling that the banquet piece was often also a warning against decadence and ostentation. No doubt the gold- and silverware, the blue jewellery box and the shells all suggest the vanities of collecting and spending money on costly, worldly goods; but other elements caution the beholder against over-indulgence. Because of their presumed qualities as an aphrodisiac, oysters were traditionally reported to lead to

sexual excess; while, for instance, melon consumed in large amounts was sometimes thought to produce insanity. By contrast, other objects in the picture imply spiritual strength (the unbroken column) and salvation through Christ (the bread, wine and grapes all have Eucharistic associations); but the Last Supper was never like this.[22]

So many of Greenaway's shots frame Dutch still-life paintings and include minor subgenres. At one point, the lovers copulate in the plucking room, a sequence that may allude to the moral narrative of a canvas such as Gerrit Dou's *A Poulterer's Shop* (illus. 81). As Erika Langmuir explains: 'Seventeenth-century texts indicate that in Dutch and German *Vogel* (bird) was often synonymous with the phallus, *vogelen* (to bird) was a euphemism for sexual intercourse, and *vogelaar* (birdcatcher) could refer to a procurer or lover.'[23] Hence, Michael and Georgina make love in the midst of 'some fifty or more dead birds . . . lined up on the cold slabs – chickens, turkeys, geese, ducks'; and when they are interrupted by a bashful kitchen hand who removes a large bird, Michael, in the best traditions of British music hall, observes, 'Someone's having goose for dinner.' And of course, the most horrifying example of *nature morte* and of the body's containment within the space of representation involves the presentation of the dead Michael, cooked in aspic, and as brown as Rembrandt's beef. By presenting this signature dish, the French chef of the restaurant 'Le Hollandais' has become a Dutch artist in his ability to bring the real into representation. It is a movement that determines the style of the film; but, as so often, the emphatic artifice of Greenaway's image tends to have the effect of curbing our identification with it.

Beginning with a shot of several dogs, including a Dalmatian whose decay was filmed in Z&OO, the camera climbs up through the scaffolding of a stage set before pausing at a curtained portal flanked by two waiters. This is the point of no return. They turn and then conduct us through the curtains where the camera pauses high above a car park adjacent to the restaurant's back entrance, which itself seems to be way below the level of the street down a long gradient. At this point two vans and a car arrive and screech to a halt, and a group of men haul out a victim, strip him, force him to eat dog excrement and then urinate over him. The whole narrative is made literally groundless by this establishing shot, its *mise-en-scène* proven physically ungraspable at the very outset. With images of scavenging dogs and back entrances, Greenaway reminds us that everything above the backside, the zone of the scatological, is a fiction; and, of course, he saves his own film from the charge of cerebrality by treating it as a body he enters from the rear end.

After the assault on the hapless Roy, Sacha Vierny's camera pans laterally past the food vans along a blue ramp, where a road sign with the name 'La Concourse' is partially obscured, revealing only 'course' (part of a meal); it also shows the neon sign 'Luna', perhaps a reminder of the tics that characterize criminal madmen, as well as an allusion to *La Luna*, Bertolucci's 1977 film about mother–son incest, the metaphorical consumption of one's own kind, a kind of familial cannibalism.[24] Continuing on its ineluctable way, the camera pans left to right again through the kitchen, a space much too voluminous for a restaurant kitchen. The camera pauses during the panning to pick up more signs (the SPICA and BOARST names), the many work surfaces for cutting and preparing food, the varied staff and many more partly obscured or hidden places: a ladder walk-up; a draped room for poultry and game, another for bread and bakery products along the back wall. It quickly becomes clear that the fourth wall, which might be expected to be behind the camera, does not exist, so the panning does not stop or go around; it merely continues, left to right, resolutely two-dimensional.

The action takes place over the course of eight days, and at the beginning of each day there is usually a period of entry into the restaurant where, after considering the *à la carte* menu, the camera pans along tables composed of still-lifes and the Hals in the background. Occasionally it comes across a wedding party and various couples, but the camera 'swallows' them up in its passage to the Spica table – the bodies arranged like Leonardo's *Last Supper*, or the parody of it in Bunuel's *Viridiana* – which is always shown with some detail of the Hals painting visible. In consequence, the self-important figures in the canvas seem to share the same space as the actors, in part because of the manner in which the colours of the painting match those of the room. Moreover, in transforming these painted figures at the Haarlem table – figures who look straight out from Hals's painting – into the watchers of its beholders, the cinema audience, Greenaway uses the canvas to position both viewer and viewed within a common space. The scene is still depicted in wide angle and showing more ceiling than floor, but here space is deceptive. We don't know the true dimensions of the Hals painting; we rarely stop for any vantage point far enough away from the Spica table to convey true distance (one rare exception is when Georgina stops at Michael's table to look at his books and we see both Albert and Richard looking at her, and the room seems enormous); and, finally, we never discover the true dimensions of the back wall until the last scene when that wall is the point of entry for Albert.

Whenever the camera pans in the opposite direction, moving from right to left to leave the restaurant, it often accentuates the event in the narrative by pulling back and up and even travelling slightly faster than the characters, so that there is both a tension of speed and an emotional distance from the characters. It is clear that such travelling movements are carefully considered by Greenaway, as is suggested by his discussion of the murderer in Prud'hon's *Divine Justice Pursuing Crime*, 'running out left, the sinister direction, against the grain of a positive left to right reading'.[25] As Alan Woods has noticed, Spica, as aggressor – attacking Patricia, harassing Michael, hectoring Richard, torturing the porter Pup – is often on the right of the screen, facing left. The disposition of processions and recessions is not simplistic but it is simplified by the set: in the book depository the lovers are given the bad news of Pup by Richard entering from right to left, and this is followed by Georgina's visit to his hospital, where she enters from left to right, a kind of ministering angel.[26] The characters traverse from right to left in order to perpetrate acts of violence (Spica, on several occasions, dragging Georgina), to have sex (Michael and Georgina; Fitch and Patricia) and finally to escape the clutches of Spica.

The lovers escape from under Albert's very nose, as Georgie says, in the van full of now putrefying meat. Naked like Adam and Eve, they are confronted by the decay of the flesh and expelled from the paradise of the restaurant. The allusion here is to the convention of the flight from Eden, in particular that depicted in Rembrandt. Later, after being hosed down by a black attendant named Eden, they take refuge in the book depository and wander nude through its dusty corridors. The colour of this place of exile is brown, the shade of a leather binding or an oak shelf, or of the lovers' flesh even; and light reflected from water plays against the ceiling. But the book depository is yet one more paradise from which they will be ejected for their naivety in thinking that physical love can be pure; in believing that they can return to the state of innocence.

The whole structure of the film is based on artificially coloured areas such as the depository; and the colours' function is not simply decorative but a structural element. The film commences in the 'dark blue' of the car park, a glacial and hostile place redolent of putrefaction and depravity, where the weak are literally pissed on and the dogs scavenge (illus. 82). From here, the film moves to the kitchens, whose predominant colour is green – 'hooker's dark green, leaf-green, emerald, faded turquoise and eau-de-Nil – like the colours of a dark wet jungle'. This is a serene work space where creativity expresses itself naturally (illus. 83). Jets of gas shoot from the hobs like sacramental flames, and the kitchen is echoic and resonant: 'the acoustics are like those of a cathedral', and so Pup will sing *Psalm 51* like a choirboy, an incarnation of innocence. Yet this quasi-mystical place also suggests a factory, not simply by dint of the honest graft that goes on here but also because of the enormous fans and ducts whose design 'may suggest the aircraft industry of the 1940s'. The dining room is carpeted in several tones of red and on the wall is the large reproduction of Hals's painting. The toilets, which are reached through a narrow corridor, are in fact immaculate, sanitized and white, bathed in what might at first glance seem to be an absence of colour until one recalls

Newton's *Opticks*. White light is promiscuous, a fusion of all the colours of the spectrum; and so they become a place where the lovers come together for the first time, until they are interrupted by the braying of Albert. Aware of the way context inevitably colours our view, Greenaway makes the hue of a costume change from red, say, to white as its wearer passes from dining room to bathroom. And in the bathroom where cleanliness and dirt coincide we have the greatest contrast – the red sash of Albert, the thief, turns white against his still black suit.

82 The blue car park, from *The Cook, The Thief, His Wife and her Lover* (1989).

However, such colour-coding is not merely pictorial. Greenaway's film develops the theme of consumption as a means of incorporating the real, a notion that is ironically addressed by the cook when he wonders whether Georgina wishes him to cook her dead lover so that she can eat him and absorb him into herself. The idea is seen more seriously in the attempt to create in the restaurant an ambitious system of visual signification, based on the peristaltic movements of the body's digestive tract. Greenaway, as we have seen, creates his film out of long travelling shots which take us through the different parts of the set. First of all, the kitchen displays the raw materials, rendered aesthetically pleasing, perhaps, by the conventions of still-life; next, the dining room, whose walls are as red as a mouth,

announces itself as the place of ingestion, of consumption; and finally, the toilet, the site of waste, of excretion, of private functions. The kitchen communicates with the dining room by a swing door which opens and closes like a mouth; and with the toilets by means of a narrow corridor, the connecting tube between the two orifices, top and bottom. And as Albert wryly observes, '. . . the pleasures are related. Because the naughty bits and dirty bits are so close together, it just goes to show you how sex and eating are related.' This is close to Freud, who in 1905 attempted to explain the origin of excremental theories of birth; and why so many believed that 'people get babies by eating some particular thing (as they do in fairy tales) and babies are born through the bowel like a discharge of faeces'.[27]

Greenaway notes: 'All the metaphors of the film are about putting things into the mouth'; and this includes putting words into others' mouths, as the self-conscious allusions to language merely reinforce the obliquities of the film. At the beginning we see letters taken out of vehicles – among them an A and an O, alpha and omega, beginning and end. Soon after, these letters are arranged to read ASPIC & BOARST, then unscrambled once again to become the sign SPICA & BORST. Later, Michael is forced to eat his books. His manner of·dying makes Georgina's demand at gunpoint that her husband eat her lover's cooked penis – the veritable phallic signifier – all the more appropriate, as this materialization of his earlier threat that he will kill Michael and eat him means that Spica is being forced to eat his words; to consume himself, conspicuously.

BIBLIOTECHNOLOGY

Michael's book depository is 'on at least the fifth floor of a nineteenth-century building – a museum, or a library'. It is oddly lifeless, almost a still-life; a place of dust and disordered piles of books and papers comparable to the *Still Life of Books* painted by de Heem (illus. 84). In this painting, a violin, a jumble of documents and assorted books – most of which have badly worn covers and seem distorted by damp – are lying on a table in the corner of a room. The tattered state of the books is the key visual trope, since anyone who believed that texts were eternal, immutable records of human experience and knowledge is reminded of the frailness and evanescence of print; of the fact that books are inanimate objects subject to the same forces of decay as any other still-life.

Set the lifelessness of books here or in the depository against some of the elements of Prospero's library.[28] Take *An Atlas Belonging to Orpheus*, full of maps of Hell used by a husband searching for his abducted wife, Eurydice: 'When the atlas is opened the maps bubble with pitch. Avalanches of hot, loose gravel and molten sand fall out of the book to scorch the library

84 Jan Davidsz. de Heem, *Still Life with Books*, 1628.

floor.' *The Book of Mythologies* is the frame for the spirits that populate the island. 'Sitting and crouching on the double spread of pages – with text and illustrations – are various mythological figures . . . accompanied by nymphs and putti who are endeavouring to turn the next huge page to free the occupants of the next chapter – fauns and hamadryads who are already struggling to get out.'[29]

Greenaway may have derived a sense of the book as a living object from some of the textual artefacts that were produced by the Dadaists and Surrealists. In 1919, writing from Buenos Aires, Marcel Duchamp sent his newly married sister Suzanne instructions about hanging a book of geometry on the balcony and exposing it to the elements. The wind, he argued, would leaf through the book, rip its pages apart and so transform it that it would turn up ever new computational problems. This sense of living mathematics is caught in Greenaway's *Harsh Book of Geometry*, which, when opened, displays 'complex three-dimensional geometrical diagrams [which] rise up out of the pages like models in a pop-up book'. The pages flicker with logarithmic numbers and figures. Angles are measured by needle-thin metal pendulums that swing freely, activated by magnets concealed in the thick paper. In the circle of André Breton – who in a text of 1924 described a dream he had of a book whose spine was made of a wooden dwarf with a long white beard, and whose covers consisted of thick, black wool – it was Georges Hugnet who commissioned some of the most fantastic book designs. Here such disparate items as corks, mirrors, butterflies and flies, cat whiskers, slate, items of laundry and garters are fastened into a dialogue with texts, manuscripts and photos. These bibliographical experiments continued into the 1960s. In 1964, a collaboration between Giacometti and Duchamp, *La Double Vue*, appeared, which included the latter's 'Clock in Profile', an illustration that obtruded from the page like a relief. Another book, *Aube à l'antipode*, illustrated by Magritte, started to sing when it was handled.[30] Each of these experiments concurs with Foucault's observation that 'Fantasies are carefully deployed in the hushed library, with its columns of books, with its titles aligned on shelves to form a tight enclosure, but within confines that also liberate impossible worlds.'[31]

So it is with Prospero's book depository. When he crosses it, each section of the library liberates pertinent objects and people which seem to merge into each other to create bizarre new combinations: 'ambiguous bacchanalian figures – wearing birettas and mitres – sit astride a giant abacus . . . two giggling nereids – playing with a sheep – swing on a library stepladder . . . a long-tailed creature sits drinking in the shadow of a tall desk . . .' (p. 52). Such glimpses imply the potency of text in determining narrative action, and nowhere is this point made more cogently than in the opening scene where Prospero is discovered naked in his bath, standing in a pool surrounded by colonnades. *The Book of Water*, whose pages have been turned before us in the film's opening shots, lies on a table beside him in the pool. Gradually its illustrations have become more animated: at first, the script tells us, only small arrows follow the movement of a diagrammed whirlpool, then at intervals 'a wave moves, a ripple-motion animates the drawing of an ebbing tide, animated colour sweeps through the black-and-white drawing of a waterfall, a real corpse is buffeted by moving water in an image of the Flood'.[32] Out of this book emerges by degrees the full howling tempest that shipwrecks the travellers returning from the wedding in Carthage; for this is an art determining life. Greenaway's version of *The Tempest* – his own text of the play – arises out of these books which seem to create the island and determine the shapes of everything that is on it.

Hence *A Book of Architecture and Other Music* operates 'like a magnificent pop-up book' whose paper models surge up accompanied by triumphant music and arrange themselves into an library complex that compromises Prospero's reference to his 'poor cell'. In creating the library, Greenaway has borrowed his iconography from well-known Renaissance architecture; notably the library steps of the entrance to Michelangelo's Biblioteca Laurenziana in Florence, a building commissioned by Cardinal Giulio in November 1523 to house the manuscripts of his uncle Lorenzo the Magnificent (cover illustration). Michelangelo hit on the idea of three flights of stairs meeting and fusing into one on a central landing. As he envisaged it, the central flight amounted to a series of overlapping oval boxes, flanked by side wings for servants when the central flight was being ceremonially used. As built by Ammanati, the stairs diverge slightly from Michelangelo's design, but retain the flowing, dream-like invention evident in his description.[33] During the filming of *Prospero's Books*, the staircase was rebuilt in a week in an Amsterdam shipyard:

85 Steps to the library, from *Prospero's Books* (1991).

Manufactured in wood and plaster to mock and imitate the stone and gesso of the original, it was gone in a day, destroyed after a meticulous three-week reconstruction to make way for another set. Maybe the original Michelangelo staircase will be gone in a millennium, to join those earlier ascents of architectural history, the ziggurats and those de-marbled, de-stoned exposed stairs of the stepped pyramids, and every hypothetical Tower of Babel that fascinated Bruegel with the vanity of reaching the impossible, of reaching Heaven, of making a stairway to God.[34]

Yet in his shooting script, Greenaway was considerably vaguer about the design of Prospero's complex, and seemed eager that it be regarded only as a micrososm of art, rather than faith: 'it is a wooden structure . . . which can be dismantled and reconstructed – sometimes with other parts . . . sometimes in a different arrangement'. The word for this 'structure' is 'theatre'; and the Globe to be precise, that 'wooden O' whose timbers were first used in 1576 to build the theatre and then carted down from Shoreditch to Southwark in the frozen winter of 1597 to create a new world for Shakespeare's company, the Chamberlain's Men, from an old one.[35] Much of the theatrical tone of *The Cook, the Thief* derived from what Greenaway described as:

classic Revenge Tragedy out of 'the theatre of blood' with its obsession for human corporeality – eating, drinking, copulating, belching, vomiting, nakedness and blood. Most particularly the model is satirical English Jacobean theatre which was invariably erotic and certainly violent'.[36]

This places rather too much stress on corporeality; but it is quite true that some of the most sensational moments on the Renaissance stage occurred when the 'eating, drinking . . . belching, vomiting' were predicated on acts of cannibalism – witting or otherwise – presented directly to the audience. For instance, in Shakespeare's Elizabethan revenge play *Titus Andronicus* the villain partakes of her son's flesh, which has been baked into a pie; while in John Marston's *Antonio's Revenge* the hero grandly uncovers a dish which contains the limbs of the villain's son. In both these cases, the avenger's real crime is one of illicit substitution; but revenge is, in any case, all to do with reversibility, with changing places; for insofar as it entails an equivalence, it figures as a principle of order, a fearful symmetry that adapts itself peculiarly well to the economy of dramatic art. Consequently, Greenaway's film about revenge represented itself as theatre, its first sequence beginning with the opening of blood-red safety curtains and its last shots ending as these drapes close, thus placing the entire film within a set of representational frames.

But in *Prospero's Books* Greenaway, in his concern to remain faithful to his textual source – a late and singular Shakespearean comedy, rather than a conventional revenge play – borrows more extensively from theatrical conventions, and not merely in the form of props. *The Book of Mythologies*, for instance, is a huge volume, open and slanted backwards like a raked stage, and is clearly intended to be the point of origin for the theatrical ideal; curtains are closed midway through the film on the masque enacted by the spirits of the isle, which Prospero directs at the betrothal of Ferdinand and Miranda; and it is against this background of curtains clearly marked 'theatre' that Prospero declaims his Epilogue in the final moments. Or consider the moment when the young lovers, Ferdinand and Miranda, are discovered playing chess (illus. 87):

MIRANDA: Sweet lord, you play me false.
FERDINAND: No, my dearest love,
    I would not for the world.

MIRANDA: Yes, for a score of kingdoms you should wrangle,
An I would call it fair play.

The discovery here, as the curtain is drawn back, is not simply that Ferdinand is attempting to cheat at chess but that Miranda is countenancing the possibility that unfair 'play' might bring its own advantages. Already she is growing into womanhood; and, as has been noted by Patricia Simons, 'If chess is performed by a mixed-sex couple, the feminine presence turns the engagement into a sexual dalliance and it becomes a destabilized game of chance and passion.'[37] As the scene is played out, the board is surrounded by several allegorical figures carrying sticks; they frame the lovers and nakedly draw attention to the clothes the young couple wear. Miranda's gown alludes to Botticelli's Primavera; while Ferdinand's clothes are modelled on those worn by the man in Rembrandt's Guild canvas since, as Greenaway notes, the effete shipwrecked Neapolitans had strong dynastic connections with the Spanish Netherlands.

Textile draperies are also used throughout as a framing device: huge, rich billows of fabric manipulated by nude bodies, or entwined with them, in the style of the great Venetian artists: 'Bellini, Giorgione and Titian might have well filled the

86 Titian, *Bacchus and Ariadne*, 1522–3.

scholarly head of the Milanese Duke with serious classical images.' One such image may have been Titian's *Bacchus and Ariadne* (illus. 86), a canvas awash with costly Venetian colours, and whose account of insular abandon carries so many resonances for Shakespeare's play. Elsewhere, Ariel in the opening moments of the film is encountered urinating over the firmament, possibly an allusion to Rembrandt's *Rape of Ganymede*, a painting which Greenaway includes in his *Flying Over Water* catalogue;[38] but, as the film continues, he comes to resemble Bronzino's Cupid, 'a curly-haired child bent on reckless dangerous impudence'. The cherubs who blow the winds are inspired by those in Botticelli's *Birth of Venus*; the sea sirens resemble Rubens's Nereids in the *Marie de' Medici* series; the gardens in which Miranda meets Alonso are those of the Alhambra; and the perpetually ripening cornfield across which they move is drawn from Bruegel's *The Harvesters*. Finally, and ironically, Prospero takes on the appearance of Leonardo Loredan, the Doge of Venice, as represented in Bellini's portrait.

Ultimately, though, it is not so much Renaissance art but language itself that is the frame around the action and the actors; since for most of the film the words do not come from the mouths of the characters Shakespeare intended:

Even a superficial reading of *The Tempest* will show that Prospero manipulates everyone, so I've taken it to the nth degree and assumed that if he manipulates them, he probably invented them. So Gielgud is not only Prospero but also Shakespeare, and you see him actually writing the *The Tempest*. So the world is created through his voice.[39]

As Prospero writes the lines of the play he speaks them aloud, 'speaking the characters so powerfully through the words', says Greenaway, 'that they are conjured before us' (p. 9). And as the storm rises in fury he mouths the first word of the play: 'Boatswain!' Tentative at first, it becomes a conjuration: the boatswain is called into being along with the captain who, in the play, calls for him. His response – 'Here Master; what cheer?' – is directed equally to Prospero, whose magic now masters him (later Ariel, explicitly conjured into Prospero's presence, gives a similar reply: 'All hail great master, grave sir, hail!') and to the master of the ship; but Greenaway is making a further subtle speculation here, and surmising that Shakespeare himself may have played the master in a cameo role. In fact, the film follows Shakespeare's text to the letter, but only in the process of writing. The first word of the text is filmed and traced in close-up. The glass inkwell, which fills the screen, punctuates the opening sentence; it contains the sap that nourishes the images and permits the spectacle to develop. The soaked mariners take shape and, in a parallel action, the naked Prospero emerges from his bath and clothes himself in his cloak, which is also his art. Constantly changing colour, it lets escape from its billowing folds a multitude of mythological creatures, along with animals, birds, plants. And if 'the world is in his cloak' (p. 52), then the quill of Prospero is also his magic spear, both weapon and wand. Once he has set into motion his mechanism of revenge, and all his images and all the characters have been arranged like marks on a map, he will exclaim, 'they are now in my power'. That last word is also the cause of a massive power surge since it is followed by the metonymic image of a quill which plants itself like an arrow in the wood of the writing table. The bottle of ink shatters and spills its contents like a pool of blood. Later, at the very point he renounces his art – and the magic he has generated – it is the goose quill that he snaps and throws to the ground, for his art which now he abjures was only ever the art of writing. And so it is his own book that he resolves to drown.

Greenaway is especially keen to follow up the implications of this aspect of the renunciation. In his version, Prospero's speech is immediately followed by a very rapid series of close-ups of his hands re-closing over two dozen books in a cloud of spray, accompanied by a tumultuous noise, perhaps the same as is heard in the stage directions when the masque is curtailed by Prospero, and by the mariners the instant they are set free.[40] The film shows us Prospero hurling his books into the sea, each volume in his library expiring in a fashion spectacularly appropriate to its nature. Finally only two books are left: the first is a thick, printed volume of plays dated 1623. All thirty-six plays are there save one – the first nineteen pages are left blank for its inclusion. It is called *The Tempest*. The folio collection is modestly bound in dull green linen with cardboard covers and the author's initials are embossed in gold on the cover – W.S; the second book, 'bound identically – but much slimmer – Prospero's unfinished *The Tempest*'. When Prospero, after a moment, throws both of them into the sea, 'the books land together on the water and Caliban surfaces – splurting and spouting water from a long underwater swim – he snatches both books and disappears again under the surface'.

At first glance, this may seem to be a perverse augmentation of the Shakespearean source. But Greenaway has heard a sonar echo between two speeches by the two old men of the play. Midway through *The Tempest*, Alonso of Naples imagines his son Ferdinand to have drowned, and so, feeling his life no longer to be worth living, imagines himself dead: 'my son i' th' ooze is bedded, and/I'll seek him deeper than e'er plummet sounded,/And with him there lie mudded' (III, iii, 101). A mournful prospect; but Ferdinand, of course, has not drowned, and he is not lying on the oozy sea-bed beyond the reach even of a plumb-line. He has come ashore on the tide to fall in love with Miranda, and will occupy her bed, in due course. Consequently, Alonso's words are echoed, perhaps deliberately, by Prospero when he abjures his rough magic: 'And deeper than did ever plummet sound/I'll drown my book'(V, i, 56-7). Just as Ferdinand returns on the tide, so the book will be restored for posterity even in the hands of Caliban; and Prospero's gesture of artistic repression for the sake of the present cannot prevent a future re-emergence of these extraordinary books, even in another medium, such as film.

7 Making an Exhibition

'I do hate cinemas, don't you?' Greenaway told *The Times* in Rome in July 1996. 'We talk about the future of multimedia, yet we still have the spectator sitting in his seat for two hours at a time watching an old-fashioned two-dimensional image.'[1] In recent years, he has vigorously pursued the possibilities of an association between cinema and new technologies and has used assignments from galleries, museums and cities throughout Europe to mount exhibitions in which he can continue to set out his cinematic and artistic interests, but in which he repeatedly demonstrates those personal excitements that cinema has failed to satisfy in him; in particular, the notion that 'Light is a genre of its own'.

A case in point was his spectacular celebration of light and sound in the Piazza del Popolo, where three great arteries entering the city of Rome meet at the Porta Flaminia. Since filming sequences of *The Belly of the Architect* there Greenaway had been fascinated by the natural focus of the Piazza, with the triumphal entry gate of Porto del Popolo, its three Baroque churches, its statuary and fountains all contributing, he claimed, to the sense of a 'magnificent 360-degree architectural amphitheatre'. Its focal point is the 3,000-year-old obelisk, brought to Rome by the Emperor Augustus after his triumphal Egyptian campaign and erected in its present site by Pope Sistus V, the late sixteenth-century pontiff who redesigned much of Rome and sought to place ancient Egyptian obelisks at the centre points of the main thoroughfares in order to create giant meridians. Greenaway took Pope Sistus's unrealized plans as the starting point for the spectacle's tenuous narrative structure, and using cinematic techniques of lighting on the piazza, allowed the narrative to follow the rhythm of day through night.

Every ten minutes, between nine p.m. and midnight, Greenaway's false dawn broke: 6,000 lamps powered by fifteen generators and choreographed by computer created light in the East, altering the obelisk from ghostly grey to rosy pink as a chorus of starlings sang out from giant loudspeakers. Then daylight fell on the church of Santa Maria del Popolo – a conscious homage to the master of chiaroscuro, Caravaggio, some of whose canvases hang in the church – and illuminated the triumphal Porta Flaminia. In due course the twin churches of Santa Maria dei Miracoli and Santa Maria in Montesano, on the other side of the vast open space, appeared, softly illuminated, their rooftop statues picked out by flashes of artificial lightning, while bells thundered out from the soundtrack. Then followed a forest fire, with billowing smoke and a red glow over the umbrella pines at the square's edge. Then dusk, with shooting stars, and sunset. This narrative recreating a Roman day lasted only ten minutes but the audience was meant to share the experience by moving round the Piazza to different vantage points. Greenaway intended the public to be walk-on actors, using the sound and light show to give a new dimension to audience participation, and he regards this as the beginning of a new kind of interactive cinematic activity.

Three years earlier, in association with the Venice Biennale, the Commune of Venice suggested to Greenaway the possibility of an exhibition at the Museo Fortuny where most of the rooms and the exterior of the thirteenth-century palace, originally known as the Palazzo Pesaro, would be made available. The title of the exhibition – *Watching Water* – he chose in deference to the city and perhaps also as a means of reparation, since *Intervals*, the short film he shot in Venice in 1969, included no images of the city's watercourses at all. Before being given to the Municipality of Venice, the building had been owned by the artist and textile designer Mariano Fortuny, whose insatiable curiosity led him to pursue an extraordinary range of disciplines.[2] He manufactured his own dyes and pigments according to the ancient methods of early masters, pulled his own etchings on the great hand-press in his library, invented his own photographic paper for developing prints, designed lamps and furniture for his home, constructed model theatres and stage sets, designed the machinery for printing his sumptuous fabrics, made dresses and even bound his own books. The beginning of Fortuny's most creative period coincided with his move in 1899 to the Palazzo Pesaro Orfei, a building full of large, open spaces in which he could give full rein to his various talents. One journalist wrote: 'Last night I entered the mysterious Palazzo and was spellbound by his magic: I passed in front of lamps as bright as suns and my body threw no shadow; I saw, spread out on the walls of the immense rooms or enclosed in dangling glass cases, many coloured hangings, brocades and damasks of which not a thread was woven. I passed into a remote, shut-up room and saw the sky, a real sky, in calm and stormy weather, extending all round a vast amphitheatre.'[3]

The main stimulus for the exhibition was a question put by Fortuny to the same journalist: 'Can you think of anything more magical than the beauty of electricity?' Like Greenaway, Fortuny was, above all, a painter fascinated by the textures of the Venetian masters – as a young man he made assiduous copies of works by Titian, Bellini and Carpaccio – so it was logical that light was the element that fascinated him most, and the one to which he first sought to bring the opportunities presented by electricity. Indeed, Fortuny revolutionized stage-lighting techniques by his championing of movable arc-lights and his indirect lighting system which he patented in 1901 and constantly refined.[4]

> If one lets a ray of sunlight into a darkened room, one will see a shaft of light piercing the air, but the room will not be lit up. If one then introduces a white leaf of paper in front of this shaft, the light will break up and illuminate the whole room; and yet the actual quantity of light entering still remains the same in both cases. This experiment proves that it is not the quantity but the quality of light that makes things visible and allows the pupil of the eye to open properly.[5]

If an artificial light source is used instead of natural light, the effect is the same; but since the source may also be movable, this offers the possibility of using lights of different colours, with the advantage that the luminosity can either remain constant or be varied at will. Fortuny later tried reflecting the light off a white surface, as in his original experiment, and achieved an effect similar to that of daylight, making it possible to illuminate any object. He then found that if this light were shone on to a surface that was not white but multicoloured and that could be moved up to or away from the light source at will, the reflected light would take on the same colours and also be controllable in its intensity. This discovery meant that it was now possible to achieve infinite degrees of dimness and brightness, as well as a vast range of colours which could change almost imperceptibly from one to another. The advantages of this kind

of stage lighting were enormous. Since it produced a diffused light, it did not cut the scenery into sections but moulded it into a coherent whole; and the endless variety of tones that could be obtained by simply changing the reflective surface meant that all manner of different effects could be achieved, permitting 'the artist to mix his colours on the stage, to paint in the theatre as if with a palette'.[6]

The connection between light waves, electrical current and water flow lay at the heart of Greenaway's exposition. In the Venetian tradition, the exterior of the Palazzo was hung with drapes, alluding to Fortuny's careers both as an artist and as a textile designer; while the upstairs rooms were decorated as though he had just vacated them. Consider the tableau (illus. 88). Paintings, including a self-portrait (1887) of Fortuny in six-teenth-century Venetian costume, hung above a table on which ornate cutlery was laid over one of his distinctive fabrics sten-cilled in silver and gold. Tiger-lilies spilled from vases. Above everything hung the electrical fittings that gave out the artifical light to illuminate Fortuny's theatre. The downstairs rooms of

88 *Watching Water,* 1993.

the Palazzo were given over to further manifestations of the electricity that Fortuny so enthused about. Here, though, the magic was at the level of televisual and cinematic images, as Greenaway installed a monitor showing a loop of *Drowning by Numbers*, a film predicated on the importance of watching water. Behind it, in some two hundred frames on the wall, covering some thirty square metres, hung the script. Further down, the basement was given over to a fantasy of 'artificial water', which Greenaway created by projecting beams across the surface of a fluid; waves of light and water. This is an obsessive technique seen throughout Greenaway's work, here designed not only to remind his audience of the artificial lighting effects developed by Fortuny but also of the accidents of illumination caused by water reflecting off the lagoon and on to the walls and bridges of Venice.

However, Greenaway's intentions went further than simply establishing a connection between his own practice and that of Fortuny:

> Here were various opportunities united to entertain the potency of real objects and extant architecture, where the visiting crowds themselves became participants as film extras on what were, in effect, prepared sets, to find their own wide shots, mid-shots and close-ups – rather than being shown them, however imaginatively – within a series of rectangular frames selected by the limited perspective of the camera. The spectator could be the selective eye, and in effect, any imaginative film invented by a viewer would be unique and valid to him or her alone.[7]

For Greenaway, the appeal of these activities emerges out of his increasing disillusionment with film – with what he calls its phoniness, fakery and pretence. Such projects as the Popolo illumination and the Fortuny installations allowed him to continue to 'make pictures', but without any need for a camera or an easel. Moreover, these light shows permitted many more angles from which to view subjects, as much as objects. In films an immobile audience has its time frame dictated by a director, but in the Piazza del Popolo or in an exhibition space visitors are free to move around at their own pace and are permitted their own 'degrees of expansion and contraction of concentration', actions that would serve only to spoil the experience of watching a film. As Greenaway explained in 1993:

I have always been fascinated about the possibilities of an expanded metacinema that borrows much from the way paintings are perceived, and I can see some possible realization of this ambition in the making and developing of exhibitions as a cultural genre . . . In the contemporary exhibition, all manner of sophisticated cultural languages can be successfully integrated, making it a form of three-dimensional cinema with stimulus for all five senses where the viewer is not passively seated, can create his or her own time-frame of attention and can (as good as) touch the objects he is viewing and certainly have a more physical/visual relationship with them.[8]

These ideas of an 'expanded metacinema' were at the forefront of his mind when, in 1993, as part of a Welsh Fellowship Award, Greenaway was commissioned by the Welsh Arts Council to mount two separate exhibitions in the principality, one in Cardiff, the other in Swansea,. The exhibition he undertook in Cardiff, *The Audience of Mâcon*, emerged, ironically enough, out of his most controversial film, *The Baby of Mâcon*, in which he took to a horrifically logical conclusion many of the illusionistic considerations he had been developing since his earliest work, and that were now beginning to emerge in his extra-cinematic activities.

In the Cardiff show one hundred large coloured portrait photographs of film extras dressed in seventeenth-century historical costume for the film were exhibited, each one in association with its own seven seconds of sound-track from the film. Each image was titled with a description such as 'theatre musician, who paid for his own costume' or 'lame mother of three daughters who all married clerics' and, most appropriately in the context of this film, 'gullible young woman who always believed what she saw on stage'. As Greenaway admitted in the exhibition catalogue, any photograph of a historical character clearly must involve degrees of forgery – 'it is impossible to film history, the characters are probably wearing contemporary underwear under their pseudo-authentic costumes, and there were no cameras in the seventeenth century'. But he goes on to claim, first, that such demands for a suspension of disbelief are endemic and essential every time a viewer enters a cinema, whatever the nature of the film projected. And, second, that all films are about history, a history that is fabricated, with its own built-in past, illusory present and so-called future (though that future is fixed and already in the past – a viewer by watching in real time just has to catch up with it). Hence, lacking any equivalent in the narrative demands of the film, each character portrait–photograph in this Cardiff exhibition also had some kind of text appended to it – often descriptive, sometimes banal, sometimes terse to the point of irony – to offer the gentlest of criticisms that in a dominant literary culture we feel at a loss to address an image unless it has a caption, a commentary or an explanatory text. And for those whose viewing habits continued to expect an idea of plot, story or narrative, a lighting strategy was devised by longtime collaborator Reinier van Brummelen to suggest a 'chronology of viewing', each picture being illuminated in time to a sound-track made up of seven-second film clips. Along with this tightly choreographed sound-and-light show, the exhibition also featured costumed actors seated in glass vitrines, one outside and one inside the gallery. And once again, the questions jostle about the figures: were they actors earning a living wage? Were they 'real' historical characters? Or just pieces of generalized human flesh?

In any case, Greenaway intended these exhibits to encourage the exhibition's visitors to question what they were looking at – to engage with the 'contradictions, confusions and multiplicity of interpretations' inherent in any image or property. The interchange of authenticity, fakery, suspension of disbelief, questionable representation and the private and public time-frame could never be argued as cogently in dramatic narrative cinema terms – yet the lighting and the setting and the aural association had all been extracted from a cinematic scenario. Some aspects of cinematic language had been nicely broken open for examination. In this respect, the exhibition formed a perfect complement to the film; for *The Baby of Mâcon* exhibits the tyrannies of representation, and, in doing so, breaks apart the illusions that are experienced in the dark.

In the film, a play is ostensibly being performed for the seventeen-year-old Prince Cosimo de Medici, nearly the last of the great Florentine Medici family, which, now heavily in debt, was on the decline. In 1661, two years after the film is set, the family were to use Cosimo's marriage to Marguerite-Louise d'Orléans to form an alliance with France; but at this stage Cosimo, last hopeful heir – heavily under the influence of counter-Reformation propaganda, especially that of his mother, Vittoria della

89 The theatre, from *The Baby of Mâcon* (1993).

Rovere – had become a sentimental religious fanatic at an early age, determined to return himself, the Medicis and the unwilling Florentine community to the Church. That Church was, however, of 'a particular Italian seventeenth-century kind – of obsessive religious iconography, reliquaries, extreme devotional pathos, melancholic introspection, ritual observances and sentimental contemplations'(illus. 89).[9]

The play staged before Cosimo and his sumptuous entourage begins with the birth of a healthy, beautiful boy to a woman well past normal childbearing age, thus mocking all the fears and prejudices of a supposedly barren and infertile community. Naturally, the child is taken to be a miracle, which is quickly seized upon as an entrepreneurial opportunity in a world of hardship and religious fanaticism – most especially by the boy's sister, an ambitious, beautiful, vain young virgin eager for material gain. She exploits the child, turning him into an exhibit for a willingly credulous public. The exhibition takes place in a long sequence in 'the very large and echoic spaces of a dilapidated cathedral, a dark, underendowed, impoverished building – one-time magnificent – now with much evidence of shoring up and unfinished reconstruction, broken masonry and crumbling statues.There is much scaffolding and many ladders.

Ropes and chains hang down from the high ceilings. But the building is gloomily impressive – there is incense, beams of orange sunlight in the gloaming and many candles.' As Greenaway suggests, this is the bizarre world of Desiderio, now the name given to a group of artists working in Naples in about 1660 who specialized in the most extraordinary, extravagant, dramatically lit interiors;[10] buildings poised between construction and destruction.

In the course of the 'exhibition' staged in acknowledgement of his status as a saint, the child is richly dressed in seven garments. Each of these – the Sash of Humility, the Vest of Chastity, the Coat of Prudence, the Robe of Piety, the Shoes of Perseverance, the Crown of Strength, the Beads of Poverty – is given a provenance and accorded a value; labelled with the cost of what Bourdieu calls 'cultural capital'. The ceremony culminates before an elaborate altarpiece, a wooden *sacra conversazione* extravagance with three main alcoves, which has been wheeled into place, like an exhibit or even an installation.[11] One of the members of Cosimo's entourage is named 'Carpaccio', and indeed the scene does recall earlier Venetian painting. But it is more likely that this *tableau vivant* is meant to recall Bellini's *Virgin and Child with Saints* (1505; Venice, S Zaccaria). The irony lies in the fact that these structures are mobile, moving in a world of broken edifices; they are temporary, unfixed, unrooted and contingent. And yet the figures that adorn the film's altarpiece seem to co-exist within the same architectural space or cast light and to be aware of each other; placed so centrally, however, the disposition in which they find themselves demands a relentless stasis, dislocation from the body.

Encouraged by a public greed for belief, the daughter decides to claim the child as her own. She egotistically wishes to identify herself with the Virgin Mary, so she imprisons her mother, buys off her father with the proceeds made through selling the child's blessings, and then attempts to seduce the son of the bishop – a scene that climaxes when the young man is gored by a sacred cow. The daughter is declared to be an unfit mother and the child is taken into the Church's direct protection where it is even more provocatively exploited than it was by the daughter. The Church now also prospers – selling by auction the various liquids of the child's body – his phlegm, tears, urine, blood, etc. – and the cathedral is lavishly repaired on the proceeds of these commodities. All of this is too much for the jealous daughter, who suffocates the child.

As punishment she is raped to death by the militia in the guard room. This scene became notorious and attracted hostility from many quarters; but in his *mise-en-scène*, Greenaway was making some central points about illusionism (illus. 90). The floor is tiled in large slabs, which make a diagonally patterned, regular chessboard; skittles have been placed at the apex of each. From the right-hand side of the room, out of the frame, a bed is hauled on to the stage. It is a four-poster, behind the curtains of which the appalling illusion of religious punishment is played out. The shadows on this makeshift screen offer a virtual view of the horrors taking place behind; we are back to the imagery of *Les Carabiniers*, of *Z&OO* or of the scene in Flavia's studio in *The Belly of an Architect*, where the lovers disappear behind the blinds and embrace. Here it is a question of artifical repugnance; and as the judicial punishment continues for over ten minutes, the period available on a 70-mm magazine, there is a change from day to night, and the altarpiece, now lit by devotional candles, is wheeled in again, to be placed in front of the bed. In the centre and largest of the three shallow arches sits the wet-nurse who is dressing and shrouding the dead child; in the left- and right-hand side of the triptych the child's sisters kneel in penance, before being pulled away by the soldiers and sent to the brothels. At this point,

> The left-hand side of the triple-arched screen is pulled open – like the door to a small chapel, or the door to a large cupboard. . . by two stage ushers – to reveal the hanged, naked body of the mother of the child.

> 1st STAGE USHER: The family is destroyed.

> 2nd STAGE USHER: The sins of the children always begin with the mother.

> As we watch, the mother's concealing hood and wig fall away, revealing her badly birthmarked face, neck and breasts.

> The stage ushers open the right-hand panel – to discover the father. He is awkwardly seated with his throat cut – the knife curiously bandaged to his hand – a poorly re-created fake suicide.

> 1st STAGE USHER: The family is destroyed.

> 2nd STAGE USHER: The sins of the children always begin with the father.

> For a moment, the stage ushers freeze, and with the 'frozen' stage figures of the mother and father, the altarpiece reflects its painterly origins.[12]

After the death of the young woman, the child is now declared a saint and the mob, eager for relics and cynical of the Church's hand in the exploitation of the infant, revolt in the cathedral at the child's funeral, and, determined that the Church will not be the sole exploiter of their local miracle and benefit from the child's reputation and relics, the crowd dismember the child's body. Hence, as Greenaway explains:

> the film distorts this theatrical event and introduces 'reality' into the much-rehearsed piece of theatrical exhibitionism. The baby that is born on stage is not the expected fake wooden doll but a real child . . . the priest's son is not an actor who feigns a bloody death but becomes a real fatality . . . the actress who plays the virgin daughter is not just obliged to act the victim of multiple rape but is a true virgin who is raped until she perishes . . . and the child saint is not a substituted

doll but a real child who is murdered and then dismembered. The 'realities' of the theatrical propositions are deliberately mocked, suggesting various reactions – first, the dividing lines between reality, artifice and theatricality, fact and fiction, are perilously thin.[13]

And what sustains the 'realities' is an illusion, a 'much-reheased piece of theatrical exhibitionism' built out of light and sound, of props and audience.

In the final analysis, we are left with an object and a display; a relic of the film, as the bishop takes a bow on the stage while the child's head stays mysteriously suspended in mid-air at breast height, emanating light.

> Behind, in the darkness, the blackwood skeleton form of the large four-poster bed that has figured so many times in the drama – stripped now of its covers and mattresses and curtains – bursts into illumination from strings of fireworks – red, orange and white – like the fireworks of a religious display in an Italian provincial town. . . the fireworks illuminate the bed's shape – it is a fiery end that parallels the fiery comet that opened the opera.

> The child's head continues to sing/chant/intone/speak its three lines throughout the fireworks . . . the fireworks end and the Singing Head closes its eyes . . . there is silence.

The moment is dominated by a light show of the kind Greenaway designed in Rome, an illumination which claims to be explosive but whose illusion, in fact, depends on the same electricity. At first glance, the child's head seems to function as a marvellous relic; a sublime verity clearly distinguishable from the miracles of fiction and fable, such as Orpheus's head singing on the stream to Hades. Yet it is an exhibit whose signification, religious or otherwise, is, like the child itself, up for grabs. It is as vacuous as the blank faces in his drawing 'Pencil Heads'(illus. 91), ready for the imprint of character; or as meaningless as those phrenological heads exhibited along with his paintings as part of his other Welsh show, *Some Organizing Principles*, heads that have no name and exist to denote orders and inevitably, beyond that, disorders of personality (illus. 92). This is the most shocking aspect of the film: the sense that it uses a single object to draw attention to its own limits. As the object that socializes those products of a human consciousness,

91 *Pencil Heads*,
1993.

92 *Some Organizing
Principles*, 1993.

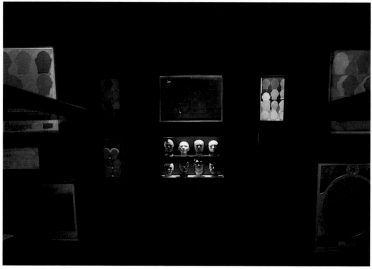

the child's head is the locus of power struggles conducted through farce, comedy, irony, transcendence, and of course, commerce. It is a space that rides on ambiguities, on unexplored assumptions, on a rhetoric that, like that of its mother, the virgin, barters the discomforts of full consciousness for the benefits of permanence and order. Greenaway shows that those who exhibit are in the paradoxical position of editing the products that extend consciousness, and so contribute, in a liberal manner, to the necessary anaesthesia of the masses – who live under the guise of religion, or entertainment, or exhibitionism.

Visitors to *Some Organizing Principles*, the exhibition Greenaway mounted at the Glynn Vivian Art Gallery in Swansea, were presented with 'a three-dimensional catalogue in sound, light and artefacts, of ways and means in which the world is measured, timed weighed, counted and numbered'. Three dimensions and three types of object: a collection of the fake texts manufactured for *Prospero's Books*, a selection of Greenaway's own paintings and some 800 historical artefacts borrowed from the rural and industrial museum collections of South Wales. Included in this last category were showcases containing ship models, natural history collections, a counter for miners going down a pit, a Second World War map of the Principality showing possible enemy attacks, scales, inkwells and letter-racks, Brecon measurement vessels, scientific equipment, games and toys, and paintings turned to display their labelled backs, 'to show how obsessive museums are with archiving'. This last 'exhibit' is significant given Greenaway's preoccupation with illusionism, and no doubt alludes to Gijsbrechts's *Reverse Side of a Painting* (illus. 93), which famously attempts to persuade the viewer to turn it the right way round. The scrap of paper marked with the number '36' may give the impression that this

93 Cornelius Gijsbrechts, *Reverse Side of a Painting*, 1670, oil on canvas.

206

canvas has been catalogued for auction. The superbly accurate rendering of the stretching frame and the texture of the canvas emphasizes give and plasticity; it functions as a substitute for the artefact. It is a surrogate exhibit, whcih draws attention to the arbitrariness of museum selection; hence the attraction for Greenaway.

However, rather than being displayed in a conventionally static manner, each of the exhibits was either picked out in turn with precisely focused stage lights, or bathed in mottled mixtures of moving coloured lights conceived and executed by Reinier van Brummelen, Sacha Vierny's lighting partner on the film sets. Greenaway claimed that in their exhibition illuminations they were, in general, seeking to create the equivalent of false perspectives by making use of 'light projections which have been – in some cases – very heavily keystoned – placing silhouettes, masks and gobos in the light beams to light impossible angles with amazing accuracy – which gives encouragement to imagine all sorts of possibilities'.[14] In the Swansea installations, however, the sense of possibility was directed against conventional practice:

> The items were given a certain attention, and even glamour, by a sympathetic system of illumination that was forever changing, putting the objects in different lights and consequently different forms of emphasis, to repudiate, in various ways, that museum insistence on neutrality which can so often be merely blandness, even sterility.

Whereas most museums begin with light and move towards darkened recesses, Greenaway prefers to start with the viewer in the dark. From this darkness, individual objects are picked out by highly focused lights, only to be plunged again into darkness when the current is cut. The result is a dramatic atmosphere with a tremendous sense of movement, which, Greenaway maintains, 'keeps the objects alive'. Here too, he is touching on a rarely considered element of exhibitions and displays – the visitor's experience of time. Seemingly less influenced by the current infatuation for interaction, he creates instead a space that is a stage for action; continually changing pools of light and dark and audiovisual prompts and enticements replace levers, buttons and touch-sensitive video monitors. There are also accompanying soundtracks, so that in the main entrance hall, for example, a loud voice counts off, 'A, 1,

B, 2, C, 3 . . .', the numbers and letters gradually moving out of synch as they are projected on to a wall and the floor.

In Swansea, these techniques were designed to highlight 'the means by which comparatively average people had used devices to measure their universe'. Yet his exhibition therefore bore very little on questions of social history, and anyone looking for evidence of how people worked, lived or struggled was likely to be frustrated, perhaps even offended, by his use of objects more as props than subjects. As with some of his film characters, he treated exhibits as signposts to ideas.

> They were exhibited, from my point of view, as properties – not invented items reproduced for the particular viewpoint of a camera, but properties with a history and a provenance, arranged, sometimes in very large numbers of the same object, as a thesaurus of source-material to be utilized at will in some unwritten hypothetical dramatic scenario of organization. Perhaps a film called indeed SOME ORGANIZING PRINCIPLES.[15]

And the main idea is the absolute necessity, and yet curiously arbitrary application, of organizing principles. 'That is what civilization is all about,' he contends; 'ordering the chaos.'

By now we know this concept is a dubious one; but Greenaway is grappling with the issue of the influence on notions of taxonomy an exhibition can exert if it is regarded as a medium such as film. Here opinions differ between those who regard the museum as a temple, a shrine to art, and those who are inclined to exploit the more academic potential of the medium. The museum environment asserts itself by neutralizing the object, severing it from its original meaning and function and putting it to a different use. On the one hand, the object is thus reduced to its visible properties; on the other, freed of its initial associations, it can serve purposes that will convey new meanings. Exhibitions have arisen out of such displacements or transfers of the objects collected out of their original environment to a different spatial setting. But can this new space be identified?

In his essay 'Valéry Proust Museum' Theodor Adorno has some characteristically pungent things to say about the ways in which museums deal with the cultural life:

> Museums are like the family sepulchres of works of art. They testify to the neutralization of culture. Art treasures are

hoarded in them, and their market value leaves no room for the pleasure of looking at them . . . Sensibility wreaks even more havoc.[16]

In other words, the museum is the place of the dead, the mausoleum of culture where the body of the past is displayed. It is a necessary concomitant of 'an institution caught in the contradictions of its culture and therefore extending to every object contained there'.[17] Adorno is suggesting that the process of making, appreciating and exhibiting art, particularly in such institutions, is an intensely political process; one that is not necessarily learnt when people visit museums, but that is fully understood and appreciated only in terms of the knowledge and received wisdom about what exhibitions are supposed to represent.[18] To one contemporary theorist, they are 'narratives which use art objects as elements in institutionalized stories that are promoted to an audience'; to another, 'they are modern ritual settings in which visitors enact complex and often deep psychic dramas about identity, dramas that the museum's stated, consciously intended programs do not and cannot acknowledge'.[19] For his part, Greenaway's curatorial activities seek to question both of these possibilities: that of narrative and that of drama.

In 1991, to celebrate 300 years of the Academy of Fine Arts in Vienna, the institution which had taught Klimt, Schiele, Kokoschka, Schwitters, Kitaj and Adolf Hitler, Greenaway was invited to stage an exhibition of cultural objects borrowed from many of the Viennese museum collections, ranging from the medical, criminal and scientific collections to the Freud Museum, the Mozarteum, the national collections of painting and the Kunsthistorisches Museum. The organizing principle of the exhibition, entitled *100 Objects to Represent the World* and held in the Semper Depot and the Hofburg Palace, was simple.

> The Americans in the *Voyager* spaceships of the 1970s had arrogantly sent a payload off into Outer Space to represent the world to any of the possible inhabitants out there who might find such a gesture interesting. You were not asked to contribute to this representation and neither was I, so what sort of world were they seeking to represent? If you and I were not consulted or represented, could their efforts be considered to have made a contribution to any picture an extraterrestrial might have of Earth?[20]

In ironic compensation of this oversight, Greenaway felt that as the new millennium approached, some form of summing-up, of stocktaking, would be useful. A roster could be organized of 'objects to represent the world'. Necessarily, the existence of the list would concentrate minds on the pressing question, 'Why is it that museum practice has arrived at certain methods of organizing subject-matter, namely, the categories of age, authorship, nationality, material and ownership, which tend to categorize and classify in ways that perhaps are no longer valuable or instructive?'

Consequently, Greenaway juxtaposed art objects of so-called high artistic reputation with items of low cultural standing, and with objects apparently lacking any cultural credentials at all. In other words, this was an exhibition whose taxonomy was subjectively subversive, seeking to undermine the five orthodox categories of taxonomy that museum culture generally sees as relevant. The catalogue introduction claimed:

> This list of 100 objects seeks to include every aspect of time and scale, masculine and feminine, cat and dog. It acknowledges everything – everything alive and everything dead. It should leave nothing out – every material, every technique, every type of every type, every science, every art and every discipline, every construct, illusion, trick and device we utilize to reflect our vanity and insecurity and our disbelief that we are so cosmically irrelevant. Since every natural and cultural object is such a complex thing, and all are so endlessly interconnected, this ambition should not be so difficult to accomplish as you might imagine.[21]

Item 30 was the *Willendorf Venus*, the fertility icon carved of bone during the early Paleolithic Age; item 43 was Mozart's apocryphal skull, recovered from the pauper's grave into which he was cast. Other exhibits were a large block of slowly melting ice, a perpetual thunderstorm – once again created by Reinier van Brummelen – a pile of coins, a dead cow, 100 daily newspapers delivered every morning by a paperboy, a pile of dust, the last judicially decapitated head in Austria, a conference table and a human tattoo. Such an arbitrarily inclusive roster was bound to contains some *coups de théâtre*, if not *coups de grâce*. Hence, one of the larger objects in the exhibition was a crashed light aircraft (illus. 94), seemingly lodged among the marble columns of the Hofburg, and representing flight, hubris,

94 Crashed plane, from *100 Objects to Represent the World*, 1991.

95 Sleep, from *100 Objects to Represent the World*, 1991.

machinery, ambition, ingenuity and failure of endeavour.[22] Other striking objects included Sleep (illus. 95) – exemplified by observing the daily slumber of a volunteer who had rearranged her sleeping habits to bed down through the day for the visitor to watch 'with some wonder at such vulnerability and much silent respect for the person's need for recuperation'. Item 33 was a Baby – presented in the exhibition every day at noon for one hour to signify new beginnings, continuity, motherhood, hope, a fresh start, vulnerability and indeed simply childhood. However, perhaps the most important of all the exhibits was the first: 'a shadow made by the viewer himself stepping into the darkness of the exhibition space as though stepping into a darkened cinema, waiting, hoping, for the film-maker to fix it eternally'.[23] As Greenaway explained later: 'Here was live specimen and dead object, installation and representation, readymade, art work and art object, stuffed specimen, reproduction, potential fake, real fake, substitute, proxy object, object by description';[24] all to present a picture of a world where all these phenomena are commonly interlacing all the time. But through these textual gaps, pauses, ellipses and other strategic interruptions in its conventions and conformisms, the obvious questions press in: 'How can an art museum's face be composed when its exhibitionist heart and mind are conflicted? How can it speak realistically when its true speech can only be surrealist, fragmentary and incomplete, full of doubt and vulnerability and poetry? And mortality.'[25]

In 1990, when Greenaway was invited to mount an exhibition using the resources of the Boymans–van Beuningen Museum in Rotterdam, he once more assumed a point of view within which the conventional museum classification in terms of periods and types of objects was disregarded. His intentions in *The Physical Self* were clear: he chose to exhibit not simply his obsession with the materiality of art – the mortal, physical condition of the human body – but also to examine precisely this relationship between the representation of the body and the role of the museum. The famous collection consists mainly of Flemish and Dutch paintings, drawings and prints; but its archives also contain sculpture, ceramics, glassware, furniture and design objects manufactured over the last five centuries. From this rich reserve, exhibits relating to the human figure were arranged in a strict chronology from conception through the stages of youth and adulthood and culminating in senility.

However, in order to relate it to a directly practical world, the exhibition archly included such functional objects and artefacts as had been expressly created for the intimate touch of the human body – 'like utensils designed to be used by the hand and mouth, bicycle seats moulded for the comfort of the buttocks, spectacle frames moulded for the fragility of the nose'. Alongside these Greenaway displayed a large collection of objects and images that also exhibited the subtle traces of the human body, from thumbprints on fourteenth-century pottery to the thumbprints of Salvador Dalí on *Couple With Heads Full of Clouds*. Each of these human traces was picked out with the beam from a powerful spotlight, in a lighting set-up designed, as ever, by van Brummelen. Elsewhere, the lighting was used to give prominence to certain elements within the canvases; for instance, paintings by Cornelis Cornelisz van Haarlem (*Bacchus and the Satyrs*) and Rubens (*The Bath of Diana*) were illuminated to suggest, respectively, fire and rippling water.

However, the most significant items in *The Physical Self* were not borrowed from the museum collection. At the various inter-sections of the exhibition, viewable from every perspective, four living human figures were exhibited in glass cases. Each had been instructed to stand, sit and lie to refer to the usual poses of the still-life class, which in turn reflected the major positions of the body in everyday life. They were male and female, old and young; some thirty people being employed in a roster, each obliged to pose for a period of no more than two hours in any one day. Over the period of the seven-week exhi-bition, this meant a considerable variety of human types and bodies and poses on show within the given parameters, for Greenaway meant these four 'classical' nudes behind perspex to serve as the lightning conductors for the whole of the exhibi-tion: to provide a real focus for all the other items that drew on the body as their source of inspiration, fascination, use and util-ity; to offer, in short, the flesh and blood of this Western cultur-al fascination to see, watch, wonder at, accommodate and commemorate the body. His chapter-by-chapter arrangement is a narrative of the body from birth to death; and the living nudes formed a link between the physicality of the viewer and that of the models used for the works on display, from van Dyck's *St Jerome* to Magritte's *On the Threshold of Liberty* and Kitaj's *Halcyon Days*. Through the nudes, he recognized the essence both of art and of the art exhibition; and, beyond this, the artifi-ciality of both.

But in this, his first major exhibition, Greenaway was also attempting to draw attention to cinema's fascination with the human body, with sex, with experience, with ageing, with vul-nerability, with provocation, even embarrassment, certainly with illusion and subjectivity. And, like a film, *The Physical Self* was arranged from an initial position of 'a darkness illuminat-ed', and offered frames, isolated images, to be seen in sequence. However, at this point the correspondence becomes more com-plicated, for if this exhibition were to be seen as cinema, the time-frame of appreciation could proceed at one speed only. There would have been no possibility of by-passing areas of lower-threshold interest, no possibility of pausing when the contemplation of a single item or idea was of paramount importance. Moreover, cinema is supposed to be a social activity, yet silence and stillness are nominally required of a visitor in front of a public screen. In the exhibition space, social activity is – and certainly was in Rotterdam – observably loquacious and interactive. Would it not be possible to engineer these sorts of valuable characteristics and reactions within the language and practice of cinema?

> From these exhibitions – all of them enjoyed by a large public – I could find an audience that was not subjected to a sedentary and very largely passive role, sitting in one place in the dark looking at the illusions created of a three-dimensional world by another's subjectivity on to a flat screen. Here was an opportunity to make an audience walk and move, be sociable in a way never dreamed of by the rigours of cinema-watching, in circumstances where many differing perspectives could be brought to bear on a series of phenomena associated with the topics under consideration. Yet all the time it was a subjective creation under the auspices of light and sound, dealing with a large slice of the cinema's vocabulary.[26]

IN THE DARK

It was precisely the need to counter the passivity of 'sitting in one place in the dark looking at the illusions created of a three-dimensional world' that recently led Greenaway to inaugurate a series of ten exhibitions on the theme of film and its language which (he envisages) will take place throughout the world in the course of the next few years. Each exhibition will be of 100 days' duration and will have as its venue the streets and public spaces of the city visited; and, in that time, each city is to become the reference point for a particular aspect of cinematic artifice. In his original prospectus, Greenaway intended in all that ten areas of film would be investigated, under the following headings: Location, Audience, Frame, Acting, Properties, Light, Text, Time, Scale, Illusion. Geneva was the chosen site for the first of these installations, with the theme 'Location'. Greenaway has argued that every film, real or imagined, has to have its setting, through which the director imparts his message and binds his audience into involvement with his vision. However, in order to encourge the Genevois to look and stare and so to make this commonplace less obvious, Greenaway turned their city into a film set and the often unsuspecting citizens into the actors, extras and audience of a ceaseless drama. Researching beforehand, he wandered through the city in search of signs and symbols, real or illusory, mystic, touristic, commercial – some viewpoints with a story to tell, others observing change and interchange, others again that sought to provoke, to raise a question. In one respect, the setting was already in place – trees, water, fine buildings, statues, proud notices of historical deeds, melancholic remnants of the past, and so forth. However, from these Greenaway chose 100 locations in the city and framed them, not through the camera but instead through a device resembling the camera obscura of former times, familiar from the devices used by Neville in *The Draughtsman's Contract*. Each framing device in Geneva was built into a white-painted wooden staircase – which actually looks more like a pulpit; and the concept was that residents would be invited to look into the 'viewfinder' through which they would discover a 'set' and so be enabled to create their own internal or imaginary film, in association with Peter Greenaway. The stairs were a symbol of ceaseless motion, a link between two points, a means of travel, an analogy of success or failure, an image of life, a metaphor for ascent and descent, rise and fall, growth and aspiration; but above all, a significant pun in a project that as ever demanded very open-eyed visual awareness: the 'stare'. Furthermore, 'a stairway is a common, powerful and very practical device for spectacle and display. It is a motif used often enough in two thousand years of painting, and indeed in a hundred years of cinema, from Eisenstein's often pastiched Odessa Steps from *Potemkin* to the going-nowhere impressive scaffolding stairs of Fellini's *8 1/2*.[27]

Erected in public parks, in quiet alleys, or in the middle of a busy road, on bridges and in museums, the stairs were placed in positions of vantage, where those who mounted them could enjoy permanent, uninterrupted viewing; and because the viewer had the opportunity and freedom to place that chosen definitive frame in the 360° range, the view could exist in a context of fourteen hours of continuously changing daylight (the exhibition was held in the spring) and ten subsequent hours of artificial lighting, 'nominally static, but always subject to variations of movement and density by wind and weather, possible moonlight and the inevitable movement of people and vehicles'. Because of this arbitrary lighting, the putative film director could transform his location, creating a new ambience: 'the late-night stranger will tread on the edges of a trance, entering a circle of magic, mystery or a moment of terror'.

Greenaway used similar imagery to describe the second *Stairs* exhibition, which was more conventional and more reliant on van Brummelen's lighting expertise. To celebrate the centenary of film in 1995, Munich commissioned Greenaway to adorn the city with suitable images. However, since he intended this installation to refer specifically to the essential act of light projection, which he feels is the dominant characteristic of cinema, he chose to beam 100 non-figurative images of the dates between 1895 and 1995, during which cinema has existed, on to screens formed out of the city's buildings. He explained:

> The strong beam of projected light with its moving shadows is to be the dominant image of the screen space, oblivious of the interruption of window and cornice, brick, stone, tile or cement-rendering – creating a rectangle with pronounced edges. Inside the magic illuminated rectangle is cinema, outside is nothing and the night.[28]

And so, as part of the *Spellbound* exhibition on art and film, held at the Hayward Gallery in London in early 1996, Greenaway took over the large gallery at the top of the Hayward to create an installation representing seventy-five days in which this 'magic illuminated rectangle' was broken down into its component parts: 'artificial light, actors, props, text, illusion, audience, time, sound, changing imagery'. Throughout each day, van Brummelen's lights flashed, screens flickered with miscellaneous disconnected images, various sound effects (including a civil airliner taking off) were played at deafening volume, interspersed with music by Patrick Mimran; and newspapers, representing the texts that might possibly be 'filmed', were arranged on perspex stands (illus. 96). Most strikingly, the props – which included such diverse items as buckets of blood to represent an abbatoir (Day 9) – were laid out on long benches marked out with grid patterns, and coordinated with the days of the exhibition; and each day, too, five live actors, chosen on a stated basis (actors, for instance, who had appeared in *Macbeth*, or whose names began with Z or who had agreed to appear nude) sat in perspex cases at one end of the auditorium (illus. 97). At the other end were banks of plush red seats for the audience. The intention, as in Geneva, was to provide a cinema in which the visitor could become a film-maker, working with a different cast and situation provided on a daily basis. However, in setting up the installations Greenaway seemed unable to rein in his ironizing of cinema. For instance, among the props assembled for the crematorium (Day 67) was a volume of Auden's *Collected Shorter Poems 1927–57* open at the lyric, 'Stop all the clocks, cut off the telephone', immortalized in the popular British film *Four Weddings and a Funeral*. And, beyond this, as Adam Mars-Jones asked, 'Is it a coincidence that "actors who have appeared in a Spielberg film" (30 April) have been assigned the props for a bordello, or that "actors who have played in a Jane Austen family" have been assigned those for a sex shop?'[29]

These props so carefully laid out on gridded display tables, or the projections on to the buildings in Munich, or the white staircases in Geneva, the maps, instruments of vision and measuring devices in Swansea, or the crashes and interruptions in Vienna, the complex wall montage in Rotterdam, typify Greenaway's installations; and, as Thomas Elsaesser has observed, they 'all evoke a number of robust antinomies around removal and unpacking, storage and retrieval, inside and outside, before and after, evidence and argument'.[30] More precisely, it seems that in each installation or exhibition Greenaway has transformed a linear narrative into a spatial sequence.

It was precisely this translation that lay at the heart of one of his most ambitious projects in recent years, the 1992 television documentary on Charles Darwin, in which, effectively, motion pictures were returned to the museum. In *Darwin*, the life and work of the nineteenth-century naturalist was condensed into eighteen densely arranged tableaux, all of which were shot on a single set (illus. 98) which may represent the study in Down House, Sevenoaks, in which Darwin produced most of his revolutionary theories of evolution and variation; but then again, as the narration suggests, the study may simply be 'a nineteenth-century writing place, which may reproduce in essence all the scholarly writing places of mid- and late nineteenth-century figures like Darwin's actual and near contemporaries: Marx, Dickens, Ruskin, Prince Albert, Shaw, H. G. Wells, Tolstoy and even Freud'.[31] In each tableau this desk occupies the centre of the frame, and, while the camera moves laterally or

96 The props, from
In the Dark, 1996.

97 The actors, from
In the Dark, 1996.

98 The study, from
Darwin (1992).

zooms in and out, it never succeeds in breaking out of the confines of this rigid insular set, much as Darwin, too, was encumbered both by persistent ill-health – possibly caused by Chagas' disease – and the fixed views of the Creationists.[32] Roland Barthes observes that, 'In theatre, in cinema, in traditional literature, things are always seen from somewhere; this is the geometric basis of representation: there must be a fetishistic subject in order to project this tableau [for] the tableau has no point of departure, no support, it is a gap.'[33]

As ever, it is the lighting, once more designed by van Brummelen, that indicates the gaps behind the exhibits; indeed, in *Darwin* light becomes the fetish, the praxis regarded with excessive, even irrational reverence. In Tableau 2, the narrator draws attention to the implications of this aspect of the 'exhibition':

> By day and night there are a great many light sources in Darwin's study: table lamps, candles, candelabras placed symmetrically. In the wall behind the desk there are shutters, dark green blinds and three sets of curtains. The lamps and the windows have these various characteristics: they make the light changeable to sympathetically suit the many moods and events in Darwin's life as he opened up new vistas for himself and for philosophical thought and for us.

By mentioning this, Greenaway ensures that the illusionistic frame is broken; because of the lighting effects, viewers can never forget that they are within an exhibition space, or that the furniture is being moved around their perception not just of Darwin's thought but of aesthetics theories too. In Tableau 10, 'In which Darwin considers some Principles in Evolution', the set has become a veritable museum of palaeontology. Fossils and skeletons fill the work benches, and between these wooden tables are led the contents of a menagerie consisting of goats, cattle and camels. As these creatures are conducted round the exhibition space, the camera moves in to Darwin's desk on which several skeletons of various primates sit. Among them – hemmed in, even – stand the clothed Darwin, on a small set of library steps (not dissimilar to those viewing devices designed for Geneva), a book open in his hands, and a naked Adam, who is, in effect, just another ape (illus. 99). The commentary, or rather the caption, observes wryly:

> Even if [Darwin's Victorian contemporaries] could agree to the evolutionary mechanism in principle, they still insisted in seeing God's hand guiding the evolutionary process until it manifests itself in its prime creation: Adam. And from Adam to the Victorian English gentleman. But standing alongside Adam did not make Darwin agree that they were both there as any part of any divine structure.

99 Adam and Darwin, from *Darwin* (1992).

They stand there only as part of a museum structure; indeed, one that was a by-product of Darwin's rebuttal of theories of polygenesis, which meant that alternative means had to be developed for establishing and representing the fractured unity of the human species. In the late nineteenth century, as far as the display of artefacts in museums was concerned, all objects of a similar nature, irrespective of their ethnographic groupings, were arranged in an evolutionary series leading from the simple to the complex.[34] If this wholesale reordering was the effect on natural history museums, what effect might Darwin's findings have had on galleries or on institutions containing works of art?

The issue is encapsulated in Tableau 7, 'In which Nineteenth-Century Attitudes to the Creation of the World are Considered'. Here the views of the creationists are set in a complex sequence of lighting effects, which lead on quite naturally to painterly allusions. Darwin stands, Adam lies on the desk; and their outstretched hands create a version of the *Creation of Adam* painted by Michelangelo on the ceiling of the Sistine Chapel. After this a rainbow is lit up behind the head of Darwin, the sign sent by God to denote a new beginning in *Genesis*; but, as was seen in *The Draughtsman's Contract*, the rainbow is also a Newtonian emblem, a sign that (as the *Opticks* proved) light is not divinely, uniquely white but promiscuous. Here, science appropriates a divine symbol and makes it its own, just as Greenaway adopts works of art following Darwinian theories. Natural selection is a narrative of survival and loss, growth and extinction, wholeness and fragmentation. On the one hand, it may suggest a final state; on the other, it also points to new departures – adaptations – in future generations.

Consider, in this respect, Tableau 16, 'In Which Darwin's Theory of Evolution is Considered Relevant to Our Present Understanding of Ourselves'. Darwin sits like the Old Testament God, his beard white, his gaze generally benign. As the tableau develops, the light is slowly dimmed, and he is approached by a crowd of people of many ages and races, a cross-section of the world (illus. 100). Of course, the image of a group watching in the dark may be inherently cinematic; but these figures are all naked, and they crouch around the inert figure of Darwin, simultaneously protecting him but also drawing protection from his figure. The narrator observes:

Since Darwin's theories suggest that the individual is the insignificant servicer of the species, then apparently the necessity to reproduce is essentially our only pertinent function. . . . Post-Darwin it is not easy to make any other human action or behaviour significant.

It is, of course, the 'necessity to reproduce' in artistic rather than biological terms that drives Greenaway throughout his work; and, consequently, this tableau, in which narrative has been reduced to space, is also an attempt to capture the shapes of Michelangelo's *Last Judgement*, painted on – even installed on – the back wall of the Sistine Chapel. In that masterpiece, a powerful, beardless Christ figure presides over a mass of risen figures on whom he is passing judgement. Unusually, saints and sinners are lumped together, without any hierarchies; all that matters to Michelangelo is the body exhibited nakedly as a body. And it is through the frequently startling representation of such bare necessities in his films, artworks, and curatorial activities that Greenaway intends to pull his viewers out of the dark and into the artificial light.

Acknowledgements

This book need not have been written. Greenaway is a film-maker who greatly enjoys explaining himself or setting out his intentions, either in interview, lecture or essay; and, as will be clear from my own accounts of his work, I am much indebted to the detailed exegeses of his films he has provided over the years. Yet for all his openness about his work, he has gained the reputation for arcaneness and difficulty; one interviewer described him recently as 'The Wizard of Odd'. As I see it, the best response to such peremptory dismissals is to try to place Greenaway's work in as broad and familiar a cultural context as possible. Consequently, I have written this short book not simply for students of 'Film Studies', but also for those who may be in the intellectual potential inherent in the conjunction of 'Cinema' and 'Art History'.

At all times during the gestation of this publication, Reaktion Books has been patient and helpful. I have benefited from discussions about Greenaway's work with the following people: Glenn Black, Richard Boyd, Kate Crane, Richard Cronin, Bob Cummings, Donald Greig, Esther Kaposi, Vassiliki Kolocotroni, Willy Maley, Deborah Pascoe, John Pitcher, Jane Rose, May Sanderson, Boyd Steenson, and Duncan Wu. Errors and misreadings that remain are, of course, my own responsibility. I would like to express my gratitude to Peter Greenaway, for his generosity both with his time and materials; and to his assistant, Eliza Poklewski Koziell, without whose help this book would have suffered. Finally, I would like to thank my parents, Sid and Joan Pascoe, for their constant support.

Filmography and Bibliography

FILMS DIRECTED BY GREENAWAY

Train (1966) 5 mins
Tree (1966) 16 mins
Revolution (1967) 8 mins
5 Postcards from Capital Cities (1967) 35 mins
Intervals (1969) 7 mins
Erosion (1971) 27 mins
H is for House (1971) 9 mins (re-edited 1978). NARRATION: Colin Cantlie, Peter
    Greenaway and his family. MUSIC: From Vivaldi's *Four Seasons*.
Windows (1975) 4 mins. NARRATION: Peter Greenaway. MUSIC: Rameau's *The Hen*.
    CALLIGRAPHY: Kenneth Breese.
Water (1975) 5 mins. MUSIC: Max Eastley.
Water Wrackets (1975) 12 mins. NARRATION: Colin Cantlie. MUSIC: Max Eastley.
    CALLIGRAPHY: Kenneth Breese.
Goole by Numbers (1976) 40 mins.
Dear Phone (1977) 17 mins. NARRATION: Colin Cantlie. CALLIGRAPHY: Kenneth
    Breese.
1–100 (1978) 4 mins. MUSIC: Michael Nyman.
A Walk Through H (1978) 41 mins. British Film Institute (BFI). PHOTOGRAPHY: Bert
    Walker and John Rosenberg. MUSIC: Michael Nyman. NARRATION: Colin
    Cantlie. CAST: Jean Williams. CALLIGRAPHY: Kenneth Breese.
Vertical Features Remake (1978) 45 mins. Arts Council of Great Britain.
    PHOTOGRAPHY: Bert Walker. MUSIC: Michael Nyman (theme music: Brian Eno).
    NARRATION: Colin Cantlie.
The Falls (1980) 185 mins. BFI. SCRIPT: Peter Greenaway. HEAD OF PRODUCTION:
    Peter Sainsbury. PHOTOGRAPHY: Mike Coles, John Rosenberg. EDITOR: Peter
    Greenaway. MUSIC: Michael Nyman (additional music by Brian Eno, John
    Hyde, Keith Pendlebury). With the voices of Colin Cantlie, Hilarie Thompson,
    Sheila Canfield, Adam Leys, Serena Macbeth, Martin Burrows.
Act of God (1981) 28mins. Thames Television. SCRIPT: Peter Greenaway.
    PRODUCER: Udi Eicler. PHOTOGRAPHY: Peter George. EDITOR: Andy Watmore.
The Draughtsman's Contract (or *Death in the English Garden*) (1982) 108 mins. BFI
    in association with Film on Four. SCRIPT: Peter Greenaway. HEAD OF
    PRODUCTION: Peter Sainsbury. PRODUCER: David Payne. PHOTOGRAPHY: Curtis
    Clark. EDITOR: John Wilson. PRODUCTION DESIGNER: Bob Ringwood. MUSIC:
    Michael Nyman. CAST: Anthony Higgins, Janet Suzman, Anne Louise
    Lambert, Hugh Fraser, Neil Cunningham.
Four American Composers (1983) 55 mins each episode. Channel 4
    Television/Transatlantic Films. Four television documentaries on John Cage,
    Robert Ashley, Philip Glass, Meredith Monk (based on the Almeida Concerts
    of September 1982). PRODUCER: Revel Guest PHOTOGRAPHY: Curtis Clark.
    EDITOR: John Wilson.
Making a Splash (1984) 25 mins. Channel 4 Television/Media Software. SCRIPT:
    Peter Greenaway. PRODUCER: Pat Marshall. MUSIC: Michael Nyman.
A TV Dante–Canto 5 (1985) Channel 4 Television (the first part of a series of 33
    Cantos to be made in collaboration with Tom Phillips). SCRIPT: Peter
    Greenaway, Tom Phillips. PRODUCER: Sophie Balhetchet. PHOTOGRAPHY: Mike
    Coles, Simon Fone. EDITOR (FILM): John Wilson. EDITOR (VIDEO): Bill Saint.
    CAST: Susan Crowley, John Mattocks, Donald Copper.
Inside Rooms–26 Bathrooms (1985) 25 mins. Channel 4 Television/Artifax
    Productions. SCRIPT: Peter Greenaway. PRODUCER: Sophie Balhetchet.

PHOTOGRAPHY: Mike Coles. EDITOR: John Wilson. MUSIC: Michael Nyman.

A Zed and Two Noughts (1985) 115 mins. BFI Production/Allarts Enterprises/Artificial Eye Productions/Film Four International. SCRIPT: Peter Greenaway. PRODUCERS: Peter Sainsbury, Kees Kasander. PHOTOGRAPHY: Sacha Vierny. PRODUCTION DESIGNER: Ben Van Os, Jan Roelfs. EDITOR: John Wilson. MUSIC: Michael Nyman. CAST: Andrea Ferreol, Brian Deacon, Eric Deacon, Frances Barber, Joss Ackland.

The Belly of an Architect (1986) 118 mins. Callendar Company/Film Four International/British Screen Hemdale/Sacis. SCRIPT: Peter Greenaway. PRODUCERS: Colin Callender, Walter Donohue. PHOTOGRAPHY: Sacha Vierny. PRODUCTION DESIGNER: Luciana Vedovelli. EDITOR: John Wilson. MUSIC: Wim Mertens, Glenn Branca. CAST: Brian Dennehy, Chloe Webb, Lambert Wilson, Stefania Casini.

Drowning by Numbers (1988) 119 mins. Film Four International/Elsevier Vendex Film. SCRIPT: Peter Greenaway. PRODUCER: Kees Kasander, Denis Wigman. PHOTOGRAPHY: Sacha Vierny. PRODUCTION DESIGN: Ben Van Os, Jan Roelfs. EDITOR: John Wilson. MUSIC: Michael Nyman. CAST: Bernard Hill, Joan Plowright, Juliet Stevenson, Joely Richardson, Jason Edwards, Nathalie Morse.

Fear of Drowning (1988) 30 mins. Allarts Enterprises (for Channel 4 TV). SCRIPT: Peter Greenaway. PRODUCER: Paul Trybits. CO-DIRECTOR: Vanni Corbellini. CAST: Peter Greenaway (Presenter) and the actors and crew of *Drowning by Numbers*.

A TV Dante: The Inferno – Cantos 1-8 (1989) 90 mins. KGP Production in association with Channel 4 TV/Elsevier Vendex/VPRO. Made in collaboration with painter Tom Phillips. CAST: John Gielgud, Bob Peck, Joanne Whalley.

The Cook, the Thief, his Wife and her Lover (1989) 120 mins. Allarts Enterprises/Erato Films/Films Inc. SCRIPT: Peter Greenaway. PRODUCER: Kees Kasander. PHOTOGRAPHY: Sacha Vierny. PRODUCTION DESIGN: Ben Van Os, Jan Roelfs. EDITOR: John Wilson. MUSIC: Michael Nyman. CAST: Michael Gambon, Helen Mirren, Richard Bohringer, Alan Howard.

Death in the Seine (1990) 40 mins. Erato Films/Allarts TV Productions/Iros Image/La Sept. PHOTOGRAPHY: Jean Penzer. PRODUCTION DESIGN: Ben Van Os. MUSIC: Michael Nyman. CAST: Jim Van der Woude, Jean-Michel Dagory.

Prospero's Books (1991) 123 mins. Allarts, Cinea, Camera One, Penta Film co-production in association with Elsevier Vendex Film, Film Four International, VPRO, Canal Plus and NHK. SCRIPT: William Shakespeare and Peter Greenaway. PRODUCER: Kees Kasander. PHOTOGRAPHY: Sacha Vierny. PRODUCTION DESIGN: Ben Van Os and Jan Roelfs. EDITOR: Marina Bobdyl. MUSIC: Michael Nyman. CAST: John Gielgud, Michael Clark, Tom Bell, Kenneth Cranham, Isabelle Pasco, Mark Rylance.

M is for Man, Music, Mozart (1991) 29 mins. BBC, AVRO, Artifax. SCRIPT: Peter Greenaway. PRODUCER: Annette Moreau. PRODUCTION DESIGN: Jan Roelfs. MUSIC: Louis Andriessen. CAST: Ben Craft, Kate Gowar, Karen Potisk.

Darwin (1992) 52 mins. Telemax Les Editions Visuelles, Allarts Enterprises, Antenne 2, Channel 4, RAI 2, Telepool, Time Warner. SCRIPT: Peter Greenaway. PHOTOGRAPHY: Reinier van Brummelen.

The Baby of Mâcon (1993) 120 mins. Allarts Enterprises, UGC-La Sept, Cine Electra II, Channel 4, Filmstiftung Nordrhein Westfalen, Canal+. SCRIPT: Peter Greenaway. PRODUCER: Kees Kasander. PHOTOGRAPHY: Sacha Vierny. PRODUCTION DESIGN: Ben Van Os and Jan Roelfs. EDITOR: Chris Wyatt. CAST: Ralph Fiennes, Julia Ormond, Philip Stone, Jonathan Lacey, Don Henderson.

The Pillow Book (1995) 123 mins. Kasander & Wigman Productions, Woodline Films and Alpha Films in association with Channel Four Films, Studio Canal Plus and Delux Productions. SCRIPT: Peter Greenaway. PRODUCER: Kees Kasander. PHOTOGRAPHY: Sacha Vierny. EDITOR: Chris Wyatt. CAST: Vivian Wu, Ewan McGregor, Yoshi Oida, Ken Ogata, Judie Ongg, Yutaka Honda.

The Physical Self Boymans–van Beuningen, Rotterdam, Netherlands, November 1990
Hundert Objekte Zeigen die Welt – 100 Objects to Represent the World Akademie der Bildenden Künste, Vienna, Austria, October 1991
Le Bruit des Nuages – Flying out of this World Louvre, Paris, France, November 1992
Watching Water Palazzo Fortuny, Venice, Italy, 12 June–12 September 1993
Some Organizing Principles Glynn Vivian Art Gallery, Swansea, UK, October 1993
The Audience of Mâcon Foto Gallery, Cardiff, UK, October 1993
The Stairs: Geneva, the Location Geneva, Switzerland, April 1994
The Stairs II: Munich, Projection Munich, Germany, October 1995
'In the Dark' – Spellbound: Art & Film Hayward Gallery, London, February 1996 (other contributors Damien Hirst, Ridley Scott, Paula Rego, Terry Gilliam, Eduardo Paolozzi, Fiona Banner, Douglas Gordon, Boyd Webb and Steve McQueen)
Cosmology at the Piazza del Popolo: a history of the Piazza from Nero to Fellini using light and sound Rome, Italy, 23–30 June 1996

ONE-MAN SHOWS

1988 Broad Street Gallery, Canterbury, UK
1989 Arcade Carcassonne, Palais de Tokyo, Paris, France
1990 Nicole Klagsbrun Gallery, New York, USA; Australia Centre of Contemporary Art, Melbourne, Australia; Ivan Dougherty Gallery, College of Fine Arts, The University of New South Wales, Paddington, Australia; Cirque Divers, Liège, Belgium; Shingawa Space T33, Tokyo, Japan; Altium, Fukuoka, Japan; Dany Keller Galerie, Munich, Germany; Video Galleriet, Copenhagen, Denmark; Kunsthallen Brandts Klaedefabrik, Odense, Denmark; Galerie Xavier Hufkens, Brussels, Belgium
1991 "If Only Film Could Do The Same", Watermans Gallery, Brentford, UK; City Art Centre, Dublin, Ireland
1992 Gesellschaft für Aktuelle Kunst Bremen, Germany; Nicole Klagsbrun Gallery, New York, USA
1994 "If Only Film Could Do The Same", Arizona State University Art Museum, Temple, Arizona
1995 "The World of Peter Greenaway", Nicole Klagsbrun Gallery, New York, USA
1996 "The World of Peter Greenaway", Le Case d'Arte, Milan, Italy; "The Tyranny of the Frame", Galerie Fortlaan 17, Ghent, Belgium; "Peter Greenaway", Mylos Art Gallery, Thessaloniki, Greece

PUBLICATIONS

Plans and Conceits ". . . of Doubtful Authenticity" (London, 1982)
The Draughtsman's Contract Bilingual edition, English and French (Paris, 1984)
A Zed and Two Noughts (London, 1986)
The Belly of an Architect (London, 1987)
Drowning By Numbers (London, 1988)
Fear of Drowning: Règles du Jeu Bilingual edition, English and French (Paris, 1988)
The Cook, the Thief, his Wife and her Lover (Paris, 1990)
Papers: Papiers Bilingual edition, English and French (Paris, 1990)
A TV Dante with Tom Phillips (London, 1990)
The Physical Self Bilingual edition, English and Dutch (Rotterdam, 1990)
Prospero's Books: A Film of Shakespeare's "The Tempest" (London, 1991)
Prospero's Subjects (Tokyo, 1992)
Hundert Objekte Zeigen die Welt – 100 Objects to Represent the World

Bilingual edition, German and English (Vienna, 1992)
Le Bruit des Nuages Bilingual edition, French and English (Paris, 1992);
    republished as *Flying out of this World* (Chicago, 1994)
Rosa (Paris, 1993)
Watching Water (Milan, 1993)
The Falls (Paris, 1993)
Some Organizing Principles Bilingual edition, English and Welsh (Swansea, 1993)
The Audience of Mâcon Bilingual edition, English and Welsh (Cardiff, 1993)
The Baby of Mâcon (Paris, 1994)
The Stairs: Geneva, the Location/ The Stairs: Genève, le cadrage Bilingual edition,
    English and French (London, 1994)
The Pillow Book (Paris, 1996)
The Stairs: Munich (London, 1995)
Flying Over Water (Barcelona, 1997)

BOOKS AND ARTICLES ON PETER GREENAWAY

Christiana Barchfeld, *Filming by Numbers: Peter Greenaway. Ein Regisseur zwischen
    Experimentalkino und Erzählkino*, German edition, Tübingen, 1993.
Agnès Berthin-Scaillet, *Peter Greenaway: Fête et Défaite du Corps*, Paris, 1992.
Daniel Caux and others, eds., *Peter Greenaway*, Paris, 1987.
Domenico De Gaetano, *Il Cinema di Peter Greenaway*, Turin, 1995.
Laura Denham, *The Films of Peter Greenaway*, London, 1993.
Bridget Elliott and Anthony Purdy, 'Peter Greenaway and the Technologies of
    Representation: The Magician, the Surgeon, their Art and its Politics', in *Art &
    Film*, Art & Design Profile No. 49, July 1996, pp. 16–23.
Bridget Elliott and Anthony Purdy, *Peter Greenaway: Architecture and Allegory*,
    London, 1997.
Jonathan Hacker and David Price, *Take Ten: Contemporary British Film Directors*,
    Oxford, 1991 [includes analysis of Greenaway's work, an interview and a
    filmography].
Detlef Kremer, *Peter Greenaways Filme: Vom Überleben der Bilder und Bücher*,
    Stuttgart, 1995.
James Park, *Learning to Dream: The New British Cinema*, London, 1984.
Brigitte Peucker, *Incorporating Images: Film and the Rival Arts*, Princeton, 1995
    [chapter 3, 'Incorporation in Greenaway', pp. 156–65].
Leon Steinmetz, *The World of Peter Greenaway*, Boston, 1995.
John Walker, *Art and Artists on Screen*, Manchester, 1993 [features sections on *The
    Draughtsman's Contract* and *The Belly of an Architect*].
David Wills and Alec McHoul, 'Zoo-logics: questions of analysis in a film by
    Peter Greenaway', in *Textual Practice*, ed. Terence Hawkes, issue 1, vol. 5, 1991.
David Wills, *Prosthesis*, Stanford, 1995 [chapter 6 on *The Belly of an Architect*].
Alan Woods, *Being Naked, Playing Dead: The Art of Peter Greenaway*, Manchester,
    1996.

References

1 ARTIFICIAL LIGHT

1 Peter Greenaway, *A Zed and Two Noughts* (London, 1986), hereafter *Z&OO*, p. 110.
2 Part of the exhibition *The Director's Eye: Drawings and Photographs by European Film-makers*, at the Museum of Modern Art, Oxford.
3 Quoted in Stephen Heath, 'The Cinematic Apparatus: Technology as Historical and Cultural Form', in *The Cinematic Apparatus*, eds. Teresa de Lauretis and Stephen Heath (London, 1980).
4 *The Early Films of Peter Greenaway* (London, 1992), p. 3.
5 *Ibid.*
6 Vernon Gras, 'Dramatising the Failure to Jump the Culture/Nature Gap: The Films of Peter Greenaway', *New Literary History*, 26 (1995), pp. 123–43; 124.
7 Adam Barker, 'A Tale of Two Magicians', *Sight and Sound* (May 1991), p. 27.
8 *Take Ten: Contemporary British Film Directors*, eds. Jonathan Hacker and David Price (Oxford, 1991), p. 210.
9 *Take Ten: Contemporary Film Directors*, p. 213; Christopher Bray, 'Always Miserable', TLS (15 October 1993), p. 18.
10 Peter Matthews, 'Continental Movies', *The Modern Review* (August–September 1993), p. 32.
11 'Viktor Shklovsky, Art as Technique', in *Russian Formalist Criticism*, ed. and trans. Lee T. Lemon and Marion T. Reis (Lincoln, Nebraska, 1965), p. 12.
12 *The Early Films of Peter Greenaway*, p. 2.
13 Peter Greenaway, *Drowning by Numbers* (London, 1988), p. 71.
14 Germaine Dulac, 'The Essence of the Cinema: The Visual Idea' (1925), in *The Avant-Garde Film: A Reader of Theory and Criticism*, ed. P. Adams Sitney (New York, 1978), p. 39.
15 Peter Greenaway, 'My Favourite Film', in *100 Years of Cinema*, supplement to *Sight and Sound* (February 1996).
16 Peter Greenaway, *The Cook, the Thief, his Wife and her Lover* (Paris, 1989), p. 51.
17 Peter Greenaway, *The Stairs 2: Munich. Projection* (London, 1996), p. 39.
18 *Ibid.*
19 Christian Metz, 'On the Impression of Reality in the Cinema', in *Film Language: A Semiotics of the Cinema*, translated by Michael Taylor (New York, 1974), pp. 3–15.
20 Peter Greenaway: *The Stairs 2*, p. 44.
21 Greenaway told an interviewer: 'It is well known that I love much Resnais and especially *Last Year at Marienbad*, a cornerstone film, which influenced much of my work. But there are other important films to me, such as Godard's *Les Carabiniers*.'
22 Peter Greenaway, *The Stairs* (London, 1994), p. 34.
23 Peter Greenaway, *The Cook, The Thief . . .*, p. 87.
24 Peter Greenaway, *The Audience of Mâcon* (Cardiff, 1993), n.p.
25 Peter Greenaway, *The Stairs*, p. 9.
26 Peter Greenaway, interview in *American Film*, vol. xvi, no. 10 (November 1991), p. 37.

27 Peter Greenaway, *The Stairs 2*, p. 43.

28 Alan Woods, *Being Naked, Playing Dead: The Art of Peter Greenaway* (Manchester, 1996), p. 78.

29 Paul Wells, 'Compare and Contrast: Derek Jarman, Peter Greenaway and Film Art', in *Art & Design Profile 49: Art & Film* (London, 1996), p. 27.

30 Gilles Deleuze, *Cinema I: The Movement-Image*, translated by Hugh Tomlinson and Barbara Habberjam (Minneapolis, 1986), pp. 5 and 23.

31 Hollis Frampton, 'The Withering Away of the State of the Art', *Circles of Confusion* (New York, 1983), p. 164.

32 Jacques Aumont, *L'Oeil interminable* (Paris, 1989). For other recent French approaches to the same topic, see *Cinéma et Peinture: Approches*, ed. Raymond Bellour (Paris, 1990); and Raymond Bellour, 'The Film Stilled', *Camera Obscura*, 24 (1990).

33 Sergei Eisenstein mentions Van Eyck, Picasso and particularly El Greco as forefathers of filmic montage; and elsewhere in his film criticism, Kandinsky, Van Gogh and Gauguin are lauded for their use of colour. Eisenstein, 'Synchronization of the Senses', p. 100, and 'Colour and Meaning', pp. 113–18, in *Film Form: Essays in Film Theory*, ed. Jay Leyda (New York, 1949).

34 Peter Greenaway, *Papers* (Paris, 1990), p. 36.

35 *Ibid.*

36 André Bazin, 'Painting and Cinema', in *What is Cinema?* translated by H. Grey (Berkeley and Los Angeles, 1967).

37 Jean-Louis Baudry, 'The Ideological Effects of the Basic Cinematic Apparatus', *Film Quarterly*, 28, no. 2 (1974–75), pp. 39–47; Jean-Louis Baudry, 'The Apparatus', *Camera Obscura*, 1 (1976), pp. 104–26; Jean-Louis Comolli, 'Technique and Ideology: Camera, Perspective, Depth of Field', *Film Reader*, 2 (1977), pp. 128–40. See also Claude Bailble, 'Programmation du regard', *Cahiers du cinéma*, 281 (1977), pp. 5–19.

38 Peter Greenaway, 'Just Place, Preferably Architectural Place', in *Projections 4 1/2* (London, 1995).

39 André Bazin, *What is Cinema?*, pp. 12, 14. Since Bazin, similar formulations have emerged. Stanley Cavell has observed in *The World Viewed* (New York, 1971): 'So far as photography satisfied a wish, it satisfied a wish not confined to painters, but the human wish, intensifying since the Reformation, to escape subjectivity and metaphysical isolation . . . Photography overcame subjectivity in a way undreamed of by painting, one which does not so much defeat the act of painting as escape it altogether: by automatism, by removing the human agent from the act of reproduction'; and Rudolf Arnheim has spoken of 'the fundamental peculiarity of the photographic medium: the physical objects themselves print their image by means of the optical and chemical action of light' and suggested that, in fact, as a result of this peculiarity, when we look at photographs, 'we are on vacation from artifice'. See 'On the Nature of Photography', *Critical Inquiry*, 1 [1974], pp. 149–61.

40 'The Myth of Total Cinema' by Bazin, in *What is Cinema?*, p. 21.

41 Stephen Heath, *Questions of Cinema* (Basingstoke, 1981).

42 Jean-Louis Comolli, 'Machines of the Visible', in *The Cinematic Apparatus*, eds Teresa de Lauretis and Stephen Heath (London, 1980), p. 141.

43 John Berger, *Ways of Seeing* (London, 1972), p. 16.

44 Paul Wells, 'Compare and Contrast', p. 27.

45 This and the following four quotes from Peter Greenaway, *Fear of Drowning* (Paris, 1988), pp. 35–41.

46 Holman Hunt to an unidentified correspondent, draft MS fragment, (Manchester, John Rylands Library). For full discussion of this painting, see *The Pre-Raphaelites* (London, 1984), pp. 94–6.

47 F.G. Stephens, *William Holman Hunt, a memoir of the artist's life* (London,

1860), pp. 19–20: 'The painter first put into practice in an historical picture, based on his own observations, the scientific elucidation of that peculiar effect which having been hinted at by Leonardo . . . was partly explained by Newton and fully developed by Davy and Brewster.' Stephens evidently means Sir Humphrey Davy and Sir Daivd Brewster.

48 In 'Just place, preferably Architectural Place', Greenaway identified 'the damp ditch in Hunt's *Hireling Shepherd*' as one of the places he would quote in 'a hypothetical *genius loci* film'.

49 For specific discussion, see Lindsay Errington, *Social and Religious Themes in English Art, 1840–1860* (University of London, PhD thesis, 1973), p. 302.

50 Leon Steinmetz, *The World of Peter Greenaway* (Boston, 1995).

51 Peter Greenaway, *Papers*, p. 83.

2 ART AND LANGUAGE

1 Quoted in Alan Woods, *Being Naked, Playing Dead* (Manchester, 1996), p. 106.

2 Peter Wollen, 'The Last New Wave: Modernism in the British Films of the Thatcher Era', in *British Cinema and Thatcherism: Fires Were Started*, ed. Lester Friedman (London, 1993), p. 44.

3 Alan Woods, *Being Naked, Playing Dead*, p. 105.

4 *Ibid.*, p. 241.

5 Marco Livingstone, 'Pluralism since 1960', in David Britt, *Modern Art: Impressionism to Post-Modernism* (London, 1989), p. 391.

6 Alan Woods, *Being Naked, Playing Dead*, p. 106.

7 R. B. Kitaj, 'On Associating Texts with Paintings', *Cambridge Opinion*, 37 (January 1964), pp. 52–3.

8 Marco Livingstone, *Kitaj* (London, 1992), p. 15. Livingstone discusses several paintings directly influenced by articles in the *Journal. Pariah* (1960), *Welcome Every Dread Delight* (1962) and *Isaac Babel Riding With Budyonny* (1962) all had as source an essay by Rudolf Wittkower entitled 'Marvels of the East: A Study in the History of Monsters', *Journal of the Warburg and Courtauld Institutes*, v (1942), pp. 159–97; and *Yamhill* and *Notes Towards the Definition of Nobody*, both completed in 1961 included the motif of a man with a padlocked mouth, discussed in Gerta Calmann, 'The Picture of Nobody: An Iconographical Study', *Journal of the Warburg and Courtauld Institutes*, xxii (1960), pp. 60–104.

9 See Frances A. Yates, 'The Art of Ramon Lull: An approach to it through Lull's Theory of the Elements', *Journal of the Warburg and Courtauld Institutes*, xxii (1959), pp.115–73, and Yates, 'Ramon Lull and John Scotus Erigena', *Journal of the Warburg and Courtauld Institutes*, xxiii (1960, January–June), pp. 1–44. These are listed by Kitaj in the 1963 catalogue, p. 5, cat. 4. The reference quoted is from p. 2 of the 1960 article.

10 Peter Greenaway, *Some Organizing Principles* (Swansea, 1993), n.p., Section 18.

11 R. B. Kitaj in *Recent British Painting: The Peter Stuyvesant Collection*, exhibition catalogue (November/December 1967), p. 21.

12 *Take Ten: Contemporary Film Directors*, eds. Jonathan Hacker and David Price (Oxford, 1991), p. 210.

13 See Pierre Bourdieu, translated by Richard Nice as 'The Aristocracy of Culture', in *Media, Culture, Society* (Oxford, 1980), pp. 225–54.

14 Terry Eagleton, 'Capitalism, Modernism, and Post-Modernism', *New Left Review*, 152 (July/August 1985), pp. 60–73.

15 Robert Brown, review of *Intervals*, *Monthly Film Bulletin* (BFI) (April 1982), p. 75.

16 On Frampton, see 'Hollis Frampton', special issue of *October*, no. 32 (Spring 1985), and Scott MacDonald, *Avant-Garde Film: Motion Studies*

(Cambridge, 1993).

17 I am indebted to Robert Brown's review of *Dear Phone*, *Monthly Film Bulletin* (BFI) (April 1982), p. 74.

18 John Grierson, 'The Course of Realism', in *Grierson on Documentary* (London, 1946), p. 70.

19 Daniel Caux and others, *Peter Greenaway* (Paris, 1987), p. 99.

20 Peter Greenaway, *Some Organizing Principles* (Swansea, 1993), n.p., Section 19.

21 Peter Greenaway, *Le Bruit des Nuages* (Paris, 1992).

22 Another major example of such a mediating device is, of course, the view-finder, an idea which Greenaway develops with greater confidence in *The Draughtsman's Contract*.

3 FIELDS OF VISION

1 On Zick, see B. Bushart, *Deutsche Malerei des Rokokos* (Königstein im Taunus, 1976); O. Metzger, *Januarius Zick* (Munich, 1981); J. Strasser, *Januarius Zick* (Munich, 1987).

2 Greenaway has admitted the connection: 'It's a small conceit, but the ratio of the film frame of *The Draughtsman's Contract*, being 1 to 1.66, is the preferred ratio of those books or drawings by Claude Lorraine of artificially realized landscapes full of trees and sheep. Perhaps *The Draughtsman's Contract* itself is like flicking through a book of drawings of landscapes – a copy-book for reference, a training manual made for profit, a self-reflexive notion, because much of the film is about how to draw a landscape with conviction. And money. Those Claude drawings, I am sure, were the result of drawing what you know and not what you see – the dilemma that tripped the draughtsman.' Alan Woods, *Being Naked, Playing Dead*, p. 228.

3 On the history of framing and viewing devices, see Aaron Scharf, *Art and Photography* (Harmondsworth, 1974), and John J. Hammond, *The Camera Obscura: A Chronicle* (Bristol, 1981); A. Hyatt Mayor, 'The Photographic Eye', *Metropolitan Museum of Art Bulletin*, 5, no. 1 (Summer 1946), pp. 15–26; and Joel Snyder, 'Picturing Vision', *Critical Inquiry*, 6 (1980), pp. 499–526.

4 Jonathan Crary, *Techniques of the Observer: On Vision and Modernity in the Nineteenth Century* (Cambridge, MA, 1992), p. 27.

5 Sir Isaac Newton, *Opticks, or a Treatise of the Reflection, Refractions, Inflections and Colours of Light* (1730; fourth edn. New York, reprinted 1952), p. 26.

6 Stephen Heath, 'Narrative Space', *Questions of Cinema* (London, 1981), pp. 19–75, especially p. 35.

7 Greenaway has described a similar light effect caught on film later. 'A favourite moment . . . happens in a wide landscape shot, when the draughtsman returning to the house in a late scene says something like, "Now, madam, in this day of changing weather . . .". At that moment a large black cloud covered the sun. It would have been impossible either to accurately forecast that sudden change in weather or, considering the wide open landscape, to have managed to make it happen by artificial light. Lighting by God.' Alan Woods, *Being Naked, Playing Dead*, p. 237.

8 Greenaway later claimed that his intentions with regard to de La Tour were really very vague: 'Where are the images that relate to de La Tour? There are some figure groupings which are perhaps blasphemously reinterpreted from a de La Tour *Nativity*. The Virgin, the Child, St Anne and Joseph seen by candlelight are now two pimps and a whore seen by candlelight. But that claustrophobic, quiet, mysterious, introspective atmosphere that you experience with de La Tour – so much less flamboyant than the other *ténébristes* – I don't see that atmosphere being so

strong in the film at all now, so I was obviously imagining it. No matter, no matter. De La Tour's light was a considerable inspiration to me when we made the film.' See Alan Woods, *Being Naked, Playing Dead*, p. 232.

9 I am indebted to the account of this painting in John Hayes, *Thomas Gainsborough* (London, 1980), p. 78.

10 William Hogarth, 'Autobiographical Notes', in *The Analysis of Beauty*, ed. Joseph Burke (Oxford, 1955), p. 219.

11 My account of this painting is indebted to Roland Paulson, *Hogarth: Art and Politics*, 3 volumes (Cambridge, 1993), iii, p. 220.

12 George Sandys, *Ovid's Metamorphoses*, English ed. (1632; repr. 1976), p. 195.

13 Quoted by Peter Wollen, 'The Last New Wave', in *Fires Were Started*, ed. Lester Friedman (London, 1993), p. 45.

4 MEDICAL EXPERIMENTS AND ART THEORY

1 Peter Greenaway, *A Zed and Two Noughts* (London, 1986), p. 17.

2 Sacha Vierny also photographed, among other films, *Hiroshima Mon Amour and Belle du Jour*. Of *Z&OO*, Greenaway recalled: 'He made a rainbow in that film that competed with the sun. And all with great economy of means and very fast. I'm sure if you gave him a lit candle and two sheets of newspaper he would come up with a solution to any film-lighting problem. He insists on two sheets – one for him to use and the other for you to read while you wait.' Interview in *Take Ten: Contemporary British Film Directors*, eds Jonathan Hacker and David Price (Oxford, 1991), p. 220.

3 'The essence of cinema is movement.' Georg Lukacs, 'Gedanken zu einer Ästhetik des Kinos', in *Kino-Debatte: Texte zum Verhältnis von Literatur und Film 1909–1929*, ed. Anton Kaes (Tübingen, 1978), p. 113.

4 Peter Greenaway, *The Falls* (Paris, 1993), p. 44.

5 Interview, *Take Ten*, p. 218.

6 *Z&OO*, p. 15.

7 David I. Hull, *Darwin and his Critics* (Cambridge, MA, 1973), p. 36.

8 Charles Darwin, *The Variation of Plants and Animals under Domestication*, 2 volumes (London, 1868), ii, pp. 26, 53.

9 *Papers*, p. 75. See also Greenaway's article on the enclosure of wild animals in zoos, *Time Out* (17–30 December 1982).

10 *Z&OO*, p. 15.

11 Charles Darwin, *The Variation of Plants and Animals*, ii, p. 23.

12 *The Autobiography of Charles Darwin, 1809–1882*, edited with appendix and notes by his granddaughter, Nora Barlow (London, 1958), p. 53. On the delay, see 'Darwin's Delay', in Stephen Jay Gould, *Ever Since Darwin* (New York, 1977), chapter 1.

13 *The Autobiography of Charles Darwin*, p. 57.

14 Peter Greenaway, *Darwin* (1992), Tableau 17.

15 Northrop Frye, 'Myth, Fiction, and Displacement', in *Fables of Identity* (New York, 1963), p. 19.

16 Peter Greenaway, 'Flight as Unnatural Inheritance', in *Le Bruit des Nuages* (Paris, 1992), pp. 44–5.

17 Stephen Heath, 'Body, Voice', in *Questions of Cinema* (London, 1981) p. 183.

18 *Z&OO*, p. 95.

19 cf. *OED*: 'In biological and botanical terms the prefix sometimes denotes the power of spontaneous movement (formerly supposed to be a distinctive characteristic of animals).'

20 For a compact account of Muybridge's legacy and the controversy surrounding his work, see 'The Representation of Movement in Photography and Art', in Aaron Scharf, *Art and Photography* (Harmondsworth, 1969).

21 For background accounts of this early cinematic technology, see C.W.

Ceram, *Archaeology of the Cinema* (New York, 1965); Michael Chanan, *The Dream that Kicks: The Prehistory and Early Years of Cinema in Britain* (London, 1980), especially pp. 54–65; Jean-Louis Comolli, 'Technique et idéologie', *Cahiers du cinema*, no. 229 (May–June 1971), pp. 4–21; Steve Neale, *Cinema and Technology: Image, Sound, Colour* (Basingstoke, 1985). For more theoretical approaches to the illusion of movement, see Joseph and Barbara Anderson, 'Motion Perception in Motion Pictures', and Bill Nichols and Susan J. Lederman, 'Flicker and Motion in Film', both in *The Cinematic Apparatus*, eds Teresa de Lauretis and Stephen Heath (London, 1980), pp. 76–95 and 96–105.

22 *The Philadelphia Times* (2 August 1885).

23 Alan Woods, *Being Naked, Playing Dead* (Manchester, 1996), p. 251.

24 Quoted in Alan Woods, *Being Naked, Playing Dead*, p. 57.

25 My account is indebted to Gordon Hendricks, *Eadweard Muybridge: The Father of the Motion Picture* (New York, 1975), p. 166; and Robert Bartlett Haas, *Muybridge: Man in Motion* (Berkeley, 1976).

26 Alan Woods, *Being Naked, Playing Dead*, p. 250.

27 Interview with Francis Bacon, in *Francis Bacon – 1971 Grand Palais*, a film by Gavin Millar for BBC TV (London, 1971). On Bacon's debt to Muybridge, see Van Deren Coke, *The Painter and the Photograph: From Delacroix to Warhol* (Albuquerque, 1972), p. 159, who suggests Muybridge sources for the following Bacon paintings: *Rhinoceros* (1952); *Study of a Nude* (1952–3); *Study for a Nude* (1951) and *Two Figures*. Hugh M. Davies, *Francis Bacon: The Early and Middle Years* (New York, 1978) has a fine discussion of Bacon's studies of dogs executed at the same period, and in what follows I am indebted to his arguments.

28 Nicolas and Elena Calas, *The Peggy Guggenheim Collection of Modern Art* (New York, n.d.), p. 227.

29 'Notes by Bacon', in *The New Decade*, exhibition catalogue (New York, Museum of Modern Art, 1955), collected in John Russell, *Francis Bacon* (London, 1964).

30 'Avec lui on retrouve ce talent particulier de Vermeer, qui parvient à fixer l'extrême pointe d'un moment: une fraction de fraction de seconde!' *Peter Greenaway*, ed. Daniel Caux and others (Paris, 1987), p. 108.

31 *Z&OO*, p. 14.

32 For background to Van Meegeren's forgeries, see Lord Kilbracken, *Van Meegeren* (London, 1966).

33 This paragraph is indebted to Bridgett Elliott and Anthony Purdy, 'Peter Greenaway and the Technologies of Representation: The Magician, the Surgeon, their Art and its Politics', in *Art & Film* (London, 1996), pp. 16–24.

34 Walter Benjamin, 'The Work of Art in the Age of Mechanical Reproduction', reproduced in *Film Theory and Criticism*, eds. Gerald Mast and Marshall Cohen, 2nd edn (New York, 1979), pp. 862–63.

35 In the discussion that follows, I am much indebted to the commentaries in Arthur K. Wheelock, *Vermeer and the Art of Painting* (New Haven, 1995).

36 For a fine account of this map see James A. Welu, 'Vermeer: His Cartographic Sources', *Art Bulletin*, 57 (1975), pp. 534–45.

37 On Vermeer's perspective, see Arthur K. Wheelock, *Vermeer*, p. 139.

38 The literature on Vermeer and the camera obscura is extensive. See in particular: Charles Seymour, 'Dark Chamber and Light-filled Room: Vermeer and the Camera Obscura', *Art Bulletin*, 46 (1964), pp. 323–31; Heinrich Schwarz, 'Vermeer and the Camera Obscura', *Pantheon*, 24 (1966), pp. 170–80; Arthur K. Wheelock Jr, *Perspective, Optics and Delft Artists Around 1650* (New York, 1977), pp. 283–301; and Arthur K. Wheelock Jr, 'Constantijn Huygens and Early Attitudes towards the Camera Obscura', *History of Photography*, 1 (1977), pp. 93–103.

1 *The Falls* (Paris, 1993), p. 46. Piero's masterpiece is also alluded to in Biography 54, where above Throper 'Castor' Fallcaster's bed there hangs a large white egg, on a long thread. Greenaway discusses the painting in the catalogue to his 1997 Barcelona Exhibition, *Flying over Water*: 'The suspended egg in this Piero della Francesca *sacra conversazione* is a mystery. Is it a symbol of fertility, some prophetic image of a spermatozoa about to fertilize the cockleshell ovum behind it? Why is the egg upside-down, hanging from its broader end? Is it a masonic emblem? Is it sheer virtuosity, plumb-lining a weight into a shadowy void to demonstrate skill? Is it a commentary on complex mathematical symmetry? Is it a Leda reference identifying God with Zeus? Is it a reference to immaculate conception and virginal birth – the fertilized egg transplanted into the Virgin's womb, thereby bypassing carnal fertilization?', *Flying over Water* (London, 1997), p. 59.

2 Peter Greenaway, *Le Bruit des Nuages*, (Paris, 1992), p. 26.

3 My translation of the following: 'Le Christ meurtri est Kracklite, le héros, la victime, la victime sacrificielle du film. Trois personnages énigmatiques discutent à l'arrière-plan du cadre – dans le film ce sont trois représentants de la mafia intellectuelle italienne. Les trois personnages achèvent leurs raileries par une ironique sentence de mort à l'encontre de Kracklite: pour la première fois, ils lui donnent à penser qu'il est, s'identifiant à Boullée, une victime du cancer de l'estomac . . . Plus tard, ivre et pris de panique, il s'écrit: "Jésus-Christ serait mort d'un cancer de l'estomac si vous Romains ne l'aviez pas crucifié d'abord." Nous ne nous sommes pas contentés de faire référence au contexte du tableau; avec le mépris et la sentence de mort c'est tout ensemble la forme et le contenu que nous avons utilisés.' *Peter Greenaway*, ed. Daniel Caux and others (Paris, 1987), p. 119.

4 John White, *The Birth and Rebirth of Pictorial Space*, 3rd edn (London, 1987). For an important account of the design of the panel, see R. Wittkower and B. A. R. Carter, 'The Perspective of Piero della Francesca's "Flagellation"', *Journal of the Warburg and Courtauld Institutes*, xvi (1953), pp. 292–302.

5 Philip Guston, 'Piero della Francesca: The Impossibility of Painting', *Art News*, 64 (1965), p. 39.

6 The most widely accepted interpretation of *The Flagellation* at present would see the episode as representing in symbolic form the turbulent state of the church following the fall of Constantinople, while the group of figures to the right depicts participants in one of the Councils (perhaps that of Mantua in 1459) charged with the task in the years immediately following of organizing a crusade aimed at halting the Turkish advance. See A. Paolucci, *Piero della Francesca* (Florence, 1989), and Maurizio Calvesi, 'La Flagellazione nel quadro storico del convegno di Mantova e dei progetti di Mattia Corvino', in *Piero della Francesca and his Legacy*, ed. Marilyn Aronberg Lavin (Hanover, NH, 1995), pp. 115–27. However, another critic has suggested that the two older men in the trio in the foreground have both lost their sons, one to the plague, the other to tuberculosis; and that 'these events brought the two fathers together and caused the commission of Piero's painting'. Hence, the young man between them 'personifies the "beloved son"', and the viewer would have been able to see a link between the suffering Son of Man inside the architectural structure and the death of the son in the outside 'real' world. Marilyn Aronberg Lavin, *Piero della Francesca: The Flagellation* (New York, 1972), p. 71.

7 Alan Woods, *Being Naked, Playing Dead*, p. 258.

8 Peter Greenaway, *The Belly of an Architect* (London, 1987), p. 99.

9 William Vaughan, *Romantic Art* (London, 1978), p. 68.

10 Peter Greenaway, *The Stairs: Geneva* (London, 1994), p. 32.

11 Peter Greenaway, *The Belly of an Architect*, p. vii.
12 Etienne-Louis Boullée, *Architecture: An Essay on Art*, translated by Sheila de Valle, reprinted in Helen Roseanu, *Boullée and Visionary Architecture* (New York, 1976), p. 82.
13 A. M. Vogt, *Boullees Newton-Denkmal, Sakralbau und Kugelidee* (Basel, 1969).
14 Richard Sennett, *Flesh and Stone: The Body and the City in Western Civilization* (London, 1994), p. 87.
15 Quoted in Helen Roseanu, *Boullée and Visionary Architecture*, p. 107.
16 *Ibid.*
17 Peter Greenaway, *Le Bruit des Nuages*, p. 9.
18 Peter Greenaway, *Le Bruit des Nuages*, p. 176.
19 Peter Greenaway, *The Belly of an Architect*, p. 135.
20 Peter Greenaway, *The Stairs: Geneva*, p. 48.
21 Peter Greenaway, *The Belly of an Architect*, p. 33.
22 For a fine and detailed account of the *mise-en-scène* of this sequence, see Alan Woods, *Being Naked, Playing Dead*, pp. 153–63.
23 For a highly idiosyncratic but convincing reading of the film, see David Wills, *Prosthesis* (Stanford, 1995), chapter 5, 'Rome, 1985'.
24 This paragraph is much indebted to Peter Greenaway's own account in *Fear of Drowning* (Paris, 1988), pp. 62ff.
25 Peter Greenaway, *Drowning by Numbers* (London, 1988), p. 61.
26 Peter Greenaway, *Fear of Drowning by Numbers*, p. 65.
27 Peter Greenaway, *Drowning by Numbers*, p. 34.
28 Peter Greenaway, *Fear of Drowning by Numbers*, p. 109.
29 *Ibid.*, p. 11.
30 For excellent accounts of the illusionism at the heart of this painting, see John Searle, '*Las Meninas* and the Paradoxes of Pictorial Representation', *Critical Inquiry*, 6 (1980), pp. 477–88; and the article in response, Joel Snyder and Ted Cohen, 'Reflections on *Las Meninas*: Paradox Lost', *Critical Inquiry*, 7 (1980), pp. 429–47.
31 Peter Greenaway, *Fear of Drowning by Numbers*, p. 31.
32 Peter Greenaway, *Drowning by Numbers*, p. 4.
33 Peter Greenaway, *Fear of Drowning by Numbers*, p. 63.
34 Peter Greenaway, *Drowning by Numbers*, p. 118.
35 Peter Greenaway, *Fear of Drowning by Numbers*, p. 25.
36 *Ibid.*, p. 43.
37 Wolfgang Stechow, *Bruegel* (London, 1990), p. 60.
38 In much of the discussion that follows I am indebted to Sandra Hindman, 'Peter Bruegel's Children's Games, Folly, and Chance', *Art Bulletin*, 63 (1981), pp. 447–75.
39 Peter Greenaway, *Drowning by Numbers*, p. 111.
40 Vernon Gras, 'Dramatising the Failure to Jump the Culture/Nature Gap: The Films of Peter Greenaway, *New Literary History*, 36 (1995), pp. 123–43.
41 Peter Greenaway, *Fear of Drowning by Numbers*, p. 9.
42 Sigmund Freud, 'The Claims of Psychoanalysis to Scientific Interest' (1913); standard edition xiii, p. 188.
43 Peter Greenaway, *Fear of Drowning by Numbers*, p. 117.
44 Peter Greenaway, *Drowning by Numbers*, p. 104.
45 Leon Steinmetz, *The World of Peter Greenaway* (Boston, 1995), p. 67.

6 THE BOOK DEPOSITORY

1 Peter Greenaway, *The Cook, the Thief, his Wife and her Lover* (Paris, 1990), p. 68.
2 *Ibid.*, p. 70.
3 Roland Barthes, *The Pleasure of the Text*, translated by Richard Miller (New York, 1975), p. 51.

4 Peter Greenaway, *Prospero's Books* (London, 1991). An alternative version of the story of Prospero, including dismemberment and mutilation of a woman who is 'opened . . . like a book', is recounted in 'Ex Libris Prospero', a brief text for *Parkett*, no. 26.

5 Derek Jarman, who filmed *The Tempest* in 1977, imagines that the volumes Prospero brought to his island were 'The Pimander and Orphic Hymns, Plotinus on the soul - *The Book of Life* (Ficino), *Conclusiones* (Pico della Mirandola), Paracelsus, Roger Bacon, *The Secret of Secrets*, a bestseller in the Middle Ages, Agrippa's *Occult Philosophy* and Dee's *Hieroglyph Monad, Shadow of Idea* (1592) by Bruno who was burnt at the stake for heresy in 1600 in the Campo de' Fiori, Rome'. *Chroma: A Book of Colour – June '93* (London, 1994), p. 75.

6 Roland Barthes, *The Pleasure of the Text.*

7 Peter Greenaway, *The Pillow Book* (Paris, 1996), p. 102.

8 *Ibid.*, p. 86.

9 *Ibid.*, p. 67.

10 On the life of St Jerome, see J. N. D. Kelly, *Jerome: His Life, Writings and Controversies* (London, 1975); and on his later reputation see Eugene F. Rice, *Saint Jerome in the Renaissance* (Baltimore, 1985).

11 Peter Greenaway, *The Physical Self* (Rotterdam, 1990), n.p.

12 *Ibid.*

13 Ezra Pound, *Canto* LXXX: 'all that Sandro knew, and Jacopo / and that Velazquez never suspected / lost in the brown meat of Rembrandt / and the raw meat of Rubens and Jordaens'.

14 Joel E. Siegel, 'Greenaway by Numbers', *City Paper* (6 April 1990), p. 22. See also Michael Walsh, 'Allegories of Thatcherism: The Films of Peter Greenaway', in *British Cinema and Thatcherism*, ed. Lester Friedman (London, 1993), pp. 255–78.

15 Jakob Rosenberg, Seymour Slive and E. H. ter Kuile, *Dutch Art and Architecture: 1600 to 1800* (Harmondsworth, 1977), p. 50.

16 For accounts of the development of *stil-leven* and a taxonomy of its various sub-forms, see Ingvar Bergström, *Dutch Still Life Painting in the Seventeenth Century*, translated by C. Hedström and G. Taylor (London, 1956), still the standard work in this area.

17 Peter Greenaway, *Fear of Drowning* (Paris, 1988), p. 45.

18 This fascination with entomology is seen also in *A Zed & Two Noughts*, where the dead animals become fly-blown before the cameras of the Deuce twins; in *Drowning by Numbers*, where flies and other insects crawl on, stick to and flap their wings against inanimate objects arranged in still-life forms; and in *Prospero's Books*, where flies crawl across *The Book of Motion*.

19 Norman Bryson considers the relation between superabundance and the Dutch still-life in 'Abundance', the third of his essays on the form in *Looking at the Overlooked* (London, 1990).

20 Quoted in Rosenberg and others, *Dutch Art and Architecture*, p. 338.

21 The best recent account of the painter and his many imitators is Sam Segal, *Jan Davidsz. de Heem und sein Kreis* (Braunschweig, 1991).

22 In my account of these symbolic associations I am indebted to Sam Segal's *A Prosperous Past: The Sumptuous Still-Life in the Netherlands 1600–1700*, ed. William B. Jordan (The Hague, 1988).

23 Erika Langmuir, *A Companion Guide to the National Gallery* (London, 1994), p. 193.

24 I owe this point to William F. Van Wert's review of the film in *Film Quarterly* (1990).

25 Peter Greenaway, *Le Bruit des Nuages* (Paris, 1992), p. 170.

26 Alan Woods, *Being Naked, Playing Dead*, p. 291.

27 Sigmund Freud, *Three Essays on the Theory of Sexuality* (1905), in *The Complete Psychological Works*, standard edition, translated by James

Strachey (London, 1953–74), vol. vii, p. 196.

28 For a Foucaultian reading of the life of books, see Peter Schwenger, 'Prospero's Books and the Visionary Page,' *Textual Practice*, 8 (1994).

29 Peter Greenaway, *Prospero's Books*, p. 57.

30 For accounts of the book as a Surrealist object, see Susi R. Bloch, 'The Book Stripped Bare', in *Artists' Books: A Critical Anthology and Source Book*, ed. Joan Lyons (Rochester, NY, 1987), pp. 133–49; and R. R. Hubert, *Surrealism and the Book* (Berkeley, 1988).

31 Michel Foucault, 'Fantasia of the Library', in *Language, Counter-Memory, Practice: Selected Essays and Interviews*, ed. Donald F. Bouchard (Ithaca, 1977), p. 90.

32 Peter Greenaway, *Prospero's Books*, pp. 20, 39.

33 See J. Ackerman, *The Architecture of Michelangelo*, 2 volumes (London, 1961); for an account critical of the conception of the stairs, see R. Wittkower, *Idea and Image* (London, 1978), pp. 11–71, where it is claimed that the vestibule's forms manifest an irreconcilable conflict.

34 Peter Greenaway, *The Stairs: Geneva* (London, 1994), p. 57.

35 A 'wooden O', *Henry V*, Prologue, 1.13. The episode is described in Samuel Schoenbaum, *William Shakespeare: A Compact Documentary Life* (London, 1978), pp. 207–8.

36 Peter Greenaway, *The Cook, the Thief . . .* (Paris, 1989), p. 7.

37 Patricia Simons, '(Check)Mating the Grand Masters: The Gendered, Sexualized Politics of Chess in Renaissance Italy,' *Oxford Art Journal*, 16 (1993).

38 Peter Greenaway, *Flying over Water* (London, 1997), p. 7.

39 Simon Garfield, 'Drowning Books by Numbers', *The Independent on Sunday Review* (28 April 1991).

40 'PROSPERO starts suddenly, and speaks; after which, to a strange and hollow, and confused noise [the figures] heavily vanish (IV, I, 138); the stage direction is echoed in the Boatswain's speech: 'with strange and several noises / Of roaring, shrieking, howling, jingling chain, / And more diversity of sounds, all horrible, / We were awak'd; straightway, at liberty (V, i, 232–5)'. For an account of the non-Shakespearean provenance of the stage directions, see John Jowett, 'New Created Creatures: Ralph Crane and the Stage Directions in *The Tempest*', *Shakespeare Survey*, 36 (1983), pp. 107–20.

7 MAKING AN EXHIBITION

1 Julia Owen, 'Romans in the Gloaming', *The Times* (4 July 1996).

2 For background to the artist, see Guillermo de Osma, *Mariano Fortuny: His Life and Work* (London, 1980). In the account of Fortuny that follows, I am much indebted to de Osma's book.

3 Corrado Tumiati, 'Il mio vicino mago', *Corriera della Sera* (6 September 1932), translated by G. de Osma.

4 The system was originally patented as 'Système d'éclairage scénique par lumière indirecte'; a few weeks later, on 26 April 1901, it was renamed 'Système de coloration, décoration et gradation scénique par lumière indirecte'.

5 Mariano Fortuny, *Eclairage Scénique: Système Fortuny* (Paris, 1904), p. 10.

6 *Ibid.*, p. 3.

7 Peter Greenaway, *The Stairs* (London, 1994), p. 20.

8 Peter Greenaway, *Some Organizing Principles* (Swansea, 1993), n.p., Section 4.

9 Peter Greenaway, *The Baby of Mâcon* (Paris, 1994), p. 5. On Cosimo II de' Medici (1642–1723) see Harold Acton, *The Last Medici* (London, 1932; third edition 1980); and E. L. Goldberg, *Patterns in Late Medici Art Patronage* (Princeton, 1983).

10 It is now generally accepted that Monsu Desiderio was the pseudonym adopted by Didier Barra, a Metzian born in 1590 who became a successful landscape and architectural painter in Naples. See M. R. Nappi, *François de Nômé e Didier Barra, l'énigma Monsu Desiderio* (Paris, 1985).

11 Greenaway discusses the form in relation to the death of Hardy in *Drowning by Numbers*: 'The box is relevant to the sacred spaces of the genre of the "Sacra Conversazione" of the fifteenth century – certainly to the paintings of Mantegna's relatives – the Bellinis – who painted perhaps the most completely realized works of the genre – where sacred figures – saints, martyrs, churchmen – are contained within an architectural framework which is two parts decorative, one part structural.' The classic account is J. Burckhardt, 'Das Altarbild', in *Beitrage zur Kunstgeschichte in Italien* (Basel, 1898), pp. 7ff, reissued as *The Altarpiece in Renaissance Italy*, translated and edited with a commentary by P. Humfrey (Oxford, 1988).

12 Peter Greenaway, *The Baby of Mâcon*, p. 108.

13 *Ibid.*, p. 3.

14 Alan Woods, *Being Naked, Playing Dead* (Manchester, 1996), p. 258.

15 Peter Greenaway, *The Stairs*, p. 23.

16 Theodor Adorno, 'Valéry Proust Museum', in *Prisms* (Boston, 1985), p. 175.

17 Douglas Crimp, 'On the Museum's Ruins', in *Postmodern Culture*, ed. Hal Foster (London, 1985), p. 43.

18 On the museum as an articulation of knowledge and power relations, see Tony Bennett, 'The Exhibitionary Complex', in *Thinking About Exhibitions*, eds Reesa Greenberg, Bruce Ferguson and Sandy Nairne (London, 1996), pp. 81–113.

19 Bruce W. Ferguson, 'Exhibition Rhetorics: Material Speech and Utter Sense', in *Thinking about Exhibitions*, eds Reesa Greenberg and others, p. 175; Carol Duncan, *The Aesthetics of Power: Essays in Critical Art History* (Cambridge, 1993), p. 192.

20 Peter Greenaway, *The Stairs*.

21 Peter Greenaway, *100 Objects to Represent the World* (Vienna, 1992).

22 In Barcelona, in spring 1997, Greenaway mounted an exhibition devoted to the Icarus myth, entitled *Flying over Water*.

23 Peter Greenaway, *The Stairs 2: Munich* (London, 1995), p. 43.

24 Peter Greenaway, *The Stairs: Geneva*, p. 17.

25 Bruce W. Ferguson, 'Exhibition Rhetorics: Material Speech and Utter Sense', in *Thinking About Exhibitions*, eds Reesa Greenberg and others, pp. 175–90.

26 Peter Greenaway, *The Stairs: Geneva*, p. 28.

27 *Ibid.*, p. 59.

28 Peter Greenaway, *The Stairs 2: Munich*, p. 51.

29 Adam Mars-Jones, *The Independent* (20 February 1996).

30 Thomas Elsaesser, 'Peter Greenaway', in *Spellbound: Art and Film*, eds Philip Dodd and Ian Christie (London, 1996).

31 Peter Greenaway, *Darwin*, Tableau 2, 'In Which Darwin Considers a Career in Medicine'.

32 See Jonathan Miller, *Charles Darwin* (London, 1986).

33 Roland Barthes, 'Diderot, Brecht, Eisenstein', reproduced in *The Responsibility of Forms* (Oxford, 1986), pp. 96–7.

34 See David K. van Keuren, 'Museums and Ideology: Augustus Pitt-Rivers, anthropological museums, and social change in later Victorian Britain', *Victorian Studies*, vol. 28 (1984).

List of Illustrations

1 'Escargot', production still from *A Zed and Two Noughts* (1985). Collection of the artist.

2 'The Snails' from storyboard for *A Zed and Two Noughts* (1985). Ballpoint pen on paper. Collection of the artist.

3 'The Snails on the Grid', production still from *A Zed and Two Noughts* (1985). Collection of the artist.

4 Publicity shot for *A Zed and Two Noughts* (1985). Photo courtesy of Steve Pike/Network.

5 J.M.W. Turner, *Rain, Steam and Speed – The Great Western Railway*, before 1844, oil on canvas. National Gallery, London.

6 *If Only Film Could Do the Same . . .*, oil and collage, 1974. Photo: Watermans Arts Centre, Brentford.

7 Agnolo Bronzino, *Andrea Doria as Neptune*, 1556, oil on canvas. Pinacoteca di Brera, Milan.

8 Kracklite as Doria as Neptune, from *The Belly of An Architect* (1987). Photo courtesy Peter Greenaway/Allarts.

9 William Holman Hunt, *The Hireling Shepherd*, 1851–2, oil on canvas. Manchester City Art Gallery. Photo: City Art Galleries, Manchester.

10 Pages from *A Framed Life*, 1988–9, mixed media on paper.

11 Pages from *A Framed Life*, 1988–9, mixed media on paper.

12 Page from *A Framed Life*, 1989, mixed media on paper.

13 Page from *A Framed Life*, 1989, mixed media on paper.

14 R. B. Kitaj, *Trout For Factitious Bait*, oil on canvas, 1965. Whitworth Art Gallery, Manchester. Photo: City Art Galleries, Manchester.

15 *Under the Ice*, 1994, mixed media on card. Collection of the artist.

16 *Vertical Features Remake: The Research*, 1974, mixed media on card. Collection of the artist.

17 *The Amsterdam Map*, 1978, mixed media on paper. Collection of the artist.

18 *Who Killed Cock Robin?*, 1978, mixed media on paper. Collection of the artist.

19 Januarius Zick, *Allegory of Newton's Service to Optics*, 1785, oil on canvas. Niedersächsische Landesgalerie, Hannover.

20 Drawing equipment, from *The Draughtsman's Contract* (1982). Photo courtesy Peter Greenaway/British Film Institute.

21 Albrecht Dürer, Perspectival apparatus, from *Unterweisung Der Messung*, Nuremberg, 1525.

22 The Draughtsman at work, from *The Draughtsman's Contract* (1982). Photo courtesy Peter Greenaway/British Film Institute.

23 The Draughtsman's grid, from *The Draughtsman's Contract* (1982). Photo courtesy Peter Greenaway/British Film Institute.

24 Homage to de la Tour (i), from *The Draughtsman's Contract* (1982). Photo courtesy Peter Greenaway/British Film Institute.

25 Georges de la Tour, *The Repentant Magdalene* (known as *Madeleine Terff*), (?)1616, oil on canvas. Musée du Louvre, Paris. Photo: Agence Photographique de la Réunion des Musées Nationaux/Hervé Landowski.

26 Homage to de la Tour (ii), from *The Draughtsman's Contract* (1982). Photo: Simon Archer; © BFI

27 Georges de la Tour, *The Repentant Magdalene*, known as *Madeleine Fabius*, (?)1616, oil on canvas. National Gallery, Washington, DC.

28 Homage to Gainsborough, from *The Draughtsman's Contract* (1982). Photo

courtesy Peter Greenaway/British Film Institute.

29 Thomas Gainsborough, (?)*Self-Portrait with his Wife Margaret*, 1746, oil on canvas. Musée du Louvre, Paris. Photo: Agence Photographique de la Réunion des Musées Nationaux.

30 Torchlight procession, from *The Draughtsman's Contract* (1982). Photo: Simon Archer; © BFI.

31 Homage to Hogarth, from *The Draughtsman's Contract* (1982). Photo courtesy Peter Greenaway/British Film Institute.

32 Hogarth, *The Lady's Last Stake*, 1758–9, oil on canvas. Albright-Knox Art Gallery, Buffalo, NY, Gift of Seymour H. Knox.

33 *Animal Game*, 1988, pencil on card.

34 Italian school, after Michelangelo, *Leda and the Swan*, sanguine, 16th century. Musée du Louvre, Paris. Photo: Agence Photographique de la Réunion des Musées Nationaux.

35 Zebra stripes, from *A Zed and Two Noughts* (1985).

36 Twins in bed, from *A Zed and Two Noughts* (1985). Photo: BFI Stills, Posters and Designs.

37 The double suit, from *A Zed and Two Noughts* (1985).

38 Eadweard Muybridge, 'Turning Around in Surprise and Running Away', Plate 73 from *Animal Locomotion*, New York, 1887. Photo: The Wellcome Institute Library, London.

39 Francis Bacon, *Dog*, oil on canvas, 1952. Museum of Modern Art, New York.

40 Van Meegeren, from *A Zed and Two Noughts* (1985). Photo: BFI Stills, Posters and Designs.

41 Katarina Bolnes, from *A Zed and Two Noughts* (1985). Photo: BFI Stills, Posters and Designs.

42 Detail from Vermeer, *The Art of Painting*, c. 1666–7, oil on canvas. Kunsthistorisches Museum, Vienna.

43 Vermeer, *Girl With a Red Hat*, c. 1665, oil on canvas. National Gallery of Art, Washington, DC, Andrew W. Mellon Collection.

44 Piero Della Francesca, *The Flagellation of Christ*, 1455–60, oil on panel. Galleria Nazionale Delle Marche, Urbino.

45 Drunken Kracklite, from *The Belly of an Architect* (1987). Photo courtesy of Peter Greenaway/Allarts.

46 Galeazzo Mondella, *The Cortège of Silenus*, pen and brown ink, sepia wash, c. 1500. Musée du Louvre, Paris. Photo: Agence Photographique de la Réunion des Musées Nationaux.

47 Terminal prognosis, from *The Belly of an Architect* (1987). Photo courtesy of Peter Greenaway/Allarts.

48 John Henry Fuseli, *The Artist Moved by the Grandeur of Antique Fragments*, c. 1778–80, chalk with sepia wash. Kunsthaus, Zürich.

49 Torso interview, from *The Belly of an Architect* (1987). Photo courtesy of Peter Greenaway/Allarts.

50 Etienne Louis Boullée, *Project for a Cenotaph to Sir Isaac Newton*, 1784, ink and wash. Bibliothèque Nationale de France, Paris.

51 Etienne Louis Boullée, *Interior View by Night*, 1784, ink and wash. Bibliothèque Nationale de France, Paris.

52 Redon, *Le Boulet (dit Le Prisonnier)*, 1886, charcoal. Musée du Louvre, Paris. Photo: Agence Photographique de la Réunion des Musées Nationaux.

53 Redon, *La Boule*, c. 1878, black crayon and stump on paper. Musée du Louvre, Paris. Photo: Agence Photographique de la Réunion des Musées Nationaux.

54 Hotel copies, from *The Belly of an Architect* (1987). Photo courtesy of Peter Greenaway/Allarts.

55 Agnolo Bronzino, *A Young Woman With her Little Boy*, 1540, oil on panel. National Gallery, Washington, DC.

56 Flavia's mural, from *The Belly of an Architect* (1987). Photo courtesy of Peter Greenaway/Allarts.

57 The white screen, from *The Belly of an Architect* (1987). Photo courtesy of Peter Greenaway/Allarts.

58 Caspasian's entry, from *The Belly of an Architect* (1987). Photo courtesy of

Peter Greenaway/Allarts.

59 Woman and child, from *The Belly of an Architect* (1987). Photo courtesy of Peter Greenaway/Allarts.

60 Girl and shadow, from *Drowning by Numbers* (1988). Photo: BFI Stills, Posters and Designs.

61 *The Skipping Girl*, 1988, pencil and ink on card.

62 Formal considerations, from *Drowning by Numbers* (1988). Photo: BFI Stills, Posters and Designs.

63 Detail from Diego Velázquez, *Las Meninas*, 1656, oil on canvas. Museo del Prado, Madrid.

64 The number count: 99, from *Drowning by Numbers* (1988). Photo: BFI Stills, Posters and Designs.

65 Pieter Bruegel, *Children's Games*, 1560, oil on panel. Kunsthistorisches Museum, Vienna.

66 Peter Paul Rubens, *Samson and Delilah*, c. 1609, oil on wood. National Gallery, London.

67 *Prospero's Books: A Catalogue*, 1989, mixed media on card.

68 Flesh and text, from *The Pillow Book* (1995). Photo: Marc Guillamot.

69 St Jerome installation at *The Physical Self*, Rotterdam, 1990.

70 Van Dyck, *St Jerome*, (?)1626, oil on canvas. Museum Boymans-van Beuningen, Rotterdam.

71 The study, from *Prospero's Books* (1991). Photo courtesy of Peter Greenaway/Allarts.

72 Antonella da Messina, *St Jerome in his Study*, c. 1475, oil on lime. National Gallery, London.

73 Georges de la Tour, *The Penitent St Jerome*, c. 1625, oil on canvas. Nationalmuseum, Stockholm.

74 Albrecht Dürer, 'St John Devours the Book (*Rev.* X, 1–5; 8–10)', engraving from *Revelation of St John*, 1498.

75 Stuffing Michael, from *The Cook, The Thief, His Wife and her Lover* (1989). Photo courtesy of Peter Greenaway/Allarts.

76 Rembrandt, *Anatomy Lesson of Dr Joan Deyman*, 1656, oil on canvas. Rijksmuseum, Amsterdam.

77 Frans Hals, *Banquet of the Officers of the Haarlem Militia Company*, 1616. Frans Halsmuseum, Haarlem. Photo: Tom Haartsen.

78 Rembrandt, *Slaughtered Ox*, 1655, oil on wood. Musée du Louvre, Paris. Photo: Agence Photographique de la Réunion des Musées Nationaux/Gérard Blot.

79 The dining room, from *The Cook, The Thief, His Wife and her Lover* (1989). Photo: Miramax Films.

80 Jan Davidsz. de Heem, *Still Life with Parrots*, 1648, oil on canvas. The John and Mable Ringling Museum of Art, Sarasota, FL.

81 Gerrit Dou, *A Poulterer's Shop*, c. 1670, oil on oak. National Gallery, London.

82 The blue car park, from *The Cook, The Thief, His Wife and her Lover* (1989). Photo: E. Serio.

83 Green kitchens, from *The Cook, The Thief, His Wife and her Lover* (1989). Photo: Miramax Films.

84 Jan Davidsz. de Heem, *Still Life with Books*, 1628, oil on wood. Koninklijk Kabinet van Schilderijen 'Mauritshuis', The Hague.

85 Steps to the library, from *Prospero's Books* (1991). Photo courtesy of Peter Greenaway/Allarts.

86 Titian, *Bacchus and Ariadne*, 1522–3, oil on canvas. National Gallery, London.

87 A game of chess, from *Prospero's Books* (1991). Photo: BFI Stills, Posters and Designs.

88 *Watching Water*, 1993.

89 The theatre, from *The Baby of Mâcon* (1993). Photo courtesy Peter Greenaway/Allarts.

90 The screen, from *The Baby of Mâcon* (1993). Photo courtesy Peter Greenaway/Allarts.

91 *Pencil Heads*, 1993, acrylic on card.

92 *Some Organizing Principles*, 1993.
93 Cornelius Gijsbrechts, *Reverse Side of a Painting*, 1670, oil on canvas. Statens Museum for Kunst, Copenhagen.
94 Crashed plane, from *100 Objects to Represent the World*, 1991.
95 Sleep, from *100 Objects to Represent the World*, 1991.
96 The props, from *In the Dark*, 1996. Photo courtesy of John Riddy.
97 The actors, from *In the Dark*, 1996. Photo courtesy of John Riddy.
98 The study, from *Darwin* (1992). Photo courtesy of Peter Greenaway/Allarts.
99 Adam and Darwin, from *Darwin* (1992). Photo courtesy of Peter Greenaway/Allarts.
100 'Tableau 16' from *Darwin* (1992). Photo courtesy of Peter Greenaway/Allarts.